LATIN AMERICA

ECONOMIC INTEGRATION AND COOPERATION BUSINESS LAW HANDBOOK

VOLUME 1

STRATEGIC INFORMATION AND AGREEMENTS

International Business Publications, USA
Washington DC, USA

LATIN AMERICA

ECONOMIC INTEGRATION AND COOPERATION BUSINESS LAW HANDBOOK

VOLUME 1 STRATEGIC INFORMATION AND AGREEMENTS

UPDATED ANNUALLY

We express our sincere appreciation to all government agencies and international organizations which provided information and other materials for this handbook

Cover Design: International Business Publications, USA

2018 Edition Updated Reprint International Business Publications, USA
ISBN 1-4330-2908-1

For additional analytical, business and investment opportunities information,
please contact Global Investment & Business Center, USA
at (703) 370-8082. Fax: (703) 370-8083. E-mail: ibpusa3@gmail.com
Global Business and Investment Info Databank - www.ibpus.com

Printed in the USA

LATIN AMERICA

ECONOMIC INTEGRATION AND COOPERATION BUSINESS LAW HANDBOOK

VOLUME 1

STRATEGIC INFORMATION AND AGREEMENTS

TABLE OF CONTENTS

LATIN AMERICA: STRATEGIC INFORMATION

Area	19,197,000 km^2 (7,412,000 sq mi)
Population	626,741,000 (est.)
Population density	31/km^2 (80/sq mi)
Demonym	Latin American
Countries	20
Dependencies	13
Languages	Mainly: Spanish and Portuguese Others: Quechua, Mayan languages, Guaraní, French, Aymara, Nahuatl, Italian, German, English, Dutch, Polish, Ukrainian, Welsh, Yiddish, Chinese, Japanese
Time zones	UTC-2 to UTC-8
Largest cities	(Metro areas) 1. Mexico City 2. São Paulo 3. Buenos Aires 4. Rio de Janeiro 5. Bogotá 6. Lima 7. Santiago 8. Belo Horizonte 9. Guadalajara 10. Monterrey

Latin America is a group of countries and dependencies in the Americas where Romance languages are predominant. The term originated in 19th century France as *Amérique latine* to consider French-speaking territories in the Americas (Haiti, French Guiana, Martinique, Guadeloupe, Saint Martin, Saint Barthélemy) along with the larger group of countries where Spanish and Portuguese languages prevailed. It is therefore broader than the terms Ibero-America or Hispanic America—though it usually excludes French Canada and modern French Louisiana.

Latin America consists of nineteen sovereign states and several territories and dependencies which cover an area that stretches from the northern border of Mexico to the southern tip of South America, including the Caribbean. It has an area of approximately 19,197,000 km^2 (7,412,000 sq mi), almost 13% of the Earth's land surface area. As of 2015, its population was estimated at more than 626 million and in 2014, Latin America had a combined nominal GDP of 5,573,397 million USD and a GDP PPP of 7,531,585 million USD. The term "Latin America" was first used in 1861 in *La revue des races Latines*, a magazine "dedicated to the cause of Pan-Latinism"

ECONOMY AND ECONOMIC DEVELOPMENTS

The Great Depression caused Latin America to grow at a slow rate, separating it from leading industrial democracies. The two world wars and U.S. Depression also made Latin American countries favor internal economic development, leading Latin America to adopt the policy of import substitution industrialization.

Countries also renewed emphasis on exports. Brazil began selling automobiles to other countries, and some Latin American countries set up plants to assemble imported parts, letting other countries take advantage of Latin America's low labor costs. Columbia began to export flowers and cocaine, becoming the world's second leading flower exporter and leading supplier of cocaine.

Economic integration was called for, to attain economies that could compete with the economies of the U.S or Europe. Starting in the 1960's with the Latin American Free Trade Association and Central American Common Market, Latin American countries worked toward economic integration.

Country	GDP (PPP) (millions)	Per capita
Brazil	2,309,138	11,892
Mexico	1,659,016	14,514
Argentina	710,690	17,382
Colombia	467,670	10,038
Venezuela	369,324	13,480
Peru	300,114	9,958
Chile	281,368	16,078
Ecuador	125,066	8,372
Dominican Republic	93,408	9,784
Guatemala	74,026	4,875
Costa Rica	54,516	12,520
Uruguay	52,111	16,019
Bolivia	51,478	5,023
Panama	48,812	12,615
El Salvador	44,845	6,919
Paraguay	36,235	5,426
Honduras	35,649	4,240
Trinidad and Tobago	26,866	19,739
Jamaica	24,637	8,747
Nicaragua	18,758	3,072
Haiti	12,431	1,167
The Bahamas	10,786	30,009
Barbados	6,300	22,744
Guyana	5,842	7,038
Suriname	5,069	8,949
Belize	2,804	8,069
Saint Lucia	2,158	12,476

Country	GDP (PPP) (millions)	Per capita
Antigua and Barbuda	1,781	21,363
Grenada	1,396	13,135
Saint Vincent and the Grenadines	1,259	11,561
Dominica	981	13,222
Saint Kitts and Nevis	925	16,218
LAC-32	6,837,162	11,770

REFORMS

Large countries like Argentina called for reforms to lessen the disparity of wealth between the rich and the poor, which has been a long problem in Latin America that retards economic growth.

Advances in public health caused an explosion of population growth, making it difficult to provide social services. Education expanded, and social security systems introduced, but benefits usually went to the middle class, not the poor. As a result, disparity of wealth increased. Increasing inflation and other factors caused countries to be unwilling to fund social development programs to help the poor.

Bureaucratic Authoritarianism

Bureaucratic authoritarianism was practiced in Brazil after 1964, in Argentina, and in Chile under Augusto Pinochet, in a response to harsh economic conditions. It rested on the conviction that no democracy could take the harsh measures to curb inflation, reassure investors, and quicken economic growth quickly and effectively. Though inflation fell sharply, industrial production dropped with the decline of official protection.

U.S. RELATIONS

After World War II and the beginning of a Cold War between the U.S. and the Soviet Union, U.S. diplomats became interested in Asia, Africa, and Latin America, and frequently waged proxy wars against the Soviet Union in these countries. The U.S. sought to stop the spread of communism. Latin Americans generally resented the U.S. superiority over them. Latin America also complained of the U.S. support to locals in overthrowing nationalist governments, and intervention through the CIA. Still, Latin America respected the U.S. during this time, and Latin American countries generally sided with the U.S., even though they complained of being neglected by the U.S.'s concern with communism in Europe and Asia, not Latin America. In 1947, the U.S. Congress passed the National Security Act, which created the National Security Council in response to America's growing obsession with anti-communism.

In 1954, when Jacobo Arbenz of Guatemala accepted the support of communists and attacked holdings of the United Fruit Company, the U.S. decided to assist Guatemalan counterrevolutionaries in overthrowing Arbenz. These interventionist tactics featured use of the CIA rather than the military, which would be used in Latin America for the majority of the Cold War in events like the overthrow of Salvador Allende. Latin America was more concerned with issues of economic development, while the United States focused on fighting communism, even though the presence of communism was small in Latin America.

Cuban Revolution

By 1959, Cuba was afflicted with slow economic growth and a corrupt dictatorship under Batista, and Fidel Castro ousted Batista that year and set up the first communist state in the hemisphere.

The U.S. imposed a trade embargo on Cuba, and combined with Castro's expropriation of private enterprises, this was detrimental to the Cuban economy.

Around Cuba, rural guerrilla conflict and urban terrorism increased, inspired by the Cuban example. The United States put down these rebellions by supporting Latin American countries in their counter guerrilla operations through the Alliance for Progress launched by President John F. Kennedy.This thrust appeared to be successful. A Marxist, Salvador Allende, became president of Chile in 1970, but was overthrown three years later. Despite riots and political instability, most Latin American countries besides Cuba adopted democracies.

Bay of Pigs Invasion

Encouraged by the Guatemala success, Kennedy, in 1960, decided to launch an attack on Cuba. The Bay of Pigs invasion was an abortive invasion of Cuba in 1961, financed by the U.S. through the CIA, to overthrow Castro. The incident proved to be very embarrassing for the new Kennedy administration.

Alliance for Progress

President John F. Kennedy initiated the Alliance for Progress in 1961, to establish economic cooperation between the U.S. and Latin America.The Alliance would provide $20 billion for reform in Latin America, and counterinsurgency measures. Instead, the reform failed because of the simplistic theory that guided it and the lack of experienced American experts who could understand Latin American customs.

Cuban missile crisis

The Cuban Missile crisis nearly brought the U.S. and the Soviet Union to war in October of 1962. Soviet premier Nikita Khrushchev had installed several missiles in Cuba that could hit most of the Eastern United States. President Kennedy decided to place a naval blockade on Cuba to prevent further Soviet shipments of missiles. In the end, Khrushchev submitted, taking missiles away. In return, Kennedy agreed never to invade Cuba, and to withdraw nuclear-arms from Turkey.

WASHINGTON CONSENSUS

The set of specific economic policy prescriptions that were considered the "standard" reform package were promoted for crisis-wracked developing countries by Washington, D.C.-based institutions such as the International Monetary Fund (IMF), World Bank, and the US Treasury Department during the 80s and 90s.

In recent years, several Latin American countries led by socialist or other left wing governments—including Argentina and Venezuela—have campaigned for (and to some degree adopted) policies contrary to the Washington Consensus set of policies. (Other Latin countries with governments of the left, including Brazil, Chile and Peru, have in practice adopted the bulk of the policies). Also critical of the policies as actually promoted by the International Monetary Fund have been some U.S. economists, such as Joseph Stiglitz and Dani Rodrik, who have challenged what are sometimes described as the "fundamentalist" policies of the International Monetary Fund and the US Treasury for what Stiglitz calls a "one size fits all" treatment of individual economies.

The term has become associated with neoliberal policies in general and drawn into the broader debate over the expanding role of the free market, constraints upon the state, and US influence on other countries' national sovereignty.

This politico-economical initiative was institutionalized in North America by the 1994 NAFTA, and elsewhere in the Americas through a series of like agreements. The comprehensive Free Trade Area of the Americas project, however, was rejected by most South American countries at the 2005 4th Summit of the Americas.

TURN TO THE LEFT

In most countries, since the 2000s left-wing political parties have risen to power. Hugo Chávez in Venezuela, Lula da Silva in Brazil, Fernando Lugo in Paraguay, Néstor Kirchner and his wife Cristina Fernández in Argentina, Ollanta Humala in Peru, Evo Morales in Bolivia, Daniel Ortega in Nicaragua, Manuel Zelaya in Honduras, Rafael Correa in Ecuador, are all part of this wave of left-wing politicians who also often declare themselves socialists, Latin Americanists, or anti-imperialists (often implying opposition to US policies towards the region). There are also some leaders who, although aren't exactly leftist, are closer to the centre-left in the political spectrum. Examples of this are Ricardo Lagos and Michelle Bachelet in Chile, Tabaré Vázquez and José Mujica in Uruguay, Laura Chinchilla in Costa Rica, and Mauricio Funes in El Salvador. A development of this has been the creation of the eight-member ALBA alliance, or "The Bolivarian Alliance for the Peoples of Our America" (Spanish: *Alianza Bolivariana para los Pueblos de Nuestra América*). In the 2010, only three countries in Latin America had right-wing presidents. These were Sebastián Piñera in Chile, Felipe Calderon in Mexico, and Juan Manuel Santos in Colombia.

THE RETURN OF SOCIAL MOVEMENTS

In 1982, Mexico announced that it could not meet its foreign debt payment obligations, inaugurating a debt crisis that would discredit Latin American economies throughout the decade.

This debt crisis would lead to neoliberal reforms that would instigate many social movements in the region. A “reversal of development” reigned over Latin America, seen through negative economic growth, declines in industrial production, and thus, falling living standards for the middle and lower classes.

Governments made financial security their primary policy goal over social security, enacting new neoliberal economic policies that implemented privatization of previously national industries and informalization of labor.

In an effort to bring more investors to these industries, these governments also embraced globalization through more open interactions with the international economy. Significantly, as democracy spread across much of Latin America, the realm of government more inclusive (a trend that proved conductive to social movements), the economic ventures remained exclusive to a few elite groups within society. Neoliberal restructuring consistently redistributed income upward while denying political responsibility to provide social welfare rights, and though development projects took place throughout the region, both inequality and poverty increased. Feeling excluded from these new projects, the lower classes took ownership of their own democracy through a revitalization of social movements in Latin America.

Both urban and rural populations had serious grievances as a result of the above economic and global trends and have voiced them in mass demonstrations. Some of the largest and most violent of these have been protests against cuts in urban services, such as the Caracazo in Venezuela and the Argentinazo in Argentina.

Rural movements have made diverse demands related to unequal land distribution, displacement at the hands of development projects and dams, environmental and indigenous concerns, neoliberal agricultural restructuring, and insufficient means of livelihood. These movements have benefited considerably from transnational support from conservationists and INGOs. The Movement of Rural Landless Workers (MST), is perhaps the largest contemporary Latin American social movement.

As indigenous populations are primarily rural, indigenous movements account for a large portion of rural social movements, including the Zapatista rebellion in Mexico, the Confederation of Indigenous Nationalities of Ecuador (CONAIE), indigenous organizations in the Amazon region of Ecuador and Bolivia, pan-Mayan communities in Guatemala, and mobilization by the indigenous groups of Yanomami peoples in the Amazon, Kuna peoples in Panama, and Altiplano Aymara and Quechua peoples in Bolivia. Other significant types of social movements include labor struggles and strikes, such as recovered factories in Argentina, as well as gender-based movements such as the Mothers of the Plaza de Mayo in Argentina and protests against maquila production, which is largely a women's issue because of how it draws on women for cheap labor.

These various social movements have continued today along with a broader political shift to the left. They are credited with raising social awareness across the globe of important issues affecting indigenous peoples in Latin America and through their work with NGOs and other international organizations. Moreover, they have provided tangible alternatives to the principles of neoliberalism, spurring constitutional changes and legislative policy while demonstrating the merits of active representative democracies.

The 2000s commodities boom caused positive effects for many Latin American economies. Another trend is the rapidly increasing importance of the relations with China.

IMPORTANT ECONOMIC DEVELOPMENTS

According to Goldman Sachs' BRIC review of emerging economies, by 2050 the largest economies in the world will be as follows: China, United States, India, Brazil, and Mexico.

On a per capita basis most Latin American countries, including the largest ones (Argentina, Mexico, Brazil, Chile, Peru, Venezuela, and Colombia), have per capita GDPs greater than that of China in 2009. As of 2010 Latin America included five nations classified as high-income countries: Argentina, Chile, Uruguay, Mexico and Panama.

The following table lists all the countries in Latin America indicating a valuation of the country's GDP (Gross domestic product) based on purchasing-power-parity (PPP), GDP per capita also adjusted to the (PPP), a measurement of inequality through the Gini index (the higher the index the more unequal the income distribution is), the Human Development Index (HDI), the Environmental Performance Index (EPI), and the Quality-of-life index. GDP and PPP GDP statistics come from the International Monetary Fund with data as of 2006. Gini index, the Human Poverty Index HDI-1, the Human Development Index, and the number of internet users per capita come from the UN Development Program. The number of motor vehicles per capita come from the UNData base on-line. The EPI index comes from the Yale Center for Environmental Law and Policy and the Quality-of-life index from The Economist Intelligence Unit. Green cells indicate the 1st rank in each category, while yellow indicate the last rank.

SOCIO-ECONOMIC PERFORMANCE INDICATORS FOR LATIN AMERICAN COUNTRIES

Country	GDP (PPP) (2012 estimates) Billions of USD	GDP per capita (PPP) (2012 estimates) USD	Income equality (2000–2010) Gini index	Poverty Index (2009) HPI-1 %	Human Develop. (2011) HDI	Envirnm. Perform. (2010) EPI	Real GDP growth (2010) %	Emissions per capita (2008) ton CO2
Argentina	732.223	18,411	48.8	3.7	0.797 (VH)	61.0	7.5	4.4

Country	GDP (PPP) (2012 estimates) Billions of USD	GDP per capita (PPP) (2012 estimates) USD	Income equality (2000–2010) Gini index	Poverty Index (2009) HPI-1 %	Human Develop. (2011) HDI	Envirnm. Perform. (2010) EPI	Real GDP growth (2010) %	Emissions per capita (2008) ton CO2
Bolivia	51.796	5,084	57.2	11.6	0.663 (M)	44.3	4.0	1.3
Brazil	2,310.998	11,767	55.0	8.7	0.718 (H)	63.4	7.5	1.9
Chile	311.546	17,482	49.1	3.2	0.805 (VH)	73.3	5.0	4.4
Colombia	519.866	10,445	58.5	7.6	0.710 (H)	76.8	4.7	1.4
Costa Rica	56.130	12,332	48.9	4.6	0.744 (H)	86.4	3.8	1.5
Cuba	111.1	9,700	N/A	4.7	0.776 (H)	78.1	1.4	2.7
Dominican Republic	95.391	9,648	48.4	9.1	0.689 (M)	68.4	5.5	2.0
Ecuador	133.825	8,952	54.4	7.9	0.720 (H)	69.3	2.9	1.9
El Salvador	48.640	8,442	46.9	14.6	0.674 (M)	69.1	1.0	1.0
Guatemala	72.958	5,071	53.7	19.7	0.574 (M)	54.0	2.4	0.8
Haiti	11.056	1,122	59.5	31.5	0.454 (L)	39.5	-8.5	0.2
Honduras	38.537	4,405	55.3	13.7	0.625 (M)	49.9	2.4	1.1
Mexico	1,849.671	15,766	51.6	5.9	0.770 (H)	67.3	5.0	3.8
Nicaragua	17.269	3,370	52.3	17.0	0.589 (M)	57.1	3.0	0.7
Panama	43.725	14,398	54.9	6.7	0.768 (H)	71.4	6.2	1.9
Paraguay	31.469	5,915	53.2	10.5	0.665 (M)	63.5	9.0	0.6
Peru	324.276	10,781	50.5	10.2	0.725 (H)	69.3	8.3	1.2
Uruguay	54.140	16,242	47.1	3.0	0.783 (H)	59.1	8.5	2.3
Venezuela	346.973	12,589	43.4	6.6	0.735 (H)	62.9	-1.3	5.2
Total	6,270.231	12,519		10.1		76.2	4	2.3

Notes: (H) High human development; (M) Medium human development; (L) Low human development

POVERTY AND INEQUALITY

Poverty continues to be one of the region's main challenges; according to the ECLAC, Latin America is the most unequal region in the world.

Inequality is undermining the region's economic potential and the well-being of its population, since it increases poverty and reduces the impact of economic development on poverty reduction.

Inequality in Latin America has deep historical roots that have been difficult to eradicate since the differences between initial endowments and opportunitites among social groups have constrained the poorest's social mobility, thus making poverty to be transmitted from generation to generation, becoming a vicious cycle. High inequality is rooted in exclusionary institutions that have been perpetuated ever since colonial times and that have survived different political and economic regimes. Inequality has been reproduced and transmitted through generations because Latin American political systems allow a differentiated access on the influence that social groups have in the decision making process, and it responds in different ways to the least favored groups that have less political representation and capacity of pressure.

Recent economic liberalisation also plays a role as not everyone is equally capable of taking advantage of its benefits. Differences in opportunities and endowments tend to be based on race, ethnicity, rurality and gender. Those differences have a strong impact on the distribution of income, capital and political standing.

According to a study by the World Bank,the richest decile of the population of Latin America earn 48% of the total income, while the poorest 10% of the population earn only 1.6% of the income. In contrast, in developed countries, the top decile receives 29% of the total income, while the bottom decile earns 2.5%. The countries with the highest inequality in the region (as measured with the Gini index in the UN Development Report) in 2007 were Haiti (59.5), Colombia (58.5), Bolivia (58.2), Honduras (55.3), Brazil (55.0), and Panama (54.9), while the countries with the lowest inequality in the region were Venezuela (43.4), Uruguay (46.4) and Costa Rica (47.2).

According to the World Bank the poorest countries in the region were (as of 2008): Haiti, Nicaragua, Bolivia and Honduras. Undernourishment affects to 47% of Haitians, 27% of Dominicans and Nicaraguans, 23% of Bolivians and 22% of Hondurans.

Many countries in Latin America have responded to high levels of poverty by implementing new, or altering old, social assistance programs such as conditional cash transfers. These include Mexico's Progresa Oportunidades, Brazil's Bolsa Escola and Bolsa Familia, and Chile's Chile Solidario.

In general, these programs provide money to poor families under the condition that those transfers are used as an investment on their children's human capital, such as regular school attendance and basic preventive health care. The purpose of these programs is to address the inter-generational transmission of poverty and to foster social inclusion by explicitly targeting the poor, focusing on children, delivering transfers to women, and changing social accountability relationships between beneficiaries, service providers and governments.

These programs have helped to increase school enrollment and attendance and they also have shown improvements in children's health conditions. Most of these transfer schemes are now benefiting around 110 million people in the region and are considered relatively cheap, costing around 0.5% of their GDP.

TRADE BLOCS

The major trade blocs (or agreements) in the region are the Union of South American Nations, composed of the integrated Mercosur and Andean Community of Nations (**CAN**). Minor blocs or trade agreements are the G3 Free Trade Agreement, the Dominican Republic – Central America Free Trade Agreement (**DR-CAFTA**) and the Caribbean Community (**CARICOM**). However, major reconfigurations are taking place along opposing approaches to integration and trade; Venezuela has officially withdrawn from both the CAN and G3 and it has been formally admitted into the Mercosur (pending ratification from the Paraguayan legislature). The president-elect of Ecuador has manifested his intentions of following the same path. This bloc nominally opposes any Free Trade Agreement (FTA) with the United States, although Uruguay has manifested its intention otherwise.

Chile has already signed an FTA with Canada, and along with Peru, Colombia and Mexico are the only four Latin American nations that have an FTA with the United States, the latter being a member of the North American Free Trade Agreement (**NAFTA**).

METROPOLITAN ECONOMIES

The following table provides estimated GDP figures for the largest metropolitan areas in Latin America in 2008.

Rank	Metropolitan area	Country	GDP (PPP) Billions of USD	Metro. pop. in 2006 Millions	GDP (PPP) per capita USD
1	Mexico City	Mexico	390	19.24	20,300
2	São Paulo	Brazil	388	18.61	20,800
3	Buenos Aires	Argentina	362	13.52	28,000
4	Rio de Janeiro	Brazil	201	11.62	17,300
5	Santiago	Chile	120	5.70	21,100
6	Bogotá	Colombia	112	7.80	15,800
7	Brasilia	Brazil	110	3.48	31,600
8	Lima	Peru	109	8.35	13,100
9	Monterrey	Mexico	102	3.58	28,500
10	Guadalajara	Mexico	81	3.95	20,500

Note: The GDP data are for 2008 while the population data are for 2006. The GDP per capita figures were obtained by dividing these two sets of data, so the results may not accurately reflect the GDP per capita for 2008.

TOURISM

Income from tourism is key to the economy of several Latin American countries. Mexico receives the largest number of international tourists, with 22.3 million visitors in 2010, followed by Argentina, with 5.2 million in 2010; Brazil, with 5.1 million; Dominican Republic, with 4.1 million;, Puerto Rico, with 3.6 million and Chile with 2.7 million.

Places such as Cancún, Galápagos Islands, Machu Picchu, Chichen Itza, Cartagena de Indias, Cabo San Lucas, Acapulco, Rio de Janeiro, Salvador, Margarita Island, São Paulo, Salar de Uyuni, Punta del Este, Santo Domingo, Labadee, San Juan, La Habana, Panama City, Iguazu Falls, Puerto Vallarta, Poás Volcano National Park, Punta Cana, Viña del Mar, Mexico City, Quito, Bogotá, Buenos Aires, Lima, Maceió, Florianópolis, Cuzco and Patagonia are popular among international visitors in the region.

Performance indicators for international tourism in Latin America

Country	International tourist arrivals 2010 x1000	International tourism receipts 2010 Millions of USD	Receipts per arrival (2)/(1) 2010 (USD/Tourist)	Receipts per capita 2009 USD	Revenues as % of exports goods and services 2003	Tourism revenues as % GDP 2003	% Direct & indirect employment in tourism 2005	World Ranking Tourism Compet. TTCI 2011	Index value TTCI 2011
Argentina	5,288	4,930	932	120	7.4	1.8	9.1	60	4.20
Bolivia	671*	279*	415	28	9.4	2.2	7.6	117	3.35
Brazil	5,161	5,919	1,146	29	3.2	0.5	7.0	52	4.36
Chile	2,766	1,636	591	98	5.3	1.9	6.8	57	4.27
Colombia	2,385	2,083	873	47	6.6	1.4	5.9	77	3.94
Costa Rica	2,100	2,111	1,005	496	17.5	8.1	13.3	44	4.43

Country	International tourist arrivals 2010 x1000	International tourism receipts 2010 Millions of USD	Receipts per arrival (2)/(1) 2010 (USD/Tourist)	Receipts per capita 2009 USD	Revenues as % of exports goods and services 2003	Tourism revenues as % GDP 2003	% Direct & indirect employment in tourism 2005	World Ranking Tourism Compet. TTCI 2011	Index value TTCI 2011
Cuba	2,507	2,080*	829*	181*	N/A	N/A	N/A	N/A	N/A
Dominican Republic	4,125	4,240	1,027	439	36.2	18.8	19.8	72	3.99
Ecuador	1,047	781	745	53	6.3	1.5	7.4	87	3.79
El Salvador	1,150	390	339	54	12.9	3.4	6.8	96	3.68
Guatemala	1,219	1,378	1,130	103	16.0	2.6	6.0	86	3.82
Haiti*	N/A	N/A	N/A	N/A	19.4	3.2	4.7	N/A	N/A
Honduras	896	650	725	82	13.5	5.0	8.5	88	3.79
Mexico	22,395	11,872	530	106	5.7	1.6	14.2	43	4.43
Nicaragua	1,011	309	305	52	15.5	3.7	5.6	100	3.56
Panama	1,317	1,676	1,272	498	10.6	6.3	12.9	56	4.30
Paraguay	465	217	466	31	4.2	1.3	6.4	123	3.26
Peru	2,299	2,274	989	76	9.0	1.6	7.6	69	4.04
Uruguay	2,352	1,496	636	428	14.2	3.6	10.7	58	4.24
Venezuela	615*	618	1,004	23	1.3	0.4	8.1	106	3.46

Note (1): Bolivia, Venezuela and Cuba, marked with * do not have all statistical data available for 2010. Data shown is for 2009

LATIN AMERICA REGIONAL INTEGRATION

The **integration of Latin America** has a history going back to Spanish American and Brazilian independence, when there was discussion of creating a regional state or confederation of Latin American nations to protect the area's newly won autonomy. After several projects failed, the issue was not taken up again until the late nineteenth century, but now centered on the issue of international trade and with a sense of Pan-Americanism due to the United States of America taking a leading role in the project. The idea of granting these organizations a primarily political purpose did not become prominent again until the post-World War II period, which saw both the start of the Cold War and a climate of international cooperation that led to the creation of institutions such as the United Nations. It would not be until the mid-twentieth century that uniquely Latin American organizations were created.

LATIC AMERICAN ORGANIZATIONS FOR ECONOMIC INTEGRATION

Trade, not politics, also served as the principal issue around which various, uniquely Latin American regional organizations were formed after mid-century. On October 14, 1951 the governments of Costa Rica, El Salvador, Guatemala, Honduras, and Nicaragua signed a new treaty creating the **Organization of Central American States** *(Organizaci6n de Estados Centroamericanos*, or *ODECA)* to promote regional cooperation, integration and unity in Central America. This led to the creation of the Central American Common Market, the Central American

Bank for Economic Integration, and the Secretariat for Central American Economic Integration (SIECA) nine years later on December 13, 1960.

Other regional trade blocs were also established in this period. The Latin American Free Trade Association (ALALC) was formed by the 1960 Treaty of Montevideo, which was signed by Argentina, Brazil, Chile, Mexico, Paraguay, Peru, and Uruguay. The signatories hoped to create a common market in Latin America and offered tariff rebates among member nations. Its main goal was to eliminate all duties and restrictions on the majority of their trade within a twelve-year period. ALALC came into effect on January 2, 1962. Inspired by the European Communities, in 1980 the ALALC was transformed into the **Latin American Integration Association** (ALADI) by the second Treaty of Montevideo to pursue the more ambitious goal of improving the economic and social development of the region through the establishment of the common market.

In 1969 the Andean Pact was founded by Chile, Bolivia, Peru, Ecuador and Colombia. In 1973, the pact gained its sixth member, Venezuela. In 1976, however, its membership was again reduced to five when Chile withdrew. Venezuela announced its withdrawal in 2006, reducing the Andean Community to four member states. The name of the organization was changed to the **Andean Community of Nations** (CAN) in 1996. In 1985 the presidents of Argentina and Brazil signed the Argentina-Brazil Integration and Economics Cooperation Program. This eventually led to the founding of **Mercosur** by Brazil, Paraguay, Uruguay and Argentina in 1991 to promote free trade and the fluid movement of goods, people, and currency. Venezuela joined Mercosur in 2012 and Bolivia is an acceding member. In 1995 Mexico, Colombia and Venezuela created the **G3 Free Trade Agreement**. Venezuela left the G3 in 2006 at the same time it left the CAN. In addition to these trade organizations, several parliamentary organizations have been created. Mercosur agreed in December 2004 to create a Mercosur Parliament, which should begin functioning in 2010. Earlier in 1987 a **Latin American Parliament** was created and is located in Panama City.

In December 2004 Mercosur and the Andean Community of Nations signed a reciprocal associate-member status agreement and issued the Cusco Declaration stating that they would create a political South American Community of Nations. The Declaration purposely invoked "Bolívar's dream," noting that it would be partially realizing his vision of uniting Latin America. The original name of the union was changed to the current one, the **Union of South American Nations** in April 2007.

Following the 2011 *Declaration de Lima*, the **Pacific Alliance** was established in 2012 by the founding members Chile, Colombia, Mexico and Peru. As of 2015, Costa Rica is in the process of joining. While membership is currently exclusively Latin American, a potential membership application by Canada is being considered favorably by some

ORGANIZATION MEMBERSHIP

For Anglo America and Latin America

Country	OAS	CELAC	ACS	Caricom	OECS	UNASUR	CAN	MERCOSUR	LAP	LAIA	LAES	RG	SICA	ALBA	PA
USA	x														o
Mexico	x	x	x	o		o			x	x	x	x			x
Guatemala	x	x	x						x	o	x	x	x		o
El Salvador	x	x	x						x	o	x	x	x		o

Country	OAS	CELAC	ACS	Caricom	OECS	UNASUR	CAN	MERCOSUR	LAP	LAIA	LAES	RG	SICA	ALBA	PA
Honduras	a	x	x						x	o	x	x	x		o
Nicaragua	x	x	x						x	o	x	x	x	x	
Costa Rica	x	x	x						x	o	x	x	x		a
Dominican Republic	x	x	x	o					x	o	x	x	a		o
Panama	x	x	x			o			x	o	x	x	x		o
Cuba	a	x	x						x	x	x	x		x	
Venezuela	x	x	x	o		x		x	x	x	x	x		x	
Colombia	x	x	x	o		x	x	a	x	x	x	x			x
Ecuador	x	x	o			x	x	a	x	x	x	x		x	
Peru	x	x	o			x	x	a	x	x	x	x			x
Bolivia	x	x				x	x	a	x	x	x	x		x	
Chile	x	x	o			x	a	a	x	x	x	x			x
Argentina	x	x	o			x	a	x	x	x	x	x			
Uruguay	x	x				x	a	x	x	x	x	x		o	o
Paraguay	x	x				x	a	x	x	x	x	x		o	o
Brazil	x	x	o			x	a	x	x	x	x	x			
Antigua and Barbuda	x	x	x	x	x									x	
Bahamas	x	x	x	x							x				
Barbados	x	x	x	x							x				
Belize	x	x	x	x							x	x	x		
Dominica	x	x	x	x	x									x	o
Grenada	x	x	x	x	x						x			o	
Guyana	x	x	x	x		x					x	x			
Haiti	x	x	x	x							x	x		o	
Jamaica	x	x	x	x							x	x			
Saint Kitts and Nevis	x	x	x	x	x										
Saint Vincent and the Grenadines	x	x	x	x	x									x	
Saint Lucia	x	x	x	x	x										
Suriname	x	x	x	x		x			x		x				

Country	OAS	CELAC	ACS	Caricom	OECS	UNASUR	CAN	MERCOSUR	LAP	LAIA	LAES	RG	SICA	ALBA	PA
Trinidad and Tobago	x	x	x	x							x				o
Montserrat				x	x										
Anguilla				a	a										
Bermuda				a											
British Virgin Islands				a	a										
Cayman Islands				a											
Turks and Caicos Islands			a	a											
Aruba			a	o											
Netherlands Antilles			a	o											
Puerto Rico				o											
U.S. Virgin Islands															
Country	OAS	CELAC	ACS	Caricom	OECS	UNASUR	CAN	MERCOSUR	LAP	LAIA	LAES	RG	SICA	ALBA	PA

IMPORTANT ORGANIZATION ASSISTING LATIN AMERICAN INTEGRATION

The post-war period has been marked by two important phenomena in the political economy of trade relations. First, globalization has changed the economic geography of the world, with increased agglomeration and larger concentrations in urban spaces and with far better and more complex transport networks that have led to cost reductions and just-in-time production methods. Second, regionalism has marked developments in the global trading system, driven by the same forces as globalization as well as by the democratization of political power and the search for stability in once-volatile areas of the world. Currently there are over 200 regional trade agreements, 90 percent notified to the WTO since 1990 (WTO 2009a).

These phenomena are in large part a result of successive efforts to establish a rules-based world trading system. Multilateral negotiations through the General Agreement on Tariffs and Trade (1947) led to the establishment of the World Trade Organization (1995), with a growing number of member countries (153 to date) and a reduction in tariffs across the world significantly expanding opportunities for countries to participate in the world economy. Latin America and the Caribbean have been active participants in both these transformational processes that have deepened considerably since the 1990s with the unilateral opening of economies and increased regional trade agreements.

Latin American and Caribbean integration is at a crossroad. After the successful development of initiatives such as the Southern Common Market (Mercosur) and the Andean Community (ANC) in the early 1990s, these processes stalled in the middle of that decade. In the case of Mercosur, after the conclusion of the transition period in 1996, this integration scheme has failed in achieving objectives such as the customs union or the deepening of regional integration. This situation got worse after 1998 when the real crisis affected the Brazilian economy. Argentina's default in 2001 and the brief crisis in Uruguay also contributed to the stagnation of Mercosur. A similar situation took place in the Andean Community. After a successful period of increased intra-regional trade from 1990 to 1996, the process has been not able to continue in the path of success. The political crisis in the two key countries of the ANC (Colombia and Venezuela) and the position of Venezuelan President Hugo Chavez towards this initiative also explain this situation.

Furthermore, the proposal of creating a Free Trade Area of the Americas (FTAA), launched at the Hemispheric Summit of Miami in 1994, also collapsed in 2003. The differences between the FTAA model proposed by the United States and that presented by Brazil and Mercosur produced a bottleneck in the negotiations. In the Ministerial Summit held in Miami in November 2003, countries decided to allow diverse modalities to promote hemispheric integration such as regional or bilateral agreements the focus of which could be less ambitious than the original FTAA proposal. In the Fourth Summit of The Americas held in Mar del Plata, Argentina, the leaders of the Americas failed to reach a consensus on hemisphere integration. The summit resulted in regional division between 29 countries, led by the United States seeking a resumption of talks toward a FTAA, and five countries (Venezuela and Mercosur: Brazil, Argentina, Paraguay and Uruguay) trying to postpone the decision.

The final document reflects two antagonistic positions about FTAA. Twenty Five "remain committed to the achievement of a balanced and comprehensive FTAA Agreement that aims at expanding trade flows ..." These countries resolved to instruct their "officials responsible for trade negotiations to resume their meetings, during 2006, to examine the difficulties in the FTAA process, in order to overcome them and advance the negotiations within the framework adopted in Miami in November 2003". By contrast, countries which opposed the FTAA, argued that "the conditions do not exist to attain a hemispheric free trade accord that is balanced and fair with access to markets that are free of subsidies and distorting practices"[1].

was the Washington Consensus and the Programs of Structural Reforms. The collapse of structural reform in countries such as Argentina and Venezuela and the narrow results in terms of improving the standard of living could be the evidence that the neo-liberal model failed. Then, it is not a surprise that regional integration, based on such a model, would have also failed.

The new left-wing governments in countries such as Argentina, Brazil, Uruguay and Venezuelan have accepted this argument and decided to promote a new model of regional integration. These countries have decided to retake some sort of public intervention in their national economic policy. Consequently, integration policy has also been reoriented and the neo-liberal bias has been reduced. The Brazilian proposal of a South American Community of Nations (SACN) is an example of this. The SACN is part of the Brazilian strategy of South American integration, but instead of concentrating exclusively on trade, it also furthers a wide development program. Brazilian government has tried to oppose a "South American agenda" to a "FTAA-US Agenda". While the latter was centered in the new issues of the international trade (investments, intellectual property, governmental procurement, etc), the Brazilian one also proposes the creation of a regional space by investing in infrastructure, energy, telecommunications and border development[2].

The government of Hugo Chavez is the most radical case in this new trend in Latin America. According to Chavez, Latin-American integration must be relaunched because its current ideological basis (neo-liberalism) is "the way to hell". In consequence, Chavez has promoted radical initiatives of economic and political integration such as the Bolivarian Alternative for the Americas (ALBA). ALBA aims to promote regional political and social integration rather than economic integration. Consequently, it would foster goals such as the formation of zones free of illiteracy, infant malnutrition, homelessness, and environmental destruction. Similarly, Chavez has fostered closer links with Mercosur and Venezuela has become a full member of this integration scheme in December 2005. Chavez has also criticized the Andean Community country decision to negotiate a free-trade agreement with the United States (known as AFTA)[3]. According to the Venezuelan government the AFTA is likely to have devastating affects on the Andean community in the political, economic and institutional spheres.

Latin America has had a long tradition of regional cooperation and integration strengthened in the 1960s through the rise of import-substituting industrialization (ISI) development strategies and the creation of the Latin American Free Trade Association (LAFTA) in South America and the Central American Common Market (CACM).[7] Briefly, ISI strategies focused on promoting infant industries through high levels of external protection, state participation, and investment regulation, with the promise of achieving export-led growth and decreased dependence on industrial countries. Regional integration provided an opportunity to deepen the potential of ISI through an increased market. This allowed the infant industries to grow in size and create production efficiencies until the achieved scale allowed them to compete. Consequently, LAFTA and CACM became the first formal attempts to harmonize trade flows and increase regional integration in Latin America.

However, ISI policies did not establish macroeconomic stability and economic growth; the first attempt at regional integration was unsuccessful due to a complicated political and economic climate. Among many factors, the region had an intrinsic tendency for national protectionism marked by tension between the state and the private sector. Trade negotiations did not provide sufficient incentives to create a rule-based system whereby the benefits accrued from increased exchange would be evenly distributed to member countries. Finally, the development of national and regional infrastructure, coupled with low levels of investment and maintenance as well as poor transport services, limited the potential gains from increased regional cooperation.

Caribbean states had a remarkably different history of economic integration, given the late independence of many of the islands from primarily Anglo-Saxon colonial rule, which stymied the first attempts at economic integration (the West Indies Federation was established in 1958 under British dictate but collapsed with the withdrawal of Jamaica in 1962.)

With independence, the Caribbean Free Trade Association was established in 1968 (modeled on the European Free Trade Association) to promote liberalized trade between its members, although few efforts were made to establish extra-regional trade relations. As a result of this, as well as of the uneven benefits accrued by its member nations, the free trade agreement was dropped in favor of the Caribbean Community (CARICOM), which was established in 1973.

In the 1990s, following what is now commonly referred to as the Debt Crisis and the structural reforms promoting trade and financial liberalization that ensued, Latin America and the Caribbean entered into a period of revived regionalism still present today. The policy framework established during this period set the stage for unilateral measures to reduce traditional barriers to trade while promoting open and competitive economies (see Devlin and Estevadeordal 2001). Furthermore, it encouraged a development strategy based on recognition of the economic and political benefits of increased cooperation and trade by securing reform through institutional and rules-based arrangements.

This cooperation initially led to an increasing number of North-South reciprocal trade agreements, followed by a rethinking of traditional approaches to integration in the region. Since 1960, a total of 37 south-south and 26 north-south bilateral and multilateral trade agreements have been notified to the WTO, and a further 17 are currently under negotiation (WTO 2009a). Simultaneously, average tariffs in the region have declined from over 40 percent in the mid1980s to about 10 percent in 2008.

Importantly, sub-regional initiatives, including MERCOSUR, CAN, and CARICOM, did not limit their agreements to trade but incorporated structural considerations to reform their institutional environment and build longer-term strategic policies to compete in the world trading system. These included agreements in standards, transport, customs cooperation, services, investment, dispute settlement, labor (except for MERCOSUR), and competition, while none included agreements concerning intellectual property rights – a clause included in all North-South trade agreements with Latin America except for the Canada-Chile agreement signed in 1997 (WB 2005). Through these measures, countries sought to enforce internal regulatory measures as well as capture the benefits of increased opportunities for export diversification, foreign direct investment (FDI), greater specialization, product differentiation, and intra-industry trade resulting from increased market access and a clear regulatory framework.

More recently, initiatives aimed at establishing a hemispheric cross-continental market, namely the Free Trade Area of the Americas (FTAA), have met with less success. These highlight the political limitations the region faces in moving forward on a common agenda for deeper integration. Equally important to note are some of the potential costs of increased regional commercial integration, such as trade and investment diversion away from other world markets, conflicts arising from asymmetric development impacts of regional integration, and, perhaps most important, the administrative and institutional strained caused by a web of different trade arrangements.

Only four of the 39 countries in Latin America and the Caribbean are not part of any regional trade agreement, while the average number of regional trade agreements per country is eight

(WTO 2009a). Complex trade agreements can increase trade costs through customs procedures, technical standards, and complex rules of origin that undermine efforts to facilitate trade between countries. A recent study by Estevadeordal and Robertson (2009) finds significant evidence of an increasing tariff effect that is consistent with trade diversion as a result of the proliferation of bilateral agreements in LAC that has coincided with declining enthusiasm for further multilateral liberalization, in this case the FTAA. These findings present a challenge to policy-makers to develop a framework where these costs are minimized and the productivity gains from increased trade and regional cooperation are better redistributed.

Among the most important challenges the region faces for the future of its integration process is the development of regional infrastructure. Given the size, complex geographical limitations, and environmentally sensitive areas of rainforest and valuable biodiversity, the region has consistently lacked quality infrastructure for regional integration. Traditional urban settlement principles that clustered along valleys and "internal regions" have prevented countries from effectively pursuing a more systematic approach to infrastructure development and long-distance land-based transport networks.

As a result of its encroaching development principles and the lack of combined land and territorial planning, the region underperforms in a series of indicators. This reflects a chronic underinvestment in new infrastructure and in maintenance of existing projects, especially in terms of its road network, the efficiency and capacity of ports, and the readiness of the airport infrastructure. In both the Logistic Performance Index (LPI) and the Enabling Trade Index, LAC ranks below the world average in terms of transport and communications infrastructure and related national and international transport shipment services. Furthermore, according to a 2007 ranking of ports, only eight out of 125 ports by total cargo volume were located in LAC while 11 made the ranking in terms of container traffic (Lloyds MIU 2009).

Recent developments in the global economy shed light on international trade trends in LAC and the role that China and India will play in driving the demand for commodities. In 2008, the global economy entered the most severe economic recession in the post-war period. The gross world product contracted by 6.25 percent (annualized) in the fourth quarter of 2008 (representing a remarkable turn of events, given the 4 percent growth a year earlier) and global activity is projected to decline by 1.3 percent in 2009 (IMF 2009b). Even countries with largely diversified export sectors and trading partners are being adversely affected by the contraction. Global production and supply chains are by and large more integrated than in the past, which has been an added shock for productive forces. In addition, given the nature of the present crisis and its roots in financial markets, the availability and affordability of trade finance, which has been substantially reduced, has further weakened prospects of recovery, although coordination from international institutions and financial centers is ongoing and could alleviate the need for long-term financing.

While LAC countries are not as reliant on foreign trade as other regions – exports as a percentage of GDP are 23 percent for the region, 10 percentage points below the world average and far from the 41 percent for the Euro area and 35 percent for East Asia – they have not been exempt from the severity of the global economic recession (WB 2009b). Commodity prices reached record peaks, expected to drop by over 33 percent compared with 2008 and recover only 3 percent in 2010. For Central American and Caribbean countries, which are net commodity importers, the overall effect of declining commodity prices on their terms of trade has been positive, enabling them to maintain healthy balances in their international reserves from the low cost of fuel imports. Their external financial linkages are generally limited, and the impact of the crisis was not as significant as in other areas of the region. Net commodity exporters with inflation-targeting regimes (Brazil, Chile, Colombia, Mexico, and Peru) have been adversely affected by declining commodity prices, causing their terms of trade to shift.

As a consequence of the crisis, the rise in protection measures further threatens recovery of world trade growth to its pre-crisis levels. In 2008, anti-dumping investigations increased by 28 percent from the year before (WTO 2009b). Many countries have adopted policies to maintain production and consumption within their national borders – usually through non-tariff trade barriers, which are easier to disguise and more difficult to sanction, and contingency measures, including increased anti-dumping measures. Although these have proved in most cases to be transitory measures and closely linked to falling economic activity, their widespread use reduces the possibility of negotiating international arrangements and limits the rapidity and depth of substantial recovery in international trade flows. The Doha round of trade talks will be difficult to revive in such an environment.

Developing countries – led by Brazil, Russia, India, and China – are feeling empowered after this most recent crisis to take a leading role in negotiations concerning the international financial architecture and world trading system. Most important, and spearheaded by Chile and Peru in the region, Asia has risen as a new player with growing importance for future trade relations with the region. Trade along the Pacific Rim is growing, with important contributions of the Asia-Pacific Economic Cooperation, which has deepened the process of integrating emerging markets in Asia and LAC. South American commodity exporters see this mostly as a new market, lifting export volumes and world prices, while Mexico and Caribbean countries perceive these linkages as an increased source of competition, especially from China and its ability to attract FDI flows.

The importance of China and India as a destination for LAC exports has increased fourfold since 1990. Trade with China has grown at an annual rate of 40 percent since 2003, the same year that the nation became Brazil's largest trading partner (Economist).[8] Lederman et al. (2007) show that, overall, the growth of China and India in world markets is an opportunity for LAC exporters and importers – accounting for up to 8 percent of LAC exports in 2004, mainly driven by China. Furthermore, the study concluded that there is no robust evidence of substitution between China's trade flows and LAC exports to third markets. As trade relations grow and China continues to play an ever more important role in the world economy, and in LAC in particular (becoming a member of the IDB in 2008), economic cooperation with China will be a source of increased value to trade relations through knowledge-sharing and technology transfers.

TWO MODELS OF REGIONAL INTEGRATION

The traditional economic debate on integration models has divided the doctrine between those who are defenders of a neo-liberal approach and those that support an interventionist model. Certainly, eclectic models have tried to combine interventionist and liberal policies, varying the character of the mixture according to the integration process. Furthermore, a centralized planning model also exists, but this one lacks empiric reference after the collapse of the communist world.

THE LIBERAL MODEL

Liberal model subscribes to the ideas of traditional theory of international trade. Considering integration as a "second best", this approach conceives custom unions like a local experience of liberalization of borders, "justifiable whereas transitory stage in which tariffs and other restrictions to trade would be gradually eliminated"4. Accordingly, regional integration would aim essentially at abolishing barriers and obstacles that prevent the free flow of goods and services between the diverse national economies. Thus, an integrated economic space would be created in which the functioning of laws of the market would allow intensifying the economic interdependence between countries. In this approach, the creation of an economic integrated space and the consequent elimination of all forms of discrimination between factors and products had to be made in a gradual way. This supposed the transit of diverse stages, from a free trade area to a total economic union, previous achievement of a customs union and common market.

For the liberal approach, economic integration has not been always synonymous of welfare. Based on the early Jacob Viner´s5 contribution on the customs unions theory, liberals make a distinction between those integration initiatives in which trade creation is promoted and those in which trade diversion predominates. Trade creation supposes the displacement of high cost producers by others of low cost producers, thus increasing of welfare in the integrated region. Trade diversion implies the substitution of low cost producers by others of high cost producers, a situation in which a loss of regional welfare takes place. As nation states are supposedly rational actors, they would further regional integration schemes in which trade creation prevails.

The analysis of the diverse theories of regional integration makes it difficult to classify the FTAA as an integration model. This is not a modality of interventionist integration, because no device of development planning, industrial programming or mechanism to mitigate the asymmetries resulting from the diverse levels of development have been included. This would allow arguing that the FTAA is based upon a classic liberal approach. Nevertheless, a more careful analysis leads to the conclusion that the FTAA proposal moves away in several aspects from the traditional liberal models. FTAA is

an example of the new regionalism predominant in the post Cold War world economic system. This new regionalism differs from previous proposals developed in the 1960s and 1970s. Though many of the premises of traditional theory of economic integration are useful to explain and understand current wave of regionalism, the analysis of this latter only based on traditional premises of customs unions theory would be a mistake.

The FTAA is based on the North American Free Trade Agreement (NAFTA) model of integration. NAFTA aims to promote the goal of free trade without intending to extend automatically to other stages of integration, such as customs union or common market. This was specifically rejected by the government of the United States due to pressures of diverse social groups, in particular special trade unions, which have rejected free movement of labor. This per se is not the real innovating issue. Other integration schemes such as the European Free Trade Association (EFTA) or the Caribbean Free Trade Area of (CARIFTA) also did not try to surpass free trade. The peculiarity of NAFTA is that the merger of a timid approach led to set up a free trade area with other ambitious economic objectives, such as the regulation of important sectors of the economies of countries' members. This makes NAFTA a scheme that goes beyond of the elimination of the tariff restrictions. FTAA aims to extend this model to the rest of the hemisphere.

THE INTERVENTIONIST MODEL

The interventionist model conceives integration like a process that goes beyond commercial issues. Its objective is the promotion of economic development and, specially, industrialization. Harry Johnson made the first contributions to surpass the narrow liberal view of economic integration. According to Johnson, economic integration could be seen as a means to promote public goods. Johnson argues that customs unions are created to protect "a collective preference in favor of the industrial sector". Economic integration is a mechanism to encourage directed investments to promote new industrial developments, capturing economies of scale and promoting competition in the industrial sector of small and relatively undeveloped economies. In addition, integration would allow the achievement of other economic objectives. By fostering industrialization, it could help countries improve their terms of trade with the rest of the world and improve their bargaining power vis-à-vis others regions.

Another important interventionist approach is represented by structuralism. For André Marchal, the utmost objective of integration is not to fuse markets but economies, through the progressive union of national economic spaces in a new economic and political organization, characterized by solidarity between its members7. Integration could not be based just on market mechanisms but also requires State intervention as director of the process. Furthermore, integration must be promoted among geographically neighboring countries with similar levels of economic development, and governments should further measures to facilitate production in scale, allow in diversification of production which in turn will promote technical progress.

Structuralism does not conceive national economies like a homogenous, harmonic and balance space, but like complex, heterogeneous and structured one. This view is very different from the liberal theory based on the idea of equilibrium and its automatic reestablishment. For that reason, states must lead a socially balanced and harmonious process through public policies. As Vacchino8 asserts, such policies can use markets and its automatism, but, also and mainly, they must promote deliberate actions and institutions. Integration must make compatible market oriented policies with States led policies and the institutions.

There have been different examples of this model in the experiences of integration in Western Europe and Latin America. In this latter region the influence of the model of integration proposed by the Economic Commission for Latin American (ECLAC) in 1960s and 1970s was important, and centered on the promotion of industrialization at regional scale. Integration was conceived like a mechanism to foster programs of industrial development that some countries had begun to develop in previous decades and that were in danger to be continued in their phase of production of capital goods, due to the narrowness of national markets. The continuation of industrialization in the regional scope, would allow creating factories with a suitable size to take advantage of the reduction in the medium costs generated by the achievement of economies of scale, thus increasing efficiency and avoiding that existed installed capacity was under-utilized. Similarly, integration would allow financing industrial join ventures that required enormous investments in capital and technologies that did not exist in most of the countries of the region.

This strategy would require a strong participation of states in the promotion of new industries and tariff protection vis-à-vis third countries. In the ECLAC´s proposal, industrial goods produced in the first stage of economic integration, must be included in a free trade regime, thus creating a regional market in which the new productions would learn to be competitive, before being exposed to extra-regional competition9.

ECLAC'S approach to open regionalism can also be conceived like an interventionist model. A tendency exists to confuse open regionalism with opening of markets in structural adjustment programs. Nevertheless, ECLAC´s version of open regionalism goes beyond commercial liberalization. This modality of regional integration was included in the Latin American debate about the issue when the old ECLAC's ideas on industrialization and regional import substitution lost relevance in the political and academic circles of the region. The Latin American version of open regionalism was delineated by ECLAC in the document "Open Regionalism in Latin American in the Caribbean: Economic Integration as Contribution to Changing Production Pattern with Social Equity" (1994). In the document is asserted that integration policies in Latin America have been dual in the last few years. On the one hand, diverse intergovernmental commercial agreements leading to create free trade areas or, in some cases, customs unions have been promoted. Other integration initiatives include objectives such as regulation of investments, intellectual property, abolition of non-tariffs barriers, and coordination of economic policies. ECLAC describes this dynamic as integration furthered by policies10.

These integration agreements are in line with a parallel process of "de facto'" integration fostered by macroeconomic and trade policies, the effect of which is the creation of similar economic conditions in the majority of Latin American countries. This has furthered regional interdependence what has been reflected in factors such as a share tendency towards the consolidation of a coherent and stable macroeconomic framework, unilateral tariff reduction, non-discriminatory promotion of exports, elimination and deregulation of obstacles to foreign investments and privatization of public firms.

ECLAC defines open regionalism as a process that results from reconciling "the interdependence that stems from preferential agreements and the interdependence which basically arises from the market signals that are produced by trade liberalization in general. What open regionalism seeks to accomplish is to make explicit integration policies compatible with, and complementary with the promotion of international competitiveness"11. In other words, by furthering open regionalism, Latin American countries would be aiming at making compatible formal integration policies with those policies leading to foster a better insertion of Latin American countries in the world economy. Thus, "open regionalism may be understood as a non-multilateral way to move towards an open international system of commerce"

In ECLAC´s ideas, regional integration could collaborate in this process of productive transformation, incorporation and diffusion of technologies available in the world. The widening of markets and increasing links between firms, sectors and institutions at subregional scale, allow the development of joint ventures helping to achieve gradually comparative advantages in sectors in which technological development and learning are facilitated by regional action. Similarly, regional integration would contribute to transform the old imports substituting industries in exporting industries to use regional market as previous phase before their penetration to global competition. Furthermore, integration can be useful in the promotion of the technological innovation. Similar tastes of population and geographic proximity would allow using regional markets like a space in which to promote technological innovations in new products at less cost and with lower degree of uncertainty than in extra-regional markets. Integration can improve the joint bargaining power of the region and help improve infrastructure and facilitation of trade, elements helping productive transformation14.

European integration can also be described like interventionist, although in a different way from that in Latin America. The objective of the European Economic Community, currently European Union, was never industrialization, a goal long time ago achieved in the old continent. Nevertheless, the European integration has promoted some policies such as protection to consumers, financial support to the less favored regions of countries members and mainly the common agricultural policy, that have implied a strong State intervention. The ideas of Thomas Biersteker on the role of the State in economy allow validating the argument on the interventionist bias of the integration model in Europe. According to Biersteker15, at least six modalities of state interventionism in the economy can be found:

The first modality tries to influence in a positive way the behavior of the private sector through fiscal policy or monetary policy.

The second regulates the behavior of deprived economic actors or organize their economic activity through policies leading to protect the environment, social security programs or labor legislation.

A third modality of intervention attempts to transform the State into mediator between capital and labor.

The fourth modality is the redistribution of social product by means of subventions or industrial policy.

The fifth is the direct production of goods and services.

The last modality of intervention of the State is in economic planning.

Accepting Biersteker's ideas, one can observe several types of interventionist policies in the European integration. The communitarian legislation to protect environment and the consumer protection policy are clearly modalities of regulating interventionism. The common agricultural policy and the regional policy are forms of redistributing interventionism. The project of construction of Airbus is an example of interventionism whose objective is the production of a particular good. Consequently, it is valid to describe to the experience of integration in Western Europe like interventionist.

Based on a categorization made by Di Filippo and Franco16, one can argue that two different conceptions about regional integration exist in the Americas. Some agreements aim at liberalizing the flow of trade and investments in the continent. These are the "Type A" agreements. By contrast, another sort of agreement is designed to promote policies beyond the liberalization of markets. Such agreements are known as "Type B". This classification can be useful to understand current integration schemes in the Americas. However, both Types A and B must be studied not only in terms of the economic model they pursue, otherwise, it would make no sense as a theoretical tool, because it would not be different from that presented in the previous section (models of integration). To understand this issue, the political and social level of these agreements must also be analyzed

In economic terms, the Type A is the empirical reference to the liberal model. The economic aspects are centred on the liberalisation of trade and factors of production as proposed by the liberal model. However, this type of agreement does not cover aspects such as coordination of macroeconomic policies, common currency, tax policy or regional policy. Notwithstanding this, type A includes the so-called trade-related issues, such as intellectual property or public procurement.

16 Armando Di Filippo and Rolando Franco "¿Qué modelo de integración regional puede contribuir a un desarrollo con equidad?", Socialis, Revista Latinoamericana de Política Social, Buenos Aires, no. 3, noviembre (2000): 45-62.

At the political level, these agreements are classic examples of intergovernmentalism. There is not a pooling of sovereignty and, consequently, security and defence issues remain at the sphere of nation-states. This intergovernmentalist approach led to a weak institutional framework, in which supranationality has been totally excluded. For this reason, the creation of a regional identity is a difficult goal to achieve.

Finally, the social dimension in this sort of agreement is just limited to the signing of labour treaties, the main objective of which is to make compulsory the execution of domestic law on the issue. These compromises aim at making compatible social cooperation with liberalisation of markets. This would imply a convergence towards a minimum social platform on social and political rights, but without any sort of compulsory legislation.

The Type B is the empirical reference of the interventionist economic model. The Type B agreements propose not only the liberalisation of trade, although free trade is important objective to be achieved. Instead these agreements foster the establishment of mechanisms leading to integrate labour and capital markets. The objective of these measures is to move toward a common market in which free movement of labour and capital would exist. Moreover, this type of agreement entails the co-ordination and harmonisation of policies such as fiscal revenues or taxes. The utmost objective is the unification of some of these policies. By the same token, these sort of agreements further a regional policy leading to aid to less developed regions thus promoting economic and social cohesion.

At the political level, a Type B agreement accepts mechanisms to pool sovereignty and, consequently, the security and defence issues could be included in a common framework, at least as long-term objective. This approach led to a relatively strong institutional framework, in which supranationality could be accepted. This could contribute to creation of a regional identity.

At the social level, co-ordination, harmonisation and unification of social policies become a possibility in these agreements. As a result, aspects such as employment policies and rights, work organization, health, hygiene and safety at work, social protection, equality between women and men, social protection, etc., are covered by the integration process.

The collapse of the strategy of industrialisation, the debt crisis in the 1980s and the most severe economic recession of the region for decades, supposedly demonstrated that interventionist model was misleading. In consequence, this latter was actually excluded from most of the national economic strategies of Latin American and Caribbean countries and it was substituted by neo-liberal ideas inspired in the structural adjustment programmes recommended by the International Monetary Fund (IMF) and the World Bank.

As a result, integration strategies in Latin America and the Caribbean have been modified and adapted to this new predominant liberal approach. This is essentially centred on the promotion of free trade, excluding any sort of policy leading to promote regional industrial development, as the old Latin American and Caribbean integration proposals in the 1960s and 1970s suggested. For neo-liberalism integration must always be subordinated to multilateral liberalisation of trade and must be oriented to foster trade creation and not trade diversion. This would validate the classical theory that considers that trade creation has positive effects on welfare, whilst trade diversion reduce welfare. Those arguments that emphasised the need for trade diversion in customs unions and those that promoted regional localisation of industries between developing countries were discarded. Integration schemes in Latin America became part of a global strategy to promote the liberalisation, without exception or reserves, of goods and services, the elimination of restrictions to foreign investments, the rejection of policies leading to promote industrialisation and the exclusion of preferential and compensatory measures to assist less developed countries or regions.

Therefore, the liberal model was quite popular in the 1990s in the region. Nonetheless, this enthusiasm with this model was severely affected by the "Real" Crisis in Brazil (1998) and particularly by the Argentina's Default in 2001. Similarly, although structural reform helps achieving a better macroeconomic environment in some countries of the region, its contribution to the solution of problems such as the regional competitiveness, the financial instability or inequity was fairly poor. Finally, since the end of last decade and, at least partially, as a result of the social effects of structural reform, new leaders have come to power in various countries with a political discourse and an economic strategy opposed, or at least critical, to the liberal model. This is case of Hugo Chavez in Venezuela, Luiz Ignácio Lula da Silva in Brazil, Néstor Kirchner in Argentina, Tabaré Vasquez in Uruguay, and more recently, Evo Morales in Bolivia. Despite the differences among them, a common denominator exists: free trade is not enough. Consequently, the liberal model that was the ideological base of the new Latin American integration is currently in crisis in many countries of the region. Obviously, such a situation has had an impact on the political support to a FTAA type of regional integration model.

IMPORTANT LESSONS

Among Latin America's integration models, MERCOSUR is a representative integration model owing to its economic size as its position behind NAFTA and EU in the world. MERCOSUR has accomplished important economic achievements until now: It created the single largest market in Latin America in which goods, services and people move relatively freely. It has contributed to social cooperation among member states in areas such as legislation, education, culture, out of political rationales. There has been, also, a development for policy coordination system in MERCOSUR. However, not only there is no adoption of a single currency which has been suggested strongly by Argentina, but also there is no particular convergence of understanding of the needs to coordinate macro-economic policies. Argentina has a very active position on this point, including the adoption of a single currency.

After several failed attempts of economic integration in Latin America such as the Latin American Free Trade Association (1960), the Latin American Common Market (1965) and the Latin American Integration Association (1979)—MERCOSUR was established in 1991.

The MERCOSUR has the objectives to create a common market following the European model, through customs union. However, its actual stage is imperfect customs union. In fact, it needs more time to countries can create regional integration system in its initial stage with their political will. However, after the creation of a regional trade bloc, the political will should pave way to institutions so that this can work for economic integration. Political will of countries for intervention is necessary to resolve any problems that need member states' mutual understanding. Minimum intervention of political will of member states is the key factor for further development of a regional trade bloc.

After the creation of an economic bloc, joint policies among member states are necessary for its functioning. The trade bloc cannot depend upon mutual understanding of states for the realization of common objectives. Common institutions in MERCOSUR are necessary. However, Brazil as the leading country was reluctant to create centralized institutions which would have resulted in increased interdependence among member-states.

As MERCOSUR has the purpose to become a common market in Latin America similar to the EU in Europe, institutionalization for functional purposes is necessary. This institutional integration is a way to guarantee authority over national governments and which will transform them into supranational institutions.

MERCOSUR was created as a strategic response to the U.S. hegemony in the Western Hemisphere when the U.S pronounced the creation of the NAFTA in 1993. In this sense, MERCOSUR was a tool to attain political objectives. To respond to globalization process in South America, both Argentina and Brazil needed to resolve their historically long rivalry at any cost. The creation of a mega bloc in North America gave strong motivation to both countries to initiate a dialogue. MERCOSUR was created with this political background to dissolve the continental security problem. In fact, after the formation of the MERCOSUR, democracy and peace were strengthened in the region.

However, behind this political implication, each member country had its own motivations. Argentina, Paraguay and Uruguay had strong expectations for economic gains through MERCOSUR than Brazil. These countries had been consistently clamoring for expanding the MERCOSUR, while Brazil has showed its strong political interests.

While the economic motive was prevalent in Argentina, Uruguay and Paraguay, there were still important dissimilarities in their perception of MERCOSUR. Argentina was the most oriented by its economic interests in the formation of MERCOSUR. Paraguay had a strong motivation for being guaranteed democracy through MERCOSUR against persistent anti-democratic pressures after over three decades of authoritarian ruling by General Alfredo Stroessner (1954-89). MERCOSUR provided protection to Paraguay for its recovery of democracy from the Stroessner dictatorship. Uruguay joined MERCOSUR to avoid the potential economic loss, since Argentina and Brazil were Uruguay's largest trade partners. With these different motives of member states of MERCOSUR, I can be certain that MERCOSUR was not established from its own initiative but from the outside pressure with the governments' political initiatives and not by economic needs. The Treaty of Asuncion in 1991 shows the purpose of MERCOSUR to establish a common market (Article 1) with following integration items: This common market shall involve: The free movement of goods, services and factors of production between countries through, inter alia, the elimination of customs duties and non-tariff restrictions on the movement of goods, and any other equivalent measures; The establishment of a common external tariff and the adoption of a common trade policy in relation to third States or groups of States, and the coordination of positions in regional and international economic and commercial forums; The coordination of macroeconomic and sectoral policies between the States Parties in the areas of foreign trade, agriculture, industry, fiscal and monetary matters, foreign exchange and capital, services, customs, transport and communications and any other areas that may be agreed upon, in order to ensure proper competition between the States Parties; The commitment by States Parties to harmonize their legislation in the relevant areas in order to strengthen the integration process.

Accordingly, MERCOSUR seeks to establish the coordination of economic and sectoral policies of member nations. In fact, MERCOSUR became the second largest trading bloc in the world behind EU in terms of deepening integration process.

The volume of intra-regional trade in MERCOSUR had increased until the beginning of 2000. Since then, the portion of intra-regional trade has become stagnant which has cast the doubt on the economic contribution of regional integration. In fact, MERCOSUR has faced several trade crises provoked by the uncoordinated macroeconomic policies among member states. These countries have common characteristics of agricultural-specialized countries in the world market. However, in inter-trade market, Brazil has more industrialized economic profile, making it more flexible in both markets. These different economic profiles practically resulted in very different political goals between Argentina and Brazil about the development plan of MERCOSUR. Argentina wants to open MERCOSUR to other countries as it needs more trade partners in Latin America owing to its heavy dependency on South American markets. This idea of expanding membership is shared with Paraguay and Uruguay. Brazil has different ideas: Even though, it agrees with the expanding membership, it wants to limit the membership to South America and deepen MERCOSUR among member states. However, at the same time, Brazil does not want to accelerate the creation of supranational institutions in MERCOSUR making the harmonization of macroeconomic policies among member states difficult. It is a very contradictory position taken by Brazil in MERCOSUR and a dilemma that practically Brazil should resolve alone.

The lack of institutional integration which has brought about lack of macroeconomic policies among nations has resulted in real economy, in prioritizing the national policies over MERCOSUR's common interests.

This tendency to place the national goals and sovereignty over MERCOSUR objectives is explicitly exemplified in one of MERCOSUR's major underlying problems: its lack of macroeconomic and exchange rate policy coordination (institutional integration), which is also directly measured through the exchange rate variability in the region—one of the nominal variables representing the extent of economic integration between members of a regional bloc.

In order for MERCOSUR to be successful as both a customs union and a common market, it must synchronize the macroeconomic policies of member nations, particularly those of Brazil and Argentina. Macroeconomic coordination between Brazil and Argentina is essential for MERCOSUR's success as Latin America's southern cone market. This is especially significant since Uruguay and Paraguay will implement monetary policies in line with these two countries to sustain positive trade relations with them.

The negative effects of the lack of coordination in macroeconomic policy in MERCOSUR were demonstrated in two important crises: Brazil's currency devaluation in 1999 and Argentina's subsequent recession and devaluation in 2001-2002.

These two events were considered most critical crises that threatened MERCOSUR's very existence since its creation in 1991. These events taught member countries how important the coordination of macroeconomic policies and synchronization of exchange rate policies among member states are for sustaining regional integration.

In January of 1999, the Brazilian government had terminated its policy of periodic small devaluation of the Real due to the accelerated loss of foreign reserves, resulting from capital outflows and trade deficits. The government made a drastic devaluation of 40% against the U.S. Dollar. This devaluation had several important negative effects on MERCOSUR. First of all, it triggered an economic recession in MERCOSUR, accompanied by the reduction in the intra-regional trade volume. As Argentinean export products were less competitive on the Brazilian market because of the Real's devaluation, the Argentinean government had suffered under strong pressure to implement protectionist measures to restrict the importation from Brazil. For example, the Menem administration decided to erect various barriers to import certain types of Brazilian steel, applying a minimum FOB export price of US$41,000 per ton on imports of Brazilian cold steel or iron laminates. In April 1999, Argentina banned Brazilian beef from entering the country and imposed prior licensing for imports of paper. The measures aimed to appease local producers who feared an influx of Brazilian products. After the change of the Brazilian exchange rate regime, Argentinean producers had lost competitiveness in the domestic market to imported products from Brazil. At the same time, Argentina had difficulty in exporting its products to Brazilian market, because of its high export prices.

The Brazilian government began engaging in similar protectionist measures, such as the requirement of prior licenses for foodstuffs, boarder sanitary controls and an import licensing system for industrial products. As Argentina depended heavily on Brazilian market for over 30% of exports, these counter-measures brought about serious impact on Argentina. This 'tit-for-tat' measures by both governments cast doubt on the sustainability of MERCOSUR.

As the economic situation improved slightly in Brazil and a new government came into power in Argentina, the two governments agreed to begin dialogue, which was the so-called 'relaunch' of MERCOSUR. In mid-2000, Fernando Henrique Cardoso and Fernando de la Rua signed an agreement to complete MERCOSUR as a customs union. The relaunch agenda included plans for a 'Little Maastricht' agreement on macroeconomic convergence plan and was perceived as the end of the serious crisis since MERCOSUR was created in March 1991.

However, as the economic situation in Argentina during 2001 was deteriorating, the relaunch program did not create the positive effects as anticipated. In March 2001 the Argentinean government decided to breach the CET, provoking a new crisis in MERCOSUR. The Minister of Economy in Argentina, Domingo Cavallo announced the 'competitiveness program' as part of an economic recovery package, raising the tariff on imports of consumer goods from outside MERCOSUR, and eliminating tariffs on imports of capital goods from outside the bloc. Both measures violated MERCOSUR agreements. The Brazilian government responded moderately in consideration of the Argentina's problems. However, Brazil refused to accept the zero reduction of import tariffs of IT and telecommunications goods as capital goods. In early April 2001, Argentina agreed to remove these goods from the list of products with a zero import rate, and Brazil formally accepted a temporary suspension of the CET. In July 2001, however, the Argentinean government violated the agreement signed in April again. Brazil now responded more strongly, suspending all bilateral negotiations and threatening to interrupt purchases of Argentinean wheat and petroleum. Bilateral tension was exacerbated by Cavallo's frequent criticism of the on-going depreciation of the Brazilian currency, as well as by his calls for MERCOSUR to be downgraded to a free trade area.

The evident worsening of the Argentinean crisis convinced the Brazilian government that if MERCOSUR was to be maintained, and more importantly, if a joint position was to be presented in the coming FTAA and WTO negotiations, it had no option but to grant Argentina the flexibility it was demanding. Following a further deal signed by the four MERCOSUR members allowing Argentina to maintain its exceptions to the CET until December 31, 2002, Brazil agreed to the introduction of the safeguards regime which Argentina had been demanding since the Brazilian devaluation of 1999. The latter would allow Argentinean sectors to obtain protection from competitive imbalances between the two countries.

Like the 2000 relaunch agenda, this new agreement was significantly vague in its scope and contents and would soon be made irrelevant by the collapse of the Argentinean economy at the end of 2001. However at the time it was signed, it constituted a joint attempt by the Argentinean and Brazilian Presidents, meeting in October 2001, to re-insert some political dynamism into the project of integration, and to dismiss growing rumors of its impending collapse. However, the economic pressures of the overvalued peso were so high that in December 2001 Argentina's currency board collapsed and the peso was devalued in January 2002.

Presidential diplomacy has played a significant and decisive role in MERCOSUR's creation and survival in the face of various critical crises. However, it was the political will of Presidents to postpone the MERCOSUR's progress to become a common market, turning it into institutional integration. In this sense, presidential diplomacy is consistently highlighted throughout MERCOSUR's most historically critical moments. MERCOSUR originated from the political will of national governments, and only thereafter generated public demand for further integration. As a result, MERCOSUR presidents have acquired the popular legitimacy and determination to intervene in MERCOSUR issues in order to promote regional integration. By delegating such power and influence on MERCOSUR to the national presidents, it is obvious that MERCOSUR presidents are sovereign as policy-crafters and decisionmakers—presiding over both MERCOSUR as an institution itself and any other regional institutions that might be created to support MERCOSUR and further integration in the region. Consequently, presidential intervention in MERCOSUR has been considered as more effective resolving mechanism on serious disputes among member states.

Presidential diplomacy reflects the will of member states not to lose national sovereignty and autonomy to MERCOSUR. They are reluctant to build community institutions that can decide and manage common policies. In particular, Brazil is against the creation of supranational institutions in MERCOSUR that can easily promote institutional integration. Even though MERCOSUR has the vision to become a common market, the founding states have no idea how to concede part of their sovereignty to MERCOSUR. This lack of common strategy on the development of institutional integration without giving up sovereignty shows lack of clear and common vision as to why MERCOSUR needs to exist. And MERCOSUR's strong reliance on presidential diplomacy to resolve any economic problem by political means, shows that the member states have more political interests than economic interests from MERCOSUR's existence.

If the member states have more economic interests than political ones, MERCOSUR should have ceased to exist during the serious crisis 1999-2001 which was mentioned above. The determination of Argentina and Brazil to maintain MERCOSUR could be explained by this political aspect. These countries frequently ignore community rules and show their willingness to postpone the attainment of objectives of MERCOSUR as a common market. As this political consideration is measured heavily, the presidential diplomacy can be accepted as *de facto* most efficient dispute settlement mechanism. As such, Argentina and Brazil could overcome their disputes without the creation of supranational institutions in MERCOSUR. Part of the reason why there exists this unwillingness to create supranational institutions that would coordinate macroeconomic policies and synchronize currency evaluation, can be the strong desire of governments not to compromise MERCOSUR. It means that they do not have confidence in MERCOSUR as a reliable organization. Consequently, MERCOSUR became a very strange integration model – searching for deep integration of common market without being a supranational institution and with strong presidential diplomacy.

In this sense, the lack of supranational institutions is one of the main reasons why MERCOSUR cannot coordinate macroeconomic policies. Without these institutions, the convergence and coordination of economic policies and national laws for the formation of common economic policies and legal order will be extremely difficult to attain. Unless MERCOSUR takes the necessary measures to reduce the role of presidential diplomacy, implement supranational institutions and coordinate macroeconomic policies among its member states, it will be practically impossible to accomplish the desired economic integration.

The experience of MERCOSUR shows us that at least three elements are important conditions for regional integration: clear objective, leadership of at least one leading country and creation of solid institutions that guarantee the shift from political will to legal community. Let us see what we have in East Asia under these criteria.

LATIN AMERICA ECONOMIC INTEGRATION - IMPORTANT DEVELOPMENTS

Regional trade agreements are playing important role for Latin American countries. The emphasis in regional agreements as a policy tool has changed quite significantly over time, with a recent boom from the mid-1980s to mid-1990s, but at present this has been challenged by a number of features of the international scenario.

Preferential trade agreements became very important in the region in recent years. Until 1991 trade preference agreements accounted for some 8% of total regional exports. By 2005 there were 68 agreements, being 51 of intra-regional preferences and 17 with countries in other regions, and affected about two-thirds of the region's total exports (ECLAC (2006)).

There are several very important sub regional initiatives that push forward the integration process in the Americas.

COMMUNITY OF LATIN AMERICAN AND CARIBBEAN STATES (CELAC)

Official languages	• Spanish • Portuguese • French • English • Dutch
Demonym	• Latin American • Caribbean
Membership	33 member states
Leaders	
• President pro tempore	Salvador Sánchez Cerén
Establishment	February 23, 2010

Area	
• Total	20,454,918 km² (7,897,688 sq mi)
Population	
• 2011 estimate	591,038,580
• Density	29/km² (75.1/sq mi)
GDP (PPP)	2014 estimate
• Total	$9.144 trillion
• Per capita	$15,175
Gini	49.6 high
HDI (2011)	▲ 0.721 high
Internet TLD	.lat

The **Community of Latin American and Caribbean States** (Spanish: *Comunidad de Estados Latinoamericanos y Caribeños, CELAC*; is a regional bloc of Latin American and Caribbean states thought out on February 23, 2010, at the Rio Group–Caribbean Community *Unity Summit*, and created on December 3, 2011, in Caracas, Venezuela, with the signature of The Declaration of Caracas. It consists of 33 sovereign countries in the Americas representing roughly 600 million people. Due to the focus of the organization on Latin American and Caribbean countries, other countries and territories in the Americas, Canada and the United States, as well as the overseas territories in the Americas of France (Overseas departments and territories of France), the Netherlands (Dutch Caribbean), Denmark (Greenland) and the United Kingdom (British Overseas Territories) are not included.

LAIA - LATIN AMERICAN INTEGRATION ASSOCIATION

Association created in August, 1980. It replaced the former LAFTA (Latin American Free Trade Association), created in 1960.

It is formed by Argentina, Bolivia, Brazil, Chile, Colombia, Cuba, Ecuador, Mexico, Paraguay, Peru, Uruguay and Venezuela. Its objectives are to create a Latin American common market in the long run and in a gradual manner, by means of tariff preferences, as well as the signing of regional agreements.

There are at present 10 preferential trade agreements in South America within LAIA comprising 45 bilateral relations and 90 tariff chronograms (Veiga/Rios (2007)). In 2006 LAIA created the Free Trade Space, aiming at facilitating market access, the adoption of common norms and disciplines, and provide support to less developed member-countries.

MERCOSUR

Association formed by Argentina, Brazil, Paraguay and Uruguay, by the Treaty of Asunción, signed in March, 1991. Associate members are Bolivia, Chile, Colombia, Ecuador and Peru. Venezuela signed a membership agreement in June, 2006, but before becoming a full member its entry has to be ratified by the national parliaments of the four original members.

Its objectives are to create a common market with free movement of goods, services and productive factors; adopt a common external policy; coordinate common positions in international forums; coordinate sector and macroeconomic policies.

Its Common External Tariff (CET) covers some 85% of intra-regional trade. Great exceptions remain the sugar and automobile sectors. The CET is effective and equal to national tariffs for 35% of total trade by Mercosur countries. From those, products stemming for 20 percentage points have zero tariffs. That is, only 15% of Mercosur adopt CET (Veiga/Rios (2007)). A number of non-tariff barriers remain in regional trade.

As from December, 2008 Brazil has announced its decision to eliminate the double charging of trade tariffs, in order to reduce costs (even at a loss of tariff revenue for some members, such as Paraguay, which depends on this item for almost 20% of its fiscal revenue). Brazil has also announced its intention to reduce the nationalized component of imports from Paraguay and Uruguay, a political decision still to be translated into technical procedures.

Mercosur has opted for remaining an inter-governmental exercise, instead of creating a supranational structure, as in the European Union and in other integration exercises in the region. This has, of course, costs and benefits. Among the former, the low degree of implementation of the common rules in Mercosur is often related to the lack of supranational entities that might impose higher degree of discipline. The benefits of the inter-governmental model, on the other hand, stem from its relative flexibility: in several critical situations this lack of institutional rigidity has allowed for changes in the negotiating process.

Mercosur has signed some 17 agreements, most of them in the 2004-2006 period. Not all of these agreements comprise trade preferences. Some are only 'base-agreements' with generic objectives and common purposes. But the total number of agreements mirrors the 'global trader' perspective adopted by Mercosur since its early days.

ANDEAN COMMUNITY OF NATIONS (ANCOM)

Association formed in May, 1969, by Bolivia, Colombia, Ecuador and Peru. Until 1996, it was known as the Andean Pact. Originally both Chile and Venezuela were member countries. The former left the Community in 1974 and the latter in 2006.

Associate members are Argentina, Brazil, Chile, Paraguay and Uruguay. Observer members are Mexico and Panama.

Its objectives are to promote the harmonic development of the member-countries in equal conditions, through integration and economic and social cooperation; to gradually form a Latin American common market; to foster sub-regional solidarity and reduce external vulnerability.

In the second semester of 2006 Venezuela decided to leave the Andean Community, based on the argument that the negotiations of Colombia and Peru with the United States would affect the essence of the Community.

The Andean Community differs from Mercosur in that there are no exceptions among the products affected by preferences, it has common norms with regard to trade mechanisms such as anti-dumping and safeguards policies and it adopts common norms also for trade in services, investment, intellectual property and competition. It has also a rather complex institutional structure.

Chile has accepted the invitation to (re)join the Andean Community as an associate member. The purpose is to form a free trade zone on the Latin American Pacific coast.

The Andean Community has negotiated trade agreements with the European Union and – in the case of Colombia and Peru – with the US, but this remains to be approved by the US Congress.

Negotiations between Mercosur and the Andean Community were completed in 2004; they are essentially bilateral trade concessions.

BOLIVARIAN ALTERNATIVE TO LATIN AMERICA AND THE CARIBBEAN (KNOWN BY ITS SPANISH ACRONYM ALBA) / PEOPLE'S TRADE AGREEMENT

The Bolivarian Alternative is an initiative led by Venezuela and Cuba, as an alternative to the FTAA negotiations. In December 2004 these two countries signed a bilateral agreement. In April 2006 Bolivia joined in the People's Trade Agreement, and in January 2007 Nicaragua joined in.

Observer members are: Antigua & Barbuda, Dominica, Ecuador, Haiti, Honduras, St Kitt & Nevis, St Vincent & Grenadines and Uruguay.

The People's Trade Agreement comprises trade facilities and complementarities in the energy sector. In January 2008 the ALBA Bank was created, adding a new dimension to the initiative.

THE SOUTH-AMERICAN UNION OF NATIONS (UNASUR)

Mercosur and the Andean Community signed in 2004 a free trade agreement which, together with Chile, Guyana and Suriname will lead to the formation of a South-American Union of Nations. It was originally (until 2007) called South-American Community of Nations (CASA in its acronym in both Spanish and Portuguese). Its members are Argentina, Bolivia, Brazil, Chile, Colombia, Ecuador, Guyana, Suriname, Paraguay, Peru, Uruguay and Venezuela.

The goal is to gradually form a free trade area in South America, as well as to provide economic complementarities among countries in the region. UNASUR represented a new model of regionalism, not focused predominantly on trade issues. Its agenda comprises other issues, such as energy integration and infrastructure, as well as social and cultural themes. Together with LAIA, these are the two exercises that comprise all South American countries.

THE G-3

The group was formed in June, 1994 and entered operation in January, 1995. Its members are Colombia, Mexico and Venezuela.

Its objectives are to eliminate trade barriers for goods and services, to promote fair competition, foster investment opportunities, protect intellectual property and foster cooperation among members.

CENTRAL AMERICAN COMMON MARKET (CACM)

Association formed in December, 1960 by El Salvador, Guatemala, Honduras and Nicaragua. Costa Rica joined the group in 1963. Its objective is to create a common market among member countries.

CACM became a free trade zone since 2001, although with the exception of some agricultural products. Efforts are being made for a common policy on investment and trade in services, trade concessions, norms for government procurement, investment, property rights, labour and environmental issues, among others.

The Common External Tariff covers 95% of the tariff lines, with an average rate of 6%. As similar to the Andean Community, CACM has a rather diversified institutional structure. Another difference with regard to Mercosur is that the members of CACM can negotiate trade agreements on an individual basis with countries from other regions.

CACM has had an intense negotiating activity in 2002-6. The CAFTA-RD (agreement with the US) was signed by all countries but Costa Rica in 2006, and submitted to a popular referendum (being approved) in this latter country in 2007. Given the importance of trade with the US (and the risk of trade diversion) one major issue raised by these agreements is to what extent the relations on a new basis with the US will affect regional integration efforts.

The rhythm of regional integration in Central America has been affected by the low output growth of the member countries, their recurrent trade deficits (compensated by remittances) and by the strong competition with Asian products both in local markets and in their main export market, the US.

LATIN AMERICAN INTEGRATION ASSOCIATION

The **Asociación Latinoamericana de Integración** (the **Latin American Integration Association**; known as **ALADI** or, occasionally, by the English acronym **LAIA**) is a Latin American trade integration association, based in Montevideo. Its main objective is the establishment of a common market, in pursuit of the economic and social development of the region. Signed on August 12, 1980, the Montevideo Treaty is an international legal framework that establishes and governs the Latin American Integration Association. It sets the following general guidelines regarding trade relations between signatory countries: pluralism, convergence, flexibility, differential treatment and multiplicity.

The **Latin American Free Trade Association** (LAFTA) was created in the 1960 Treaty of Montevideo by Argentina,Brazil, Chile, Mexico, Paraguay, Peru, andUruguay. The signatories hoped to create a common market in Latin America and offered tariff rebates among member nations. LAFTA came into effect on January 2, 1962. When the trade association began, it had seven members and its main goal was to eliminate all duties and restrictions on the majority of their trade within 12 years. By the late 1960s, the area of LAFTA had a population of 220 million and produced about $90 billion of goods and services annually. It also had an average per capita gross national product of $440.

The goal of the LAFTA is the creation of a free trade zone in Latin America. It should foster mutual regional trade among the member states, as well as with the US andCanada, the Pacific Union, the African Union, and the European Union. To achieve these goals, several institutions are foreseen:

- the council of foreign ministers
- a conference of all participating countries
- a permanent council

The LAFTA agreement had important limitations: it only refers to goods, not to services, and it does not include a coordination of policies. Compared to the European Union, the political and economic integration was very limited.

By 1970, LAFTA expanded to include four more Latin American nations: Bolivia,Colombia, Ecuador, and Venezuela. It now consisted of 11 nations. In 1980, LAFTA reorganized into the Latin American Integration Association (ALADI). LAFTA brought many new positive changes to Latin America. With LAFTA in place existing productive capacity could be used more fully to supply regional needs, industries could reduce costs as a result of potential economies through expanded output and regional specialization, and attraction to new investment occurred as a result of the regional market area.

Although LAFTA has brought many constructive results, like other FTAs, it has also brought problems to individual nations and to Latin America as a whole. Some of the problems which individual countries face are the way they are grouped together by their economic strengths according to LAFTA. The grouping was originally Argentina, Brazil, and Chile in one group, Colombia, Chile, Peru, Uruguay, and Venezuela in the second group, and the last group which included Bolivia, Ecuador, and Paraguay. There is a problem in this classification because it ignores the great economic and other differences between the countries. Problems which Latin America faced as a whole had to do with many of the nations in the continent being underdeveloped. The Free Trade Agreement was seen as a way of the countries having greater economic interactions among each other and thus improving the economic state of the poorer nations.

Any Latin-American country can join the 1980 Montevideo Treaty. Cuba was the last to accede, becoming a full member on August 26, 1999. In addition, ALADI is also open to all Latin American countries through agreements with other countries and integration areas of the continent, as well as to other developing countries or their respective integration areas outside Latin America. ALADI is now the largest Latin-American group of integration. It is responsible for regulations on foreign trade which includes regulations on technical measures, sanitary regulations, environment protection measures, quality control measures, automatic licensing measures, price control measures, monopolistic measures, as well as other measures. These regulations are put into place in order for trade to be even handed amongst members of ALADI.

The ALADI promotes the creation of an area of economic preferences in the region, aiming at a Latin American common market, through three mechanisms:

- Regional tariff preference granted to products originating in the member countries, based on the tariffs in force for third countries
- Regional scope agreement, among member countries
- Partial scope agreements, between two or more countries of the area

Either regional or partial scope agreements may cover tariff relief and trade promotion; economic complementation; agricultural trade; financial, fiscal, customs and health cooperation; environmental conservation; scientific and technological cooperation; tourism promotion; technical standards and many other fields. As the Montevideo Treaty is a "framework treaty", by subscribing to it, the governments of the member countries authorize their representatives to legislate through agreements on the economic issues of greatest importance to each country.

A system of preferences — which consists of market opening lists, special cooperation programs (business rounds, preinvestment, financing, technological support) and countervailing measures on behalf of the landlocked countries — has been granted to the countries deemed to be less developed (Bolivia, Ecuador and Paraguay), to favour their full participation in the integration process. As the institutional and normative "umbrella" of regional integration that shelters these agreements as well as the subregional ones (Andean Community, MERCOSUR, G-3 Free Trade Agreement,Bolivarian Alternative for the Americas, etc.) the Association aims to support every effort to create a common economic area.

LATIN AMERICAN ECONOMIC SYSTEM

The **Latin American and the Caribbean Economic System**, officially known as **Sistema Económico Latinoamericano y del Caribe (SELA)**, is an organization founded in 1975 to promote economic cooperation and social development betweenLatin American and the Caribbean countries. In the early 1990s, its representatives consisted of members from 28 countries and took part in the General Agreement on Tariffs and Trade (GATT) negotiations, which led to a new global agreement on restrictions on trade and established the World Trade Organization (WTO).

This area includes activities for evaluation, promotion and diversification of economic relations between Latin America and the Caribbean as a whole, with other world regions, countries and their groupings, and consultation and coordination with economic negotiations and international trade interest to Member States. In that sense, the work contains, among others:

- Ongoing monitoring and design of an agreed position of the region to economic negotiations, financial, monetary and trade being carried out in the relevant multilateral organizations.

- Monitoring developments and systematic analysis of the impact of external debt and international financial flows on the economies of Member States, and the impact they have on the development and integration of the technology gap and technology transfer.

- Analysis and development of policy proposals to advance relations between Latin America and the Caribbean as a whole, and other nations in particular.

Intra-regional Relations

Latin America and the Caribbean as a whole, is composed of subregions that are interrelated through mechanisms of integration and cooperation that generate economic and trade interdependencies in turn contribute progressively to a process of continental integration contributing to social welfare and poverty reduction. SELA's actions to support this process include:

- Activities aimed at contributing to complementarity, convergence and coordination of subregional integration processes, with special assistance to countries with smaller economies and relatively less developed.

- Monitoring and evaluating the impact of specific decisions taken by Heads of State and Government of Latin America and the Caribbean have on the process of regional integration and cooperation.

- Activities aimed at promoting development and sustainable growth with social inclusion of the economies of the region, through exchange of experiences and information on public policy and social economic development and promote cooperation and integration in special efforts to consolidate a regional financial architecture, based on the integration of Latin America and the Caribbean.

- Analysis and discussion of new forms of regional integration and cooperation have emerged recently in the region, its potential for complementarity and its impact on the regional integration process.

- Analysis, organization and processing of policy proposals for strengthening economic and trade relations between the countries of the region, including mechanisms for trade facilitation and promotion of competition, among others.

- Maintenance and updating of databases: Trade flows between countries of the region, and between these subregions, public policies on poverty in the region and the Summit of Heads of State and Government of the region within a portal that provides updates on major events in the process of economic, social and integration of the countries of the region.

Economic and Technical Cooperation

SELA is the focal point of economic and technical cooperation between countries of the region and hosts the annual "Meeting of International Cooperation Directors of Latin America and the Caribbean", which allows it to act as a forum for regional consultation and coordination among Member States in this field. Its main activities in this area are:

- Identification of areas of cooperation through mutual agreement among Member States, with a sense of complementarity between the projects conceived and evaluation of tenders and requests for technical cooperation among countries in the region.

- Provision of technical assistance to countries with smaller economies and less developed.

- Exchange of experiences and information on national policies, particularly the most successful, for the benefit of Member States and as benchmarks for the development of horizontal cooperation.

- International cooperation for development instititucional of Small and Medium Enterprises (SMEs) in the region.

The Latin American Council represents SELA's policy-making body and meets once a year. The main administrative body is the secretariat, located in Caracas, Venezuela.

International relations scholar Sheldon Liss, in*Diplomacy and Dependency: Venezuela, the United States, and the Americas* (1978) described the initial objectives of SELA:

> SELA, composed of twenty-five member states, and to which Venezuela contributes the largest share (17 per cent) of the budget, hopes to: restructure international commerce in basic commodities in order to raise developing states' export values, improve trade conditions, stimulate industrial development, control foreign-based transnational corporations, create Latin American multinational companies which will use to better advantage the human, technological, and financial resources of the area, sponsor organizations to process and market raw materials, improve the negotiating power of the member states, and plan joint economic strategies.
>
> SELA members deem it likely that Venezuelan oil wealth will permit them easy access to petrodollars for use as finance capital. (pp 271, 2.)

PUBLIC POLICIES ON POVERTY IN LATIN AMERICA AND THE CARIBBEAN

The Permanent Secretariat of SELA, through its network of Information and Knowledge Center and Digital Information and Knowledge Development Association (CDA-SELA) has made available its Member States and the general public, the database of Policies Public (Programs, Projects and Services) and combat-oriented poverty reduction in Latin America and the Caribbean.

Through this database is intended to systematize the information on public policies aimed at poverty reduction identified in the 28 Member States of SELA and include policies identified in the other countries in the region. The aforementioned is based on systematic content analysis of documentary material in the public domain located in the official Web sites and other informational materials available on the Web.

The main purpose of this database is to provide information regarding policies, strategies, programs and projects aimed at reducing poverty in the region. More specifically, with this tool: i) provides, in particular, public managers active in the fight against poverty in the region, information on policies, strategies, programs and projects implemented in Latin America and the Caribbean; ii) to release and share experiences that can be replicated in several national contexts in the region, and iii) in particular, serve as a reference source, without attempting to replace the official source of information which is sent to you via the address of the (s) page (s) or Web / document (s) e (s) in question (s).

Initially, information was systematized by using the conceptual categories contained in the typology of anti-poverty social policies, published in the "Summary of social programs to overcome poverty in Latin America. Economic Commission for Latin America and the Caribbean (ECLAC). Statistical studies and prospective series, No. 20 (2003) ". Subsequently, the categories and lines of action referred to in the above type have been updated and enriched from key documents published in the region on the matter. Below are listed the categories and the respective lines of action are currently being used in the database.

ORGANIZATION OF AMERICAN STATES

The **Organization of American States(OAS**, or, as it is known in the three other official languages, **OEA**) is a regional international organization, headquartered in Washington, D.C.,United States. Its members are the 35 independent states of the Americas.

In the words of Article 1 of the Charter, the goal of the member nations in creating the OAS was "to achieve an order of peace and justice, to promote their solidarity, to strengthen their collaboration, and to defend their sovereignty, their territorial integrity, and their independence." Article 2 then defines eight essential purposes:

- To strengthen the peace and security of the continent.
- To promote and consolidate representative democracy, with due respect for the principle of nonintervention.
- To prevent possible causes of difficulties and to ensure the pacific settlement of disputes that may arise among the member states.
- To provide for common action on the part of those states in the event of aggression.
- To seek the solution of political, judicial, and economic problems that may arise among them
- To promote, by cooperative action, their economic, social, and cultural development.
- To eradicate extreme poverty, which constitutes an obstacle to the full democratic development of the peoples of the continent.

- To achieve an effective limitation of conventional weapons that will make it possible to devote the largest amount of resources to the economic and social development of the member states.
- Over the course of the 1990s, with the end of the Cold War, the return to democracy inLatin America, and the thrust toward globalization, the OAS made major efforts to reinvent itself to fit the new context. Its stated priorities now include the following:
- Strengthening democracy: Between 1962 and 2002, the Organization sent multinational observation missions to oversee free and fair elections in the member states on more than 100 occasions. The OAS also works to strengthen national and local government and electoral agencies, to promote democratic practices and values, and to help countries detect and defuse official corruption.
- Working for peace: Special OAS missions have supported peace processes inNicaragua, Suriname, Haiti, and Guatemala. The Organization has played a leading part in the removal of landmines deployed in member states and it has led negotiations to resolve the continent's remaining border disputes (Guatemala/Belize;Peru/Ecuador). Work is also underway on the construction of a common inter-American counter-terrorism front.
- Defending human rights: The agencies of the inter-American human rights system provide a venue for the denunciation and resolution of human rights violations in individual cases. They also monitor and report on the general human rights situation in the member states.
- Fostering free trade: The OAS is one of the three agencies currently engaged in drafting a treaty aiming to establish a continental free trade area from Alaska to Tierra del Fuego.
- Fighting the drugs trade: The Inter-American Drug Abuse Control Commission was established in 1986 to coordinate efforts and crossborder cooperation in this area.
- Promoting sustainable development: The goal of the OAS's Inter-American Council for Integral Development is to promote economic development and combating poverty. OAS technical cooperation programs address such areas as river basin management, the conservation of biodiversity, preservation of cultural diversity, planning for global climate change, sustainable tourism, and natural disaster mitigation.

ORGANIZATIONAL STRUCTURE

The Organization of American States is composed of a Organization of American States General Secretariat, the Permanent Council, the Inter-American Council for Integral Development, and a number of committees.

The General Secretariat of the Organization of American States consists of sixsecretariats.

- Secretariat for Political Affairs
- Executive Secretariat for Integral Development
- Secretariat for Multidimensional Security
- Secretariat for Administration and Finance
- Secretariat for Legal Affairs

- Secretariat for External Relations
- The various committees of the Organization of American States include:
- The Committee on Juridical and Political Affairs
- The Committee on Administrative and Budgetary Affairs
- The Committee on Hemispheric Security
- The Committee on Inter-American Summits Management and Civil Society Participation in OAS Activities

COMMUNITY OF LATIN AMERICAN AND CARIBBEAN STATES (CELAC)

The **Community of Latin American and Caribbean States** (Spanish: *Comunidad de Estados Latinoamericanos y Caribeños, CELAC*, Portuguese:*Comunidade de Estados Latino-Americanos e Caribenhos*, French:*Communauté des États Latino-Américains et Caribéens*) is the name of a regional bloc of Latin American and Caribbeannations created on February 23, 2010, at the Rio Group–Caribbean Community*Unity Summit* held in Playa del Carmen,Quintana Roo, Mexico. It consists 33 sovereign countries in the Americas, and totals roughly 600 million people. Absent of the bloc are: Canada, France, theNetherlands, the United States, British andDanish dependencies in the Americas.

CELAC is an example of a decade-long push for deeper integration within the Americas. CELAC is being created to deepen Latin American integration and to reduce the once overwhelming influence of the United States on the politics and economics of Latin America, and is seen as an alternative to the Organization of American States (OAS), the regional body organised largely by Washington in 1948, ostensibly as a countermeasure to potential Soviet influence in the region.

CELAC is the successor of the Rio Groupand the *Latin American and Caribbean Summit on Integration and Development*(CALC). In July 2010, CELAC selectedPresident of Venezuela Hugo Chávez andPresident of Chile Sebastián Piñera, as co-chairs of the forum to draft statutes for the organization

MEMBER STATES

CELAC comprises 33 countries speaking five different languages:

Eighteen Spanish-speaking countries (56% of the area, 63% of the population)

Argentina	Dominican Republic	Nicaragua
Bolivia	Ecuador	Panama
Chile	El Salvador	Paraguay
Colombia	Guatemala	Peru
Costa Rica	Honduras	Uruguay
Cuba	Mexico	Venezuela

One Portuguese-speaking country (42% of the area, 34% of the population)

- Brazil

One French-speaking country (0.1% of the area, 1.6% of the population)

- Haiti

Twelve English-speaking countries (1.3% of the area, 1.1% of the population)

Antigua and Barbuda	Guyana
Bahamas	 Jamaica
Barbados	Saint Lucia
Belize	Saint Kitts and Nevis
Dominica	Saint Vincent and the Grenadines
Grenada	Trinidad and Tobago

One Dutch-speaking country (0.8% of the area, 0.1% of the population)

- Suriname

Twelve countries are in South America, which accounts for 87% of the area and 68% of the population.

On February 23, 2010, Latin American leaders at the 23rd Rio Group summit in Playa del Carmen, Quintana Roo, Mexico, said they were forming an organisation of the Latin American and Caribbean states. Once its charter was developed, the group was formally established in July 2011, at a summit in Caracas. The bloc will be the main forum for political dialogue for the area, without the United States or Canada.

In an interview in February 2010, President Evo Morales of Bolivia said, "A union of Latin American countries is the weapon against imperialism. It is necessary to create a regional body that excludes the United States and Canada. ...Where there are U.S. military bases that do not respect democracy, where there is a political empire with his blackmailers, with its constraints, there is no development for that country, and especially there is no social peace and, therefore, it is the best time for prime ministers of Latin America and the Caribbean to gestate this great new organization without the United States to free our peoples in Latin America and the Caribbean."

At the 23rd Rio Group summit, President Hugo Chávez of Venezuela said, "Now here, in Mexico, a document, a commitment, the creation of a body of Latin America and the Caribbean, without the USA, without Canada (...) Now we can say from Latin America, from Mexico (...) we have revived the dream and project of Bolívar." Mexican President Felipe Calderón added, "We decided, for the first time, to form the Community of Latin American and Caribbean States as a regional space consisting of all states."Calderon said, "We cannot remain disunited; we cannot successfully take on the future based on our differences; now it's up to us to unite without discounting the things that make us different ... to unite based on our similarities, which far outweigh our differences." Brazilian President Luiz Inácio Lula da Silva said it is "A historic fact of great significance."

President Rafael Correa of Ecuador said that the Community of Latin American and Caribbean States "can be much more effective than other instances to solve ourselves, with our own strengths, our own visions, our conflicts."

The announcement prompted debate and discussion across Latin America and the Caribbean about whether it's more beneficial to have close ties with U.S. and Canada or to work independently.

Raúl Zibechi, writing for Mexico's centre-left *La Jornada* newspaper said, "The creation of the Community of Latin American and Caribbean States is part of a global and continental shift, characterised by the decline of U.S. hegemony and the rise of a group of regional blocs that form part of the new global balance."

An editorial in Brazil's conservative *Estadao* newspaper said, "CELAC reflects the disorientation of the region's governments in relation to its problematic environment and its lack of foreign policy direction, locked as it is into the illusion that snubbing the United States will do for Latin American integration what 200 years of history failed to do."

CELAC's inaugural summit was due to be held in mid-2011, but was postponed because of the ill-health of Hugo Chavez, president of the host nation, Venezuela. The summit was instead held on 2 and 3 December 2011 in Caracas. It primarily focused on the global economic crisis and its effects on the region. Several leaders, including presidents Cristina Fernandez, Dilma Rousseff and Juan Manuel Santos, encouraged an increase in regional trade, economic development, and further economic cooperation among members in order to defend their growing economies.

Chavez, and other leaders such as Rafael Correa and Daniel Ortega, expressed hope that the bloc would work to further Latin American integration, end U.S. hegemony and consolidate control over regional affairs.

Chavez, citing the Monroe Doctrine as the original confirmation of U.S. interference in the region, openly called for CELAC to replace the OAS: "As the years go by, CELAC is going to leave behind the old and worn-out OAS." Correa called for a new human rights commission to replace theInter-American Commission on Human Rights. Other leaders argued that the organisation should be used as a tool to resolve regional disagreements and uphold democratic values, but not as a replacement of the OAS. Santos stated that he would like to see dialogue within the group over whether existing counter-drug regulations should be revised. The president of the Latin American Parliament(Parlatino) said he expects that Parlatino will become the main legislative institution of CELAC. Amongst the key issues on the agenda were the creation of a "new financial architecture," sanction for maintaining the legal status of coca in Bolivia and the rejection of the Cuban embargo by the U.S.

INDICATORS

Country	Area (km²)	Population 2010	GDP (PPP) (Intl. $) 2010	GDP (PPP) per capita (Intl. $) 2010	DI 2011	Income inequality 1993-2009 (latest available)
Antigua and Barbuda	440	88,000	1,843,968,171	20,954	N/A	N/A

Country	Area (km²)	Population 2010	GDP (PPP) (Intl. $) 2010	GDP (PPP) per capita (Intl. $) 2010	DI 2011	Income inequality 1993-2009 (latest available)
Argentina	2,780,400	40,412,000	647,063,721,324	16,012	6.84	44.5
Bahamas, The	13,880	343,000	10,888,721,245	31,746	N/A	N/A
Barbados	430	274,000	5,297,753,009	19,423	N/A	N/A
Belize	22,970	345,000	2,301,088,112	6,670	N/A	53.1
Bolivia	1,098,580	9,929,000	48,148,878,092	4,849	5.84	56.3
Brazil	8,514,880	194,946,000	2,185,420,845,946	11,210	7.12	54.7
Chile	756,090	17,113,688	270,041,323,664	15,779	7.54	52.1
Colombia	1,141,750	46,295,000	437,617,194,004	9,453	6.63	55.9
Costa Rica	51,100	4,659,000	53,898,146,703	11,569	8.10	50.7
Cuba	109,890	11,258,000	N/A	N/A	3.52	N/A
Dominica	750	68,000	834,075,050	12,266	N/A	N/A
Dominican Republic	48,670	9,927,000	92,818,322,619	9,350	6.20	47.2
Ecuador	256,370	14,465,000	116,118,648,441	8,028	5.64	49.3
El Salvador	21,040	6,193,000	41,293,984,350	6,668	6.47	48.3
Grenada	340	104,000	1,098,711,751	10,565	N/A	N/A
Guatemala	108,890	14,389,000	68,850,068,676	4,785	5.86	55.9
Guyana	214,970	755,000	2,590,945,640	3,432	6.05	44.5
Haiti	27,750	9,993,000	11,099,543,831	1,111	4.00	59.2
Honduras	112,490	7,600,000	29,814,254,443	3,923	5.84	57.0

Country	Area (km²)	Population 2010	GDP (PPP) (Intl. $) 2010	GDP (PPP) per capita (Intl. $) 2010	DI 2011	Income inequality 1993-2009 (latest available)
Jamaica	10,990	2,702,000	20,733,561,970	7,673	7.13	45.5
Mexico	1,964,380	113,423,000	1,651,879,443,740	14,564	6.93	48.3
Nicaragua	130,370	5,789,000	16,864,971,066	2,913	5.53	40.5
Panama	75,420	3,517,000	47,858,729,220	13,608	7.08	51.9
Paraguay	406,750	6,454,000	33,440,004,694	5,181	6.40	52.4
Peru	1,285,220	29,076,000	277,318,296,283	9,538	6.59	48.1
Saint Kitts and Nevis	260	52,000	872,843,179	16,785	N/A	N/A
Saint Lucia	620	174,000	1,885,828,125	10,838	N/A	42.6
Saint Vincent and the Grenadines	390	109,000	1,207,357,443	11,077	N/A	N/A
Suriname	163,820	525,000	3,984,075,762	7,664	6.65	52.9
Trinidad and Tobago	5,130	1,341,000	34,515,498,575	25,739	7.16	40.3
Uruguay	176,220	3,357,000	47,360,806,596	14,108	8.17	45.3
Venezuela	912,050	28,834,000	352,720,687,228	12,233	5.07	44.8
CELACa	20,413,300	573,251,688	6,517,682,298,953	11,370	6.35	49.6

[a] CELAC total used for indicators 1 through 3; CELAC weighted average used for indicator 4; CELAC unweighted average used for indicators 5 through 12.

Note: The colors indicate the country's global position in the respective indicator. For example, a green cell indicates that the country is ranked in the upper 25% of the list (including all countries with available data).

POLITICAL DECLARATION OF PUNTA CANA - V CELAC SUMMIT

Punta Cana, Dominican Republic January 25th, 2017

We, the Heads of State and Government of the Community of Latin American and Caribbean States (CELAC), gathered on the occasion of the Fifth Summit of the CELAC, held in Punta Cana, Dominican Republic, on January 25th, of the present year (2017);

Determined to continue advancing in unity and diversity and in Latin American and Caribbean integration, for the benefit of our region and for the wellbeing of our peoples; we reaffirm the validity of the historical heritage of the Community, comprised of the Rio Group and the Latin American and Caribbean Summit on Integration and Development (CALC), as well as the Political Declarations, Special Declarations, Communiqués and Plans of Action adopted by the previous CELAC Summits, including the Caracas Foundational Summit, the Unity Summit of Latin America and the Caribbean and the convergence process that gave way to CELAC.

Aware that the CELAC is the mechanism for agreement, unity and political dialogue in all of Latin America and the Caribbean, we ratify this space as one for the promotion of the common interests of our peoples.

Reiterating that dialogue and political agreement on the basis of reciprocal trust between our governments and respect for our differences are indispensable for further advancement towards political, economic, social and cultural integration of the Community, based on equilibrium between the convergence and the diversity of our countries; in formulating our own solutions to promote and maintain peace, inclusive and sustainable development of our peoples in order to achieve complete eradication of hunger and poverty, and promotion of the regional agenda in global forums and cooperation with other States, Regions and International Organizations, as defined among the objectives of CELAC at the Unity Summit of Latin America and the Caribbean, held at the Riviera Maya in February 2010.

Reiterating the unrestricted respect for and full adhesion to the Purposes and Principles of the Charter of the United Nations and International Law, in particular the respect to sovereignty, territorial integrity, and non-interference in internal affairs of the states,

dialogue among nations, peaceful settlement of disputes, and prohibition of the threat or use of force. We consider as a priority the strengthening of the multilateralism.

Committed to achieving sustainable development in its three dimensions -economic, social and environmental, in a balanced and integrated way, as agreed in the 2030 Agenda for Sustainable Development, with proposals for regional and global challenges, seeking common solutions for the benefit of our peoples, leaving no one behind, for which it is essential to have adequate financial resources.

Recognizing the importance of promoting and implementing public policies aimed at creating strategies for growth according to the characteristics of each country, in a balanced, inclusive, sustainable, innovative and secure manner.

Reaffirming that the historical process of consolidation, preservation and the full exercise of democracy in our region is irreversible, does not admit interruptions or retreats and will continue to be marked by respect for the essential values of democracy; access to power and its exercise in accordance with the rule of law; and respect for the constitutional faculties of the various State powers and constructive dialogue between them; the holding of free, transparent, informed and sustained elections in universal and secret suffrage as an expression of the people's sovereignty, citizen participation, social justice and equality, the fight against corruption, as well as respect for all public freedoms recognized in international instruments.

Committed to the promotion, protection and respect of all Human Rights, without any discrimination, as a fundamental basis for sustaining the democratic life of our nations. We underline the importance of implementing measures aimed at promoting and protecting the rights of vulnerable people, including indigenous and Afro-descendant peoples, migrants, persons with disabilities and women. At the same time, we will promote gender equality, decent work and will work to eradicate child labor in our region as part of actions aimed at prioritizing the rights of children and adolescents as subjects of law.

We convene the following:

INTERNATIONAL PEACE AND SECURITY

1. We reaffirm our commitment to the consolidation of Latin America and the Caribbean as a Zone of Peace, formally proclaimed during the II Summit of

CELAC, held in Havana, in January, 2014, and as a reference for interstate relations, and that contributes to the environment of mutual respect and confidence building among CELAC member States. Likewise, we emphasize the call for all States to respect the assertions of the Proclamation in their relations with Latin America and the Caribbean, aimed at the settlement of disputes by peaceful means and the recognition of the right of States to have their own political, economic, social and cultural system as an indispensable basis for promoting peace and harmony in the region.

2. We support the process of national dialogue in the Bolivarian Republic of Venezuela between the Government and the opposition, with the accompaniment of the Secretary General of UNASUR, Ernesto Samper, ex-presidents José Luis Rodríguez Zapatero, Leonel Fernández, Martín Torrijos, and the special representative of his Holiness Pope Francis. We urge the Parties to work towards achieving concrete results, as well as to comply, without delay, with the agreements reached so far, guarantee continuity of the process and resume the talks in good faith and with a constructive commitment and with full adhesion to the rule of Law, human rights and democratic institutionality, especially the separation of power within the framework of the constitution and the legislation of the Bolivarian Republic of Venezuela and under the principle of respect for non intervention in the internal affairs of States.

3. We highlight the character of a zone free of nuclear weapons in our region, established in the pioneering Tlatelolco Treaty, whose 50th anniversary will be celebrated in February 14th, in Mexico, within the framework of the 25th Session of the General Conference of the Agency for the Prohibition of Nuclear Weapons in Latin America and the Caribbean (OPANAL).

4. We reaffirm the urgent need to move towards the main objective of general and complete disarmament, under strict international control, and achieving a total prohibition and elimination of nuclear weapons. In that regard, we reiterate our intention to join in and actively participate in the negotiation that will begin in 2017 within the framework of the United Nations of a legally binding universal instrument that prohibits nuclear weapons in a transparent, irreversible and verifiable manner within a temporary framework agreed upon at the multilateral level and that leads to their total elimination.

5. We reiterate our deep rejection to acts of terrorism in all its forms and manifestations, including its funding, whatever motives may drive it, wherever and whomever has

committed them, as well as our concern for violent extremism, which may lead to terrorism.

6. Highlight the importance of Information and Communication Technologies (ICT), including the Internet, as tools to foster peace, human well being, development, knowledge, social inclusion and economic growth. We reaffirm the peaceful use of ICT, and urge the international community to avoid and refrain from carrying out unilateral measures which are incompatible with the purposes and principles of the United Nations Charter, the Universal Declaration of Human Rights and International Law, such as those with the objective of subverting societies or creating situations with the potential of fostering conflicts among states. At the same time, we stress, in regard to the use of ICT the need to not infringe on the individuals right to privacy.

7. We make a call to reach a fair, stable and lasting solution to the conflict between Israel and Palestine, in accordance with the relevant resolutions of the United Nations.

COERCIVE MEASURES

8. We reiterate our rejection to the application of unilateral coercive measures contrary to international law, including the lists and certifications that affect the countries in Latin America and the Caribbean.

9. We reiterate that the contents of paragraph 13 of the Political Declaration approved in Quito, 2016, as well as from the Special Communiqué of the 3rd CELAC Summit (Belen, 2015) and the Special Communiqué of March 26th, 2015, on unilateral actions against the Bolivarian Republic of Venezuela, and we believe the Executive Order of the United States of America, originally approved on March 9th, 2015 should be rescinded.

10. We welcome the progress in the relations between the Governments of Cuba and the United States of America and, in that context, the visit by the President of the United States of America to Cuba in March 2016. We reaffirm our call to the United

States government to unconditionally put an end to the economic, commercial and financial blockade it has imposed on the sister nation for more than five decades and is still in force. We urge the President of the United States, to use his broad executive powers to substantially change the application of the blockade.

NAVAL BASE OF THE UNITED STATES OF AMERICA IN GUANTANAMO

11. We believe that the return to the Republic of Cuba of the territory that the United States Naval Base occupies at Guantanamo, as it has been repeatedly claimed by the Cuban people and government, should be a relevant element of the process of normalization of relations between both countries, through a bilateral dialogue that adheres to International Law.

TRANSPARENCY AND THE FIGHT AGAINST CORRUPTION

12. We reiterate our commitment to strengthening mechanisms that allow us to prevent, detect, sanction and combat corruption, to improve efficiency and transparency in public administration, to promote accountability at all levels, as well as citizen participation in the oversight of public affairs and access to information, in accordance with national legislations and international conventions signed by States.

CITIZEN SECURITY AND THE FIGHT AGAINST TRANSNATIONAL ORGANIZED CRIME

13. We recognize the importance of strengthening cooperation, both between States and with societies in reducing and preventing crime related violence, as well as in combating transnational organized crime and its various manifestations for the benefit of development.

14. In that sense, we reaffirm our commitment to promote police and judicial cooperation, and to strengthen inter-agency cooperation mechanisms in the field of internal security, including digital security matters, in accordance with the adopted international obligations and the legal system of each country.

FOOD SECURITY, NUTRITION AND ERADICATION OF HUNGER

15. We reiterate our commitment to the implementation of the CELAC Plan for Food and Nutrition Security and the Eradication of Hunger 2025 (SAN-CELAC), in accordance with the Special Declaration on Food Security, Nutrition and Eradication of Hunger. We will continue to undertake efforts to obtain concrete results that allow significant improvements in the quality of life of our peoples.

FINANCING FOR DEVELOPMENT

16. In accordance with the Special Declaration on "Financing for Development", we advocate to continue working towards obtaining a proper environment for sustainable development and for overcoming challenges that financing for development presents. In this regard, we reiterate our call for developed countries to comply with the commitment to allocate 0.7% of their Gross National Product for Official Development Assistance (ODA), while reaffirming the agreed upon commitments as part of the Monterrey Consensus (2002), the Doha Declaration (2008) and the Addis Ababa Action Plan (2015). Likewise, we commit to continue promoting the use of criteria that utilize multidimentional indicators for the accurate measurement of the complex and diverse realities of development of the region.

TAX COOPERATION

17. Recognizing the need of fostering international tax cooperation, strengthening regulatory frameworks, promoting the interests of developing countries in international fora and supporting inter-governmental initiatives to contest tax evasion and avoidance, corruption and money laundering, which undertaking certain practices, create incentives for the illicit transfer of assets that cause negative effects on global economy, particularly for developing countries.

SUSTAINABLE URBAN DEVELOPMENT

18. We welcome the New Urban Agenda approved at the United Nations Conference on Housing and Sustainable Urban Development (Habitat III) that was held in Quito from the 13th to the 20th of October of 2016, and we commit to support its follow-up and review process. In this regard, we reaffirm our commitment to

sustainable urban development and, with the common ideal of a city for all, shared in the New Urban Agenda, in terms of equality in the use and enjoyment of cities and human settlements, seeking to promote integration and ensure that all inhabitants, both present and future generations, without discrimination of any kind, can create and live in just, safe, healthy, accessible, affordable, resilient and sustainable cities and settlements, in order to promote prosperity and quality of life for all. We highlight the efforts of some national and local governments to enshrine this ideal, known as "the right to the city", in their laws, political declarations and charters.

GENDER EQUALITY

19. We affirm our commitment to promote gender equity and equality, as well as the advancement of women, as necessary conditions to achieve full exercise and enjoyment of fundamental freedoms, as well as human rights in order to achieve the goals and targets for Sustainable Development of the 2030 Agenda, implementing actions for its incorporation as central and cross-cutting axes of the policies, strategies and actions of the States.

20. We commit to eradicate all forms of violence against women, adolescents and girls, to promote their political and economic empowerment by eliminating all social barriers, approving and strengthening public policies and laws on gender equality to promote gender equality, to ensure full access to education and justice, as well as economic and financial autonomy, and political participation and representation, in accordance with the Special Declaration on the Promotion of Gender Equality and Equity and Eradication of Violence against Women.

EDUCATION

21. We reaffirm our commitment to the implementation of public policies that aim to ensure at all levels the universal and free coverage of an inclusive, tenured and quality education, with a gender and intercultural perspective, without discrimination, that respects the creative skills and ancestral knowledge and the respect to the knowledge of other cultures, so that everyone develops capacities of critical thinking, logical, creative and innovative reasoning.

22. We will promote the active participation of families and communities in the different stages of the educational process, as well as the establishment of strategic alliances between the institutions of education systems, which strengthen academic mobility within the region and the mutual recognition of diplomas, while respecting national realities and legislations.

YOUTH

23. We acknowledge that young people constitute a significant segment of our populations, we commit to providing increased opportunities and equipping them with the necessary skills and knowledge to achieve their desired goals and to facilitate their full participation in decision-making processes in the sustainable development of our societies.

PROMOTION OF INFORMATION AND COMMUNICATION TECHNOLOGIES FOR HUMAN DEVELOPMENT

24. We recognize that Information and Communication Technologies (ICT), including the Internet, are important tools for promoting peace, human well-being, development, knowledge, social inclusion, growth and economic development within the framework of the Knowledge Society through the massive use of ICTs. Therefore, we highlight the

need to conceive and carry out policies and strategies in order to close the digital divide between different countries and regions, while preserving the multicultural and diversity manifestations of the region.

25. We promote the universalization of inclusive access to Information and Communication Technologies (ICTs), as important tools to democratize the access to knowledge to strengthen education processes through the development of diverse knowledge, abilities, dexterities and values; likewise, we will encourage the promotion of research and innovation, promoting the development of the personal, professional capacities and potentialities of the population.

DISASTER RISK MANAGEMENT

26. Aware of our region's vulnerability to climate change and natural and man-made disasters of natural and anthropic origin, including the Small Island Developing

States, and Low Lying Coastal States, countries of the Central American isthmus, and those who suffer the effects of El Niño and La Niña and Landlocked Developing States of the region, we recognize the importance of strengthening the implementation of the Sendai Framework for Disaster Risk Reduction 2015-2030 and the fulfillment of all its goals in the region. This will contribute to the prevention and substantial management of the risk of disasters and the losses caused by them, in lives, means of subsistence, and health, as well as economic, physical, social, cultural and environmental assets of individuals, enterprises, communities and countries.

27. We highlight the need to establish common strategies to strengthen coordination on disaster risk reduction, humanitarian assistance and rehabilitation, building on the mandates of Sendai and the guiding principles of International Humanitarian Assistance adopted by resolution 46/182 of the United Nations General Assembly. In this regard, we emphasize the need for convergence between the multiple coordination spaces in the region and the need for them to be part of the regional and global strategies for disaster risk reduction agreed in the Sendai Framework for Disaster Risk Reduction 2015-2030.

27. BIS. We underscore the need and importance of contributing to the success of the 5th Regional Platform for Disaster Risk Reduction in the Americas, to be held in Montreal, Canada, on March 2017, as well as the 5th Global Platform Session for Reducing the Disaster Risk, to be held in Cancun, Mexico, from 22 to 27 May 2017.

CLIMATE CHANGE, ENVIRONMENT AND BIODIVERSITY

28. We call for the attainment of the highest political commitment to combat climate change as an urgent priority. In this sense, we welcome the entry into force of the Paris Agreement, applicable to the signatory States and Parties, under the United Nations Framework Convention on Climate Change, on the 4th of November, 2016. We invite all signatory countries that have not submitted their respective instruments of ratification and/or adhesion, to do so as soon as possible.

29. We recognize the importance of strengthening mitigation and adaptation actions, in accordance with the United Nations Framework Convention on Climate Change

and the Paris Agreement, which includes best practices of local communities and indigenous peoples, to face the adverse effects of climate change, in accordance with the principle of common yet differentiated responsibilities and respective capabilities. Likewise, we reaffirm the importance of the means of implementation for developing countries to carry out their climate actions. Taking into consideration that our countries are located in a region highly vulnerable to the impact of climate change, we call on developed countries to fulfill their commitments on the matters of financing, with new and additional resources, technology and capacity building, including the full implementation of the Green Climate Fund of 100 billion dollars annually for developing countries from 2020 onwards.

30. We will continue to promote regional measures to encourage the protection of ecosystems, reduce deforestation and degradation, the conservation and sustainable use of biodiversity and species of wild flora and fauna threatened by international trade. We commend the recent progress in promoting synergy among the biodiversity conventions, including the possibility of promoting this objective through public policies and National Plans, in particular the National Biodiversity Strategies and their action plans within the framework of the Strategic Plan for Biological Diversity 2011-2020 and the Aichi Targets.

CHEMICAL SUBSTANCES AND WASTE

31. We continue to work towards the environmentally sound management of chemicals and of all wastes, throughout their life cycle, as well as to promote technical capacities, exchange of experiences, transfer of technology and resource mobilization to ensure synergies in existing processes and initiatives within the countries of the region.

WORLD DRUG PROBLEM

32. We reaffirm that the world drug problem is a common and shared responsibility that should be addressed in accordance with the 1961 Single Convention on Narcotic Drugs as amended by the 1972 Protocol, the 1971 Convention on Psychotropic Substances, the 1988 United Nations Convention against Illicit Trafficking in Narcotic Drugs and Psychotropic Substances, which constitute the

cornerstone of the international drug control system and other relevant international instruments, in a multilateral environment and a more intense and effective international cooperation; it demands an integrated, multidisciplinary, balanced, sustainable and broad approach, respectful of human rights, and based on scientific evidence, with measures that are mutually reinforced. We commend the celebration of the 30th Special Session of the United Nations General Assembly, dedicated to the World Drug Problem, held in April 2016, in New York, and we take note of the results of said Meeting, and we underline our joint commitment to effectively address and counter the World Drug Problem.

DEVELOPMENT OF INNOVATION, SCIENCE AND TECHNOLOGY

33. We recognize that Science, Technology and Innovation are cross-cutting themes in national and regional development plans and that their momentum allows us to build knowledge societies that increase the productive, sustainable and competitive capacities of our countries.

34. We underline the importance for our States to promote collaboration with a view to creating and producing technologies as tools for fostering entrepreneurship, innovation and scientific and economic development, aimed at identifying and finding competitive solutions to local, national and regional problems.

35. We emphasize that the means of implementation contained in the Sustainable Development Goals, including the mobilization of financial resources, as well as capacity

building and the transfer to developing countries of environmentally sound technologies under favorable conditions, and even under concessional and preferential conditions, are essential to the implementation of the 2030 Agenda for Sustainable Development, constitute an integral part of it, and are of equal importance as the other Objectives and targets.

CULTURE

36. We ratify the importance of the promotion of the right to culture and its value in order to obtain more equitable societies and the responsibility of States in adopting the necessary measures for the full realization of said objective.

37. Convinced that the CELAC is the ideal space for the expression of our identity and rich cultural diversity, we welcome the decision of the United Nations General Assembly to declare 2019 as the International year of Indigenous Languages, and we commit ourselves with the implementation of programs for the recovery, conservation, development, learning and dissemination of the different indigenous languages that are part of our cultures.

38. Recalling that cultural diversity is indispensable for peace and security at the local national and international levels, we commit ourselves to adopt measures to protect cultural expressions and its contents, taking into consideration, among others, the Project for Operational Guidelines for the Implementation, in the digital environment of the 2005 UNESCO Convention on the Promotion and Protection of the Diversity of Cultural Expressions.

COOPERATION

39. We recognize that the Declaration of Santiago, the Special Declaration of Havana on International Cooperation, and the CELAC Conceptual Framework for International Cooperation will guide cooperation at the community level through the construction of a South-South and Triangular Policy, and through the identification of other alternative financing and technical support mechanisms that support the initiatives and priorities defined by our countries.

40. We welcome the mandate established in the Santo Domingo Declaration of the First Meeting of Ministers of Foreign Affairs of CELAC-EU, which entrusts senior officials to reflect on the challenges related to the implementation of the 2030 Agenda, bi-regional cooperation, including the topic of graduation.

41. We emphasize the need for the CELAC Quartet to consider the follow-up of the special resolution on cooperation with the Republic of Haiti as a permanent point of discussion with extra-regional partners, with the aim to facilitate the implementation of the projects presented by the countries in the framework of the Cooperation Plans and Permanent Mechanisms on cooperation and agreed political dialogue. In this regard, at the IV Meeting of the Working Group on International Cooperation, held in Santo Domingo on 12 and 13 January, 2017, it was approved to form an Ad Hoc Group to carry out a diagnosis on the

cooperation needs of the Republic of Haiti and to prepare an indicative document that coordinates efforts and resources to streamline the support given.

42. We agree to continue working with the regional and sub-regional integration mechanisms in the area of cooperation, in order to establish procedures that improve coordination and dialogue at all levels.

43. We commit, within this framework, to be mindful of the special needs of the more vulnerable member States of our community.

TRADE

44. Taking into account the need for a non-discriminatory, fair trade system, based on clear, attainable and inclusive norms, we recognize the value of advancing towards the integration and complementarity of our economies, promoting public and private alliances and the participation of all sectors of society committed to the full development of our nations, fostering mechanisms that substantially increase interregional and extra-regional trade, in conformity with the established laws and uses.

45. We consider that unity is the basis to face, in a coordinated fashion, the challenges in a constantly changing world, rapid transformations and globalization, as well as the risks and uncertainties that surround the economy of the region and globally, among which is the volatility of the international financial market and protectionism. In this context, we express our determination to take appropriate measures to anticipate, avoid or mitigate possible effects on our economies and unemployment.

46. We highlight the need to strengthen the capacities and the role of micro, small and medium enterprises (SMEs) to participate in international commerce.

47. We welcome the 11th WTO Ministerial Conference to be held in Buenos Aires in December, 2017, committing to work together to obtain a package of results that will strengthen the multilateral trading system for the benefit of our peoples.

MIGRATION

48. We share a comprehensive vision of international migration based on a human rights approach that rejects the criminalization of irregular migration, as well as all forms of racism, xenophobia and discrimination against migrants, recognizes the contributions of migrants in the countries of origin and destination, and we reiterate our commitment to promote an orderly, regular and secure migration.

49. We are committed to participate actively in the preparatory process for the Intergovernmental Conference that will consider the Global Migration Pact in 2018 and welcome the offer of Mexico to organize a preparatory meeting.

50. We welcome the decision of some Governments to eliminate discriminatory and selective migration policies that affect migration flows in the region, and urges the elimination of such mechanisms in accordance with the Special Declaration on Migration and Development.

TRANSNATIONAL AND HUMAN RIGHTS

51. We recall the United Nations Guiding Principles on Business and Human Rights, adopted by the United Nations Human Rights Council through Resolution 17/4 of June 2011, and Resolution 26/9 of June 2014, which established the open-ended intergovernmental working group on transnational business and other business

enterprises with respect to human rights. And likewise take note of Resolution 32/10 on Business and Human Rights, of June 2016, by the United Nations Human Rights Council, the 1st and 2nd Sessions of the Open-Ended Working Group on Transnational Business and other Business Enterprises with respect to human rights, held from the 6th-10th July 2015, and from 24th -28th October, respectively, in the Human Rights Council and the 3rd Meeting of the Working group to be held in 2017.

DECOLONIZATION

52. We reiterate the Latin American and Caribbean character of Puerto Rico and, in taking note of the decisions on Puerto Rico adopted by the Special Committee on Decolonization of the United Nations, we reaffirm that it is a matter of interest to

the CELAC. In this sense, we commend the amnesty recently granted by the United States of America to the independence leader Oscar Lopez Rivera.

53. The member countries of the CELAC commit ourselves to continue working within the framework of International Law, and in particular, of Resolution 1514 (XV) of the General Assembly of the United Nations of December 14th, 1960, in order to ensure that the region of Latin America and the Caribbean is a territory free of colonialism and colonies.

54. We reiterate the strongest regional support for the legitimate rights of the Argentine Republic in the dispute over sovereignty over the Malvinas, South Georgia and South Sandwich Islands and the surrounding maritime areas, as well as the continuing interest in the dispute being resolved by the Peaceful settlement and negotiation, in accordance with Resolution 2065 (XX) and subsequent resolutions on the Malvinas question of the General Assembly of the United Nations and the Special Committee on Decolonization.

RELATIONS WITH EXTRA-REGIONAL PARTNERS

55. We reiterate that the extra-regional relations of the CELAC constitute mandates of the Declarations and Plans of Action, and must be carried out in accordance with The Proclamation of Latin America and the Caribbean as a Zone of Peace.

56. We welcome the meetings held at the 71st session of UNGA with The Republic of India, Korea, Turkey and the Russian Federation which have allowed us to assess progress and explore the potential for further development of these relations. In this context, we welcome the establishment of the Permanent Mechanism for Political Dialogue and Cooperation of the CELAC with the Republic of India which took place during the Meeting of the Quartet of Foreign Ministers of the CELAC and India on September 22nd 2016 in New York; and we reiterate our will to advance in the implementation of the agreements stipulated in said Mechanism.

57. We value the implementation of the Permanent Mechanism for Political Dialogue and Cooperation with the Russian Federation, expressed in the Meeting of the Expanded Quartet of Ministers of Foreign Affairs of CELAC with the Minister for Foreign Affairs of the Russian Federation, in the city of Sochi, Russia, on

November 14, 2016, during which the guidelines for the cooperation to be developed under this framework were established.

58. We highlight the progress made in the CELAC's relations with the European Union, the holding of the First Meeting of Foreign Ministers of Foreign Affairs of CELAC-EU, in

Santo Domingo, Dominican Republic, on October 25th and 26th, 2016, where the Declaration of Santo Domingo and the Assessment of Programs and Actions were adopted, and the Agreement Establishing the EU-CELAC Foundation was signed.

59. We welcome the initiative of the Government of the Republic of Korea to implement the first Korea-CELAC cooperation project with the implementation of the Workshop on Capacity-building for the Internationalization of SMEs in Latin America and the Caribbean, on December 9th, 2016 in Santiago de Chile, which resulted from the Tripartite Academic Seminar Korea-CELAC-ECLAC, “Exploring Strategies for Economic Cooperation between the Republic of Korea and Latin America and the Caribbean”, held in the same country on April 11th, 2015.

60. We appreciate the readiness of the People's Republic of China to continue advancing in the implementation of the Cooperation Plan 2015-2019 of the CELAC-China Forum, by implementing the activities agreed for 2016 and we reiterate our willingness to continue to strengthen it.

PARTICIPATION IN INTERNATIONAL FORA

61. We will continue to strengthen consultation and coordination among CELAC Member States in the United Nations and other multilateral fora, in order to continue to speaking out as a region, where appropriate, and without prejudice to existing coordinating groups, on issues of interest and relevance to the Community's Member States, as well as to submit, when feasible and required, joint initiatives adopted by consensus.

62. We welcome the election and appointment of the Republic of Ecuador as President of the Group of 77 during 2017.

MULTILATERALISM AND REFORM OF THE UNITED NATIONS

63. We reiterate the importance of strengthening multilateralism and, in that regard, the commitment to the comprehensive reform of the United Nations system. We underscore the importance of deepening intergovernmental efforts to promote the necessary reform of the Security Council, including its work methods, with a view to transform it into a transparent, representative, democratic and effective body in keeping with evolution occurred in the United Nations and international relations in the last 71 years. We also consider it fundamental to revitalize the General Assembly and the Economic and Social Council.

STRENGTHENING OF THE COMMUNITY OF LATIN AMERICAN AND CARIBBEAN STATES (CELAC)

64. We welcome the progress made in implementing the agreements reached at the Summits of Heads of State and Government, Meetings of Ministers of Foreign Affairs, Sector and National Coordinators, and commit to promote, through concrete measures, the agreements adopted.

65. We will continue to strengthen the relationship with ECLAC as a contribution to the work of the Pro Tempore Presidencies and the Community as a whole.

66. We adopt the CELAC 2017 Action Plan, with a view to contributing to the development and progress of our peoples.

67. We are thankful for the support given by member countries for having hosted the sectoral meetings, which we detail below, in compliance with the CELAC 2016 Action Plan: 1st Meeting of the Working Group and 2nd Ministerial Meeting on Education, on April 20th and 21st in the city of San Jose, Costa Rica; 2nd Meeting of Ministers of the Environment or other High-Level National Authorities Related to Climate Change, on June 24th in Panama City, Panama; The 4th Ministerial Meeting of Culture, on October 6th and 7th, in the city of Santa Cruz, Bolivia; the 5th Meeting of the CELAC on Migration and the 10th Meeting on Migration CELAC-EU, from November 8th to 11th in the city of Santiago, Chile; the 3rd Ministerial Meeting on Family Agriculture, on November 9th, 10th and 11th, in the

city of San Salvador, El Salvador; and the 5th Energy Ministerial Meeting, on November 25th in the city of Quito, Ecuador.

68. We welcome the sister Republic of El Salvador in assuming the Pro Tempore Presidency of our Community for the year 2017 and we commit ourselves to give all the necessary support for the development of a successful administration.

69. We ratify the mandates of the Special Declaration on the Upcoming Pro Tempore Presidencies of CELAC 2017, 2018 and 2019, adopted in New York on 22nd September of 2016 and thank the Plurinational State of Bolivia for hosting the Pro Tempore Presidency of CELAC in 2019.

70. We value and appreciate the great work and effort made by the Dominican Republic during its presidency, in compliance with the mandates emanating from the 2016 Plan of Action and its implementation.

71. We thank the Government and People of the Dominican Republic for their warm hospitality and excellent organization, as well as for the successful hosting of the 5th Summit of Heads of State and Government of CELAC, in Punta Cana, Dominican Republic, January 25th, 2017.

Punta Cana, Dominican Republic, January 25th, 2017

FREE TRADE AREA OF THE AMERICAS

The **Free Trade Area of the Americas** (**FTAA**) (Spanish: *Área de Libre Comercio de las Américas* (ALCA), French: *Zone de libre-échange des Amériques* (ZLÉA), Portuguese: *Área de Livre Comércio das Américas* (ALCA), Dutch: *Vrijhandelszone van Amerika*) was a proposed agreement to eliminate or reduce the trade barriers among all countries in the Americas but Cuba. In the last round of negotiations, trade ministers from 34 countries met in Miami, United States, in November 2003 to discuss the proposal. The proposed agreement was an extension of the North American Free Trade Agreement (NAFTA) between Canada, Mexico and the United States. Opposing the proposal were Cuba, Venezuela, Bolivia, Ecuador, Dominica, Nicaragua and Honduras (all of which entered the Bolivarian Alternative for the Americas in response), and Argentina, Chile and Brazil.

Discussions have faltered over similar points as the Doha Development Round of World Trade Organization (WTO) talks; developed nations seek expanded trade in services and increased intellectual property rights, while less developed nations seek an end to agricultural subsidies and free trade in agricultural goods. Similar to the WTO talks, Brazil has taken a leadership role among the less developed nations, while the United States has taken a similar role for the developed nations.

Talks towards the establishment of the Free Trade Area of the Americas began with the Summit of the Americas in Miami on December 11, 1994, but the FTAA came to public attention during the Quebec City Summit of the Americas, held in Canada in 2001, a meeting targeted by massive anti-corporatization and anti-globalization protests. The Miami negotiations in 2003 met similar protests, though perhaps not as large. The last summit was held at Mar del Plata, Argentina, in November 2005, but no agreement on FTAA was reached. Of the 34 countries present at the negotiations, 26 pledged to meet again in 2006 to resume negotiations, but no such meeting took place.

In previous negotiations, the United States has pushed for a single comprehensive agreement to reduce trade barriers for goods, while increasing intellectual property protection. Specific intellectual property protections could include Digital Millennium Copyright Act-style copyright protections, similar to the U.S.-Australia Free Trade Agreement. Another protection would likely restrict the reimportation or cross-importation of pharmaceuticals, similar to the proposed agreement between the U.S. and Canada.

Brazil has proposed a measured, three-track approach that calls for a series of bilateral agreements to reduce specific tariffs on goods, and a hemispheric pact on rules of origin and dispute resolution processes. Brazil seeks to omit the more controversial issues from the agreement, leaving them to the WTO.

The location of the FTAA Secretariat was to have been determined in 2005. The contending cities are: Atlanta, Chicago, Galveston, Houston, San Juan, and Miami in the United States; Cancún and Puebla in Mexico; Panama City, Panama; and Port of Spain, Trinidad and Tobago. The U.S. city of Colorado Springs also submitted its candidacy in the early days but subsequently withdrew. Miami, Panama City and Puebla served successively as interim secretariat headquarters during the negotiation process.

The failure of the Mar del Plata summit to set out a comprehensive agenda to keep FTAA alive has meant that there is little chance for a comprehensive trade agreement in the foreseeable future.

MEMBERSHIP

The following countries have been allowed membership of the Free Trade Area of the Americas :

Antigua and Barbuda	Dominican Republic	Panama
Argentina	Ecuador	Paraguay
Bahamas	El Salvador	Peru
Barbados	Grenada	Saint Kitts and Nevis
Belize	Guatemala	Saint Lucia
Bolivia	Guyana	Saint Vincent and the Grenadines
Brazil	Haiti	Suriname
Canada	Honduras	

Chile	Jamaica	Trinidad and Tobago
Colombia	Mexico	United States
Costa Rica	Nicaragua	Uruguay
Dominica		Venezuela

A vocal critic of the FTAA is Venezuelan president Hugo Chávez, who has described it as an "annexation plan" and a "tool of imperialism" for the exploitation of Latin America. As a counterproposal to this initiative, Chávez has promoted the Bolivarian Alternative for the Americas (*Alternativa Bolivariana para las Américas*, ALBA), vaguely based on the model of the European Union, which makes emphasis on energy and infrastructure agreements that are gradually extended to other areas finally to include the total economic, political and military integration of the member states Also, Evo Morales of Bolivia has referred to the US-backed Free Trade Area of the Americas, as "an agreement to legalize the colonization of the Americas."

On the other hand, the presidents of Brazil, Luiz Inácio Lula da Silva, and Argentina, Cristina Fernández de Kirchner, have stated that they do not oppose the FTAA but they do demand that the agreement provide for the elimination of US agriculture subsidies, the provision of effective access to foreign markets and further consideration towards the needs and sensibilities of its members.

One of the most contentious issues of the treaty proposed by the United States is with concerns to patents and copyrights. Critics claim that if the measures proposed by the US were implemented and applied this would prevent scientific research in Latin America, causing as a consequence more inequalities and technological dependence from the developed countries. On the issue of patents, some critics of the FTAA, such as Canadian activist Maude Barlow, have accused the US of attempting to patent Latin America-made inventions. On the left-wing Council of Canadians web site, Barlow wrote: "This agreement sets enforceable global rules on patents, copyrights and trademark. It has gone far beyond its initial scope of protecting original inventions or cultural products and now permits the practice of patenting plants and animal forms as well as seeds. It promotes the private rights of corporations over local communities and their genetic heritage and traditional medicines."

On the weekend of April 20, 2001, the 3rd Summit of the Americas was a summit held in Quebec City, Canada. This international meeting was a round of negotiations regarding a proposed Free Trade Area of the Americas.

The FTAA missed the targeted deadline of 2005 as planned. This followed the stalling of useful negotiations of the World Trade Organization Ministerial Conference of 2005. Over time, some governments not wanting to lose a chance of hemispheric trade expansion moved in the direction of establishing a series of bilateral trade deals. The heads however have planned a future summit called the Sixth Summit of the Americas in Cartagena, Colombia in 2012

Latin America and the Caribbean present complex trade integration architectures. Today there are four customs union projects at different stages of completion (MERCOSUR, the Andean Community, the Central American Common Market and CARICOM) plus several other Preferential Trade Agreements (PTAs) linking these integration schemes among themselves and with the countries (Mexico, Chile, Cuba, Panama and the Dominican Republic) that are not full members of any of them.

PTAs in the region are extremely varied. At one end are old-style "economic complementation agreements" that cover only trade in goods and which essentially consist of the reduction of tariffs (not their elimination) for a limited range of products. At the other end are free trade agreements (FTAs) which eliminate tariffs for nearly all products and also cover issues such as services, investment, government procurement, competition policy and intellectual property. There are also numerous "intermediate" types of PTAs.

One consequence of this fragmented architecture is that the benefits that could flow from having a single, integrated economic space (such as larger production scales, reduced transaction costs for both regional and extra-regional traders, and increased formation of regional value chains) are only partly realized. Moreover, although most intra-regional trade is already theoretically tariff-free, numerous non-tariff barriers persist, both within trading blocs and between them. As a result of these and other problems (such as poor infrastructure and red tape at the borders), intra-regional trade accounts for less than 20% of total Latin American trade, compared to about two thirds in the European Union (EU), almost 50% in NAFTA and about 40% in Asia.

Much can be done within the region to both encourage greater intra-regional trade and increase synergies between its integration architecture and the multilateral trading system. In most cases this involves designing mechanisms to promote convergence among PTAs and to reduce discrimination. One possibility is reducing the actual number of PTAs, for example by replacing the many existing bilateral PTAs by a smaller number of larger agreements. Another alternative, in principle less politically complicated, is to establish links between existing PTAs. In the case of trade in goods, this can be done through cumulation of origin, following the example set by the EU in its agreements with the Mediterranean countries.

A third alternative would be to reduce discrimination within each PTA. This in turn can be done in several ways:

- **Extending certain concessions to non-members on a Most Favoured Nation (MFN) basis.** This is usually more feasible in areas such as services, investment or intellectual property (where commitments tend to reflect a country's general regulatory framework) than in others like tariffs or government procurement, where preferential treatment (i.e. discrimination) is precisely the goal pursued through a PTA. Nevertheless, even in the case of tariffs, countries that have liberalized over a certain percentage of their total imports through PTAs could voluntarily extend that treatment to non PTA partners on an MFN basis.

- **Extending concessions to selected non-members, in particular relatively less developed countries.** This is a variant of the above: If countries A and B have a PTA, and country C (relatively less developed than both A and B) faces trade diversion in the markets of A, B or both as a result of the agreement, then A and B could agree to extend PTA benefits unilaterally to C (either across the board or in the sectors where C's exports face trade diversion).

- **Open membership clauses**, allowing non-members to accede to a PTA if they are prepared to undertake commitments comparable/equivalent to those assumed by current members. Here the EU enlargement process is the main historic example (although admittedly EU membership involves much more than trade commitments), while the current negotiations of the Trans Pacific Strategic Partnership Agreement (TPP) is another.

In 2006, and responding to the request of the Presidents of all South American countries, the Secretariats of MERCOSUR, the Andean Community and the Latin American Integration

Association (ALADI) jointly presented concrete proposals for the convergence of PTAs in the region. These included, inter alia, modalities for the acceleration of tariff phase-outs; harmonisation of rules of origin, customs procedures and sanitary and phytosanitary regimes; and a single safeguard regime. At the time ECLAC supported these proposals and suggested going further in some areas, for example moving towards cumulation of origin among the ten South American countries; focusing more effort on trade facilitation; and eliminating antidumping and safeguard measures for intraregional trade. Nevertheless, to this date no concerted action has been taken in response to either set of proposals.

Currently there are no region-wide convergence efforts underway in Latin America and the Caribbean. However, the negotiations announced in November 2010 towards a comprehensive economic integration agreement between its two largest economies, Brazil and Mexico, could — if successful — serve as a catalyst for the convergence of the different PTAs within the region. Another initiative pointing in the same direction is the ongoing process whereby Mexico and the five Central American countries aim to merge the three FTAs currently linking them into a single association agreement.

Summing up, Latin American regionalism does not appear to have resulted in substantial discrimination against extra-regional partners. This is partly due to widespread unilateral trade liberalization, especially in the 1990s, and more recently to the growing number of PTAs with partners such as the US, EU and Asian countries. A successful conclusion of the Doha Round would further reduce scope for such discrimination. The main shortcoming of Latin American regionalism is not having created more intra-regional trade. Rationalization of the region's integration architecture would go a long way towards that goal. More generally, it would help the region as a whole become more internationally competitive and make trade with it easier for outside partners by increasing transparency and reducing transaction costs.

CENTRAL AMERICAN INTEGRATION SYSTEM

Central American Integration System (Spanish: ***Sistema de la Integración Centroamericana***; **SICA**) is the economic, cultural and political organization of Central American states since February 1, 1993. It was on December 13, 1991, however, when all the countries of the ODECA (Spanish: **Organización de Estados Centroamericanos**; **ODECA**) signed the Protocol of Tegucigalpa which extended the earlier cooperation in search for regional peace, political freedom, democracy and economic development. The headquarters of the General Secretariat of SICA are located in the Republic of El Salvador.

In 1991, the institutional framework of SICA included the States of Guatemala, El Salvador, Honduras, Nicaragua, Costa Rica and Panama. Belize joined in 2000 as full member, while the Dominican Republic became an associated state in 2004. More recently, Mexico, Chile and Brazil became part of the organization as regional observers; while the Republic of China, Spain, Germany and Japan became extrarregional observers. The SICA has a standing invitation to participate as observers in the sessions of the United Nations General Assembly and maintains permanent offices at UN Headquarters.

Four countries, Guatemala, El Salvador, Honduras, and Nicaragua, are going through a process of political, cultural, and migratory integration and have formed a group called The Central America Four or *CA-4*, which has introduced common internal borders. Belize, Costa Rica, Panama and Dominican Republic join the *CA-4* only in matters of economic integration and regional friendship.

CENTRAL AMERICAN COURT OF JUSTICE

Between November 14, and December 20, 1907, following a proposal made by Mexico and the United States, five Central American nations – Costa Rica, El Salvador, Guatemala, Honduras and Nicaragua – took part in the Central American Peace Conference in Washington, D.C, sponsored by United States President Theodore Roosevelt's Secretary of State, Nobel Prize winner Elihu Root. The five nations, which had all previously been Spanish colonies had sought on numerous prior occasions, with great difficulty, to form a political alliance. The earliest attempt was the Federal Republic of Central America, and the most recent such effort had taken place 11 years earlier, with the founding of the Republic of Central America.

Nations ended the Conference by signing a peace treaty, one aspect of which created the Central American Court of Justice *(Corte de Justicia Centroamericana)*. The signatories agreed that the convention creating the Court would remain in effect for ten years, beginning at the time of the last ratification. All communications between the signatories were made through the government of Costa Rica. The Court was composed of five judges, one each from each member state. For the period of its functioning the Court heard ten cases, five of which were brought by private individuals and declared inadmissible, and three of which were started by the Court's own initiative. The court operated for 10 years, until April 1918, from its headquarters in Costa Rica, at which point it dissolved. Its members had sought without success from March 1917, when Nicaragua gave a notice of termination from the agreement, to continue the arrangement.

Several explanations for the treaty's failure exist:

- The court lacked an effective system of judicial procedure.
- The judges were not free to act independently of their respective governments.
- The court had been given a jurisdiction too broad to satisfy its member states.

ORGANIZATION OF CENTRAL AMERICAN STATES

Following the end of World War II, a new interest in integrating the Central American governments began. On October 14, 1951, 33 years after the dissolution of the CACJ, the governments of Costa Rica, El Salvador, Guatemala, Honduras, and Nicaragua signed a new treaty creating the Organization of Central American States *(Organización de Estados Centroamericanos*, or *ODECA)* to promote regional cooperation, integrity and unity in Central America. The following year, December 12, 1952, ODECA's charter was altered to create a new Central American Court of Justice (this time called the *Corte Centroamericana de Justicia*, or *CCJ)*, without the time limitation of its previous incarnation.

The Charter of San Salvador was ratified by all the governments of Central America, and on August 18, 1955 the foreign ministers held their first meeting in Antigua Guatemala. There ensued the Declaration of Antigua Guatemala, which decreed that subordinate organizations should be formed under ODECA, to help establish systems of organization and procedure so there would be no restrictions to free intercourse, to economic cooperation, to better sanitary conditions for member nations, and to continued progress in the "integral union" of the Central American nations.

The Central American Common Market, the Central American Bank for Economic Integration, and the Secretariat for Central American Economic Integration (SIECA) were established between five nations of Central America on December 13, 1960 in a conference in Managua. These nations ratified the treaties of membership the following year. Costa Rica joined the CACM in 1963. Panama is conspicuous by absence. Then organization froze in 1969 with the war between Honduras and El Salvador. In 1973, ODECA was suspended and progress in regional integration came to a standstill.

It was not until 1991 that the integration agenda was completed with the creation of the SICA, which provided a clear legal base to avoid discrepancies between the member states. The SICA membership includes the 7 nations of Central America plus the Dominican Republic, a state that is part of the Caribbean. Central America already has several supranational institutions such as the Central American Parliament, the Central American Bank for Economic Integration and the Central American Common Market. The current Central America trade block is organized by the General Treaty for Economical Integration signed October 29, 1993 (Guatemala Protocol). The CACM has succeeded in removing duties on most products moving among the member countries, and has largely unified external tariffs and increased trade within the member nations. The bank has 5 non-regional members: Argentina, Colombia, Mexico, Taiwan and Spain.

PROSPECTS FOR A CENTRAL AMERICAN CURRENCY UNION

Trade with the US—the region's largest trading partner—is the most important source of income for Central America. More than half of Central American exports are destined for the US. Remittances annually add up to billions of dollars as well. This concentration of trade with the US points to the potential benefits of reduced transaction costs and greater efficiency of a common currency. Yet, at the same time retaining their own currencies is a priority for individual countries. A weaker domestic currency means cheaper exports and a more dynamic and competitive export industry.

A new currency is unlikely and a dollarization of the region is perhaps the only possibility.The emergence of a new common currency would also be troubled by the available regional institutions' lack of effectiveness, resources and relevance; thus, governments have rarely delegated responsibilities to them. A regional central bank would also have to be established and it's not clear how this would be done.The currency union undertaking—a process that would require frequent and consistent political commitment—has not found priority in the regional agenda. Regional efforts are focused on security problems and social issues such as combating drug trafficking and organized crime, improving education, meeting energy needs, crafting natural disaster prevention measures, etc.

In terms of Robert Mundell's Optimum Currency Area criteria, Central America does not fulfill important prerequisites for a union and is arguably not the site of an optimum currency area. Though the region as a whole enjoys a high degree of factor mobility, diversified composition of output, price and wage flexibility, and important financial integration it also fails to meet important criteria. The lack of business cycle synchronization, high and dissimilar levels of public sector debt, diverging inflation rates, and the lack of high levels of intraregional trade are some deficiencies.

CENTRAL AMERICAN PARLIAMENT

The parliament was created with the vision to be a modern renewal of the historic Federal Republic of Central America which existed from 1823 to 1840. Costa Rica is the only one of the original five states not to join Parlacen, but in its place are two new contributors: Panama (which was once part of Colombia, or rather New Granada, and so was not one of the original Central American states) and the Dominican Republic. It has its more recent origins in the Contadora Group, a project launched in the 1980s to help deal with civil wars in El Salvador, Guatemala and Nicaragua. Although the Contadora was dissolved in 1986, the idea for Central American Integration remained, and its works were taken by the Esquipulas Peace Agreement, which, among other acts, agreed to the creation of the Central American Parliament. Members return 20-22 directly elected deputies to the Parliament. In spite of its efforts to promote the Esquipulas Agreement, Costa Rica has not yet ratified and is consequently not represented in the Parlacen. Parlacen has been seen by some, including former President of Honduras, Ricardo Maduro as a white elephant.

CENTRAL AMERICAN COURT OF JUSTICE

The current mission of the CCJ is to promote peace in the region and unity between its member-states. Today's Court has jurisdiction to hear cases:

- between member States
- between a member state and a non-member state which agrees to the Court's jurisdiction
- between states and any natural or legal person who is a resident of any member state
- regarding the integration process between Central American Integration System's (*SICA*) organs and member states or natural or legal persons

The Court may also offer consultation to the Supreme Courts of the region. In 2005, the Court ruled that Nicaraguan congressional reforms, which took control of water, energy and telecommunications services away from President Enrique Bolaños were "legally inapplicable", possibly further inciting the Nicaraguan political crisis. As of July 2005, the CCJ has made 70 resolutions since hearing its first case in 1994.

SYSTEM BODIES

- Central American Bank for Economic Integration (*Banco Centroamericano de Integración Económica, BCIE*)

- Central American Common Market (CACM; *Mercado Común Centroamericano, MCCA*)
- Central American Court of Justice (CCJ)
- Central American Parliament (*Parlamento Centroamericano, PARLACEN*)
    - Plenum
    - Board of Parliament
    - Secretariat
- Presidents Summit
    - Comité Consultivo (CC-SICA)
    - Council of Ministers of Foreign Affairs
    - Executive Committee (CE-SICA)
    - Vice Presidents Summit
    - Secretariat General (SG-SICA)

ORGANIZATION OF IBERO-AMERICAN STATES

The **Organization of Ibero-American States** (Portuguese: *Organização dos Estados Ibero-americanos*; Spanish:*Organización de Estados Iberoamericanos*; formally *The Organization of Ibero-American States for Education, Science and Culture*) is anintergovernmental organization, comprising the Portuguese- and Spanish-speaking nations of America and Europe, plusEquatorial Guinea in Africa.

The Organization of Ibero-American States for the Education, Science and Culture (OEI) is an international organization for inter-governmental cooperation between the Latin American countries in the field of education, science, technology and culture in the context of the integral development, democracy and regional integration.

The Members of plenary session and observers are all American, European and African: Argentina, Bolivia, Brazil,Colombia, Costa Rica, Cuba, Chile,Dominican Republic, Ecuador, El Salvador,Guatemala, Equatorial Guinea, Honduras,Mexico, Nicaragua, Panama, Paraguay,Peru, Portugal, Puerto Rico, Spain,Uruguay and Venezuela.

The seat of its General Secretariat is inMadrid, Spain, and it maintains regional offices in Argentina, Brazil, Colombia, El Salvador, Spain, Mexico and Peru, with field offices in Chile, Honduras, Nicaragua and Paraguay.

The financing of the OEI and its programs are covered by obligatory quotas and voluntary contributions by the governments of the member states and by the contributions by institutions, foundations and other organizations interested in improvement of the educational quality and in scientific and cultural development. The Honorary President of the organisation is His Majesty King Juan Carlos I of Spain.

The OEI was founded in 1949 under the title of the Office of Latin American Education and with the character of an international agency, as a result of the 1st Latin American Education Congress in Madrid. In 1954, the 2nd Latin American Congress of Education took place in Quito, and it was decided to transform the OEI into an intergovernmental organization, integrated by sovereign States, and it was so constituted on the 15 of March 1957 at the 3rd Latin American Congress of Education celebrated in Santo Domingo; they subscribed the first Statutes of the OEI, effective until 1985.

In 1979 the Congress met for the 4th Latin American of Education in Madrid; in 1983 the 5th took place in Lima, and in May 1985 it held an Extraordinary Meeting of the Congress in Bogotá, in that it was decided to change the old name of the OEI to the present one, keeping the abbreviations and extending its objectives. This modification affected only the name of its organ of Government, the Latin American Congress of Education, became the General Assembly. In December 1985, during the Meeting of the Directive Council in Panama, its members acted as plenipotentiaries of their respective States and in plenary sessions, powers of the General Assembly, subscribed the present Statutes of the OEI, which replaced the statutory text of 1957 and they approved the Organization Regulations.

Since the I Latin American Conference of Government and Chiefs of State (Guadalajara, 1991), the OEI has promoted the Conferences of Ministers of Education, as instances of preparation for the summits, and for the execution of the educative, scientific and cultural programs delegated to it.

AIMS AND OBJECTIVES

The Organization of Ibero- American States for the Education, Science and the Culture, make the principles that are based on and fulfilling its obligations in agreement with the Statutes, it established the following general aims:

- To contribute to fortify the knowledge, mutual understanding, integration, solidarity and peace between the Latin American peoples to spread education, science, technology and culture.
- To foment the development of education and the culture like vélida and viable alternative for construction of peace, by means of the preparation of the human being for the exercise responsible for the freedom, the solidarity and the defense of the human rights, as well as to support the changes that they make possible a right society month for Iberoamé rich.
- To collaborate permanently in transmission and interchange of the integration experiences economic, political and cultural produced in the countries European and Latin American, that constitutes the two areas of influence of the Organization, as well as in any other aspect susceptible to serve for the development of the countries.
- To collaborate with the Members in objective to obtain that the educative systems fulfill a triple approach: humane, developing the formation é tica, integrate and harmonize the new generations; of democratization, assuring the equality educative opportunities and the social fairness; and productive, preparing for the life of the work and favoring labor insertion.

- To collaborate in the diffusion of one culture that, without forgetting the idiosyncrasies and the peculiarities of the different countries, incorporate the codes of modernity to allow assimilation of global advances in science and the technology, revaluing the own cultural identity and taking advantage of the answers that they arise from his accumulation.
- To facilitate the relations between science, technology and society in the Latin American countries, analyzing the implications of the development scientist-knowledge from one social perspective and increasing to its valuation and the understanding of its effects by all the citizens.
- To promote the entailment of the plans of education, science, technology and culture and the plans and socioeconomic processes that persecute a development to the service of man, as well as an equitable distribution of products cultural, technological and scientific.
- To make and promote programs of lateral cooperation between the Member States and of between the States and of other regional institutions.
- To contribute to the diffusion of languages Spanish and Portuguese and to the improvement of all and techniques of its education, as well as to his conservation and preservation in the cultural minorities residents in other countries. To foment the education at the same time bilingual to preserve the multicultural identity of the communities of Ibero-America, expressed in the multilingualisms of its culture.

STRUCTURE

The government of the OEI consists of the three following organs:

General Assembly

The General Assembly, that is the supreme authority of the Organization; be integrated by Representatives or Official delegations the Member States.

It is, also the legislative instance that it establishes the general policies of the OEI, studies, it evaluates and it approves the Plan of Activities of the Organization, the Program and Global budget and fixes the quotas annual, and meets to choose to Secretary General by the corresponding period.

Directive Council

The Directive Council is the organ delegated by the General Assembly for the control of the government and of Administration of the OEI. Be integrated by the Ministers of Education of the States Members or by their representatives and is presided over by the Minister of Education of the country in which there is of to hold the next meeting of the General Assembly.

Its main mission is the one to consider and to approve the report of activities, the Program and Budget biennial and financial statement of the Organization.

General Secretariat

The General Secretariat is delegated organ permanent of the General Assembly for executive direction of the OEI and shows its presentation in relations with the Governments, the international organizations and with other institutions. Té has to its position the direction; cnica and administrative of the Organization and the execution of the programs and projects.

The General Secretariat is structured internally by a system of flexible organization, adapted to the policies, the strategies and the Plan of Activities.

MEMBER STATES

Andorra

Argentina

Bolivia

Brazil

Chile

Colombia

Costa Rica

Cuba

Dominican Republic

Ecuador

El Salvador

Equatorial Guinea

Guatemala

Honduras

Mexico

Nicaragua

Panama

Paraguay

Peru

Portugal

Puerto Rico

Spain

Uruguay

Venezuela

RIO GROUP

The **Rio Group** is an international organization of Latin American and someCaribbean states. It was created on 18 December 1986 in the Brazilian city of Rio de Janeiro by means of the Declaration of Rio de Janeiro, signed by Argentina, Brazil, Colombia, Mexico, Panama, Peru, Uruguay and Venezuela (the members of theContadora Group and the Contadora Support Group). To some extent it was perceived by some observers as an alternative body to the Organization of American States during the Cold War, since that body was dominated by the United States.

The Rio Group does not have a secretariat or permanent body, and instead relies on yearly summits of heads of states.

Current member states/organizations in alphabetical order by column:

Argentina	Dominican Republic	Mexico
Belize	Ecuador	Nicaragua
Bolivia	El Salvador	Panama
Brazil	Guatemala	Paraguay
Chile	Guyana	Peru
Colombia	Haiti	Suriname
Costa Rica	Honduras	Uruguay
Cuba	Jamaica	Venezuela

MERCOSUR

Headquarters	Montevideo
Largest city	São Paulo
Official languages	3 Guarani Spanish Portuguese
Ethnic groups	60% White (includingArab diaspora) 34% Multiracial(Pardo, mestizo, etc.) 5% Black 1% Asian andAmerindian[1]
Membership	4 Argentina Brazil Paraguay Uruguay
Government	Intergovernmental
- Presidency	Argentina (pro tempore)
	Establishment
- Treaty of Asunción	26 March 1991

- Protocol of Ouro Preto	16 December 1994
	Area
- Total	12,781,179 km² (2nd[1]) 4,934,841 sq mi
	Population
- 2008 estimate	267,386,382 (4th[1])
- Density	20.86/km² (154th[1]) 54/sq mi
GDP (PPP)	estimate
- Total	U$ 2.895 trillion (5th[1])
- Per capita	U$ 14,858 (70th[1])
HDI (2007)	0.827 (high) (50th[1])
Currency	4 Argentine peso (ARS) Brazilian real (BRL) Paraguayan guaraní (PYG) Uruguayan peso (UYU)

[1] If Mercosur considered as a single entity.

Mercosur or **Mercosul** (Spanish:*Mercado Común del Sur*, Portuguese:*Mercado Comum do Sul*, Guarani:*Ñemby Ñemuha*, English: Common Southern Market) is an economic and political agreement among Argentina,Brazil, Paraguay and Uruguay. Founded in 1991 by the Treaty of Asunción, which was later amended and updated by the 1994 Treaty of Ouro Preto. Its purpose is to promote free trade and the fluid movement of goods, people, and currency. The official languages areGuaraní, Portuguese and Spanish. It has been updated, amended, and changed many times since. It is now a full customs union. Mercosur and theAndean Community of Nations are customs unions that are components of a continuing process of South Americanintegration connected to the Union of South American Nations.

Mercosur origins trace back to 1985 when Presidents Raúl Alfonsín of Argentina and José Sarney of Brazil signed the *Argentina-Brazil Integration and Economics Cooperation Program* or**PICE** (Portuguese: Programa de Integração e Cooperação Econômica Argentina-Brasil, Spanish: Programa de Integración y Cooperación Económica Argentina-Brasil). The program also proposed the Gaucho as a currency for regional trade.

Venezuela signed a membership agreement on 17 June 2006.

The founding of the Mercosur Parliamentwas agreed at the December 2004 presidential summit. It should have 18 representatives from each country by 2010, regardless of population.

Bolivia, Chile, Colombia, Ecuador andPeru currently have associate member status.

MEMBER STATES

Member states. Map doesn't highlight Venezuela (full member pending on Paraguay's ratification).

Mercosur is composed of 4 sovereign member states: Argentina, Brazil, Paraguay, and Uruguay.

Venezuela will become the fifth full member country after Paraguay's congress ratification; all other members have ratified Venezuela's full membership.

Directly subordinated to the Common Market Group, the Work Subgroups draw up the minutes of the decisions to be submitted for the consideration of the Council, and conduct studies on specific Mercosur concerns. Currently, the Work Subgroups are the following: Commercial Matters; Customs Matters; Technical Standards; Tax and Monetary Policies Relating to Trade; Land Transport; Sea Transport; Industrial and Technology Policies; Agricultural Policy; Energy Policy; Coordination of Macroeconomic Policies; and Labor, Employment and Social Security Matters. Meetings. The meetings of the Work subgroups will be held quarterly, alternating in every member state, in alphabetical order, or at the Common Market Group Administrative Office. Activities will be carried out by the Work Subgroups in two stages: preparatory and conclusive. In the preparatory stage, the members of the Work Subgroups may request the participation of representatives from the private sector of each member state. The decision-making stage is reserved exclusively for official representatives of the member states. The delegations of representatives from the private sector in the preparatory stage of the Work Subgroup activities will have a maximum of three representatives for each member state directly involved in any of the stages of the production, distribution or consumption process for the products that fall within the scope of the subgroup's activities.

OBJECTIVES

The Southern Common Market promotes:

The free transit of produced goods, services and factors among the member states. Among other things, this includes the elimination of customs rights and lifting of nontariff restrictions on the transit of goods or any other measures with similar effects;

Fixing of a common external tariff (CET) and adopting of a common trade policy with regard to nonmember states or groups of states, and the coordination of positions in regional and international commercial and economic meetings;

Coordination of macroeconomic and sectorial policies of member states relating to foreign trade, agriculture, industry, taxes, monetary system, exchange and capital, services, customs, transport and communications, and any others they may agree on, in order to ensure free competition between member states;

The commitment by the member states to make the necessary adjustments to their laws in pertinent areas to allow for the strengthening of the integration process. The Asunción Treaty is based on the doctrine of the reciprocal rights and obligations of the member states. Mercosur initially targeted free-trade zones, then customs unification, and finally a common market. The common market will allow (in addition to customs unification) the free movement of manpower and capital across the member nations, and depends the grating of equal rights and duties to all member countries. Because member states will implement the trade liberalization at different speeds, during the transition period the rights and obligations of each party will initially be equivalent but not necessarily equal. In addition to the reciprocity doctrine, the Asunción Treaty also contains provisions for the most-favored nation concept. This concept is that after the common market is formed, member nations are to automatically extend to the other members any advantage, favor, entitlement, immunity or privilege granted to a product originating from or intended for countries that are not party to the Latin American Integration Association (ALADI).

STRUCTURE

The Asunción Treaty and Ouro Preto Protocol established the basis for the institutional Mercosur structure, creating the Common Market Council and the Common Market Group, both of which are to function at the outset of the transition phase. As provided for in this Treaty, before establishing the common market the member nations must call a special meeting in order to determine the definitive institutional structure for the public agencies managing Mercosur, as well as define the specific functions of each agency and the decision making process.

Common Market Council

The Council is the highest-level agency of Mercosur with authority to conduct its policy, and responsibility for compliance with the objects and time frames set forth in the Asuncion Treaty. The Council is composed of the Ministers of Foreign Affairs and the Economy (or the equivalent) of all five countries. Member states preside over the Council in rotating alphabetical order, for 6-month periods. Meetings: Councilmembers shall meet whenever necessary, but at least once a year. The presidents of the member nations shall partake of the annual Common Market Council meeting whenever possible. Decision Making: Council decisions shall be made by consensus, with representation of all member states.

Common Market Group

The Group is the executive body of Mercosur, and is coordinated by the Ministries of Foreign Affairs of the member states. Its basic duties are to cause compliance with the Asuncion Treaty and to take resolutions required for implementation of the decisions made by the Council. Furthermore, it can initiate practical measures for trade opening, coordination of macroeconomic policies, and negotiation of agreements with nonmember states and international agencies, participating when need be in resolution of controversies under Mercosur. It has the authority to organize, coordinate and supervise Work Subgroups and to call special meetings to deal with issues of interest. Composition: The Common Market Group shall be made up of four permanent members and four alternates from each member state, representing the following public agencies: (i) the Ministry of Foreign Affairs; (ii) the Ministry of Economy, or the equivalent (from industry, foreign affairs and/or economic coordination); and (iii) the Central Bank. The members of the Common Market Group appointed by a given member state will constitute the National Section of the Common Market Group for that particular nation. Meetings: The Common Market Group will meet ordinarily at least once every quarter in the member states, in rotating alphabetical order. Special meetings may be freely called at any time, at any previously scheduled place. The meetings will be coordinated by the Head of the Delegation of the host member state. Decision Making: Common Market Group decisions shall be made by consensus, with the representation of all member states. The official Mercosur languages will be Portuguese and Spanish, and the official version of all work papers will be prepared in the language of the country hosting the meeting.

ADMINISTRATIVE AND SOCIOECONOMIC

The Administrative Office will keep documents and issue the Mercosur official bulletin in both Portuguese and Spanish, and will also be charged with communicating the activities of the Common Market Group so as to allow for the maximum disclosure of decisions and the relevant documentation. The Socioeconomic Advisory Forum is consultative by nature, and represents the various socioeconomic sectors of the member nations.

Work Subgroups

Directly subordinated to the Common Market Group, the Work Subgroups draw up the minutes of the decisions to be submitted for the consideration of the Council, and conduct studies on specific Mercosur concerns. Currently, the Work Subgroups are the following: Commercial Matters; Customs Matters; Technical Standards; Tax and Monetary Policies Relating to Trade; Land Transport; Sea Transport; Industrial and Technology Policies; Agricultural Policy; Energy Policy; Coordination of Macroeconomic Policies; and Labor, Employment and Social Security Matters. Meetings. The meetings of the Work subgroups will be held quarterly, alternating in every member state, in alphabetical order, or at the Common Market Group Administrative Office. Activities will be carried out by the Work Subgroups in two stages: preparatory and conclusive. In the preparatory stage, the members of the Work Subgroups may request the participation of representatives from the private sector of each member state. The decision-making stage is reserved exclusively for official representatives of the member states. The delegations of representatives from the private sector in the preparatory stage of the Work Subgroup activities will have a maximum of three representatives for each member state directly involved in any of the stages of the production, distribution or consumption process for the products that fall within the scope of the subgroup's activities.

Joint Parliamentary Committee

The Committee will have both an advisory and decision-making nature, with powers to submit proposals as well. It will be competent, inter alia, to: follow up on the integration process and keep the respective Congresses informed; Take the necessary steps for the future instatement of a Mercosur parliament; Organize subcommittees to examine matters relating to the integration process; Submit its recommendations to the Common Market Council and Group as to how the integration process should be conducted and Southern Common Market formed; Make the adjustments necessary to harmonize the laws of the different member states and submit them to the respective Congresses; Establish relationships with private entities in each of the member states, as well as international agencies and bureaus so as to obtain information and specialized assistance with matters of interest: Establish relationships targeting cooperation with Congresses of the nonmember nations and entities involved in regional integration schemes; Subscribe to cooperation and technical assistance accords with public and/or private entities whether domestic, supranational or international. The Committee will be composed of a maximum of 64 acting parliamentary members, 16 per member state, and an equal number of alternates, appointed by the Congress to which they pertain, and with a term of office of at least two years. The meetings shall be conducted by a directors' board consisting of four Presidents (one for each member state). The Committee will ordinarily meet twice a year, and extraordinarily whenever summoned by any of its five Presidents. Meetings are to be held in the territory of each member state on a successive and alternating basis. Decision Making: Meetings of the Joint Parliamentary Committee will only be valid when attended by parliamentary delegations from all member states. Decisions by the Joint Parliamentary Committee will be made by consensus vote of the majority of the members accredited by the respective Congresses of each member state. Portuguese and Spanish are the official languages of the Joint Parliamentary Committee.

Trade Commission

The Trade Commission will assist the Mercosur executive body, always striving to apply the instruments of common trade policy agreed to by the member states for operation of the customs unification. Additionally, the commission should also follow up on the development of issues and matters related to common trade policies, the intra-Mercosur trade and trade with other countries. The commission will have five actual members and four alternates, with each member nation's indicating a member. The Trade Commission shall exert every effort to apply common trade policy instruments such as: Trade agreements with other countries or international entities; Administrative/commercial product lists; Final adaptation system for Mercosur customs unification; Origin system; Free-trade zone system, special customs areas and export processing zones; System to discourage unfair trade practices; Elimination and harmonization of tariff restrictions; Nonmember country safeguard systems; Customs coordination and harmonization; Consumer protection systems; and Export incentive harmonization.

Furthermore, the trade commission should speak out regarding the issues raised by the member states regarding application and compliance with common offshore tariffs and other common trade policy instruments. The commission shall meet at least once a month, as well as whenever asked to by the Mercosur executive agency or by a member state. The commission can take decisions entailing administration and application of trade policies adopted under Southern Common Market, and whenever necessary submit proposals to the executive body regarding regulation of the areas under its authority; additionally, it can propose new guidelines or modify those in existence in Mercosur trade and customs matters. In this respect, the trade commission can propose a change in the import duty on specific items under common external tariffs, including cases referring to development of new Mercosur production activities. In order to better achieve its objectives, the trade commission can create technical committees targeting direction and supervision of the work it engages in. It can also adopt internal operating regulations. Proposals and decisions of the trade commission will be taken by a consensus of the representatives indicated by each member nation. Any disputes ensuing from the application, interpretation or compliance with the acts issued by the trade commission are to be referred to the Mercosur executive body, and should be resolved using the directives set forth in the Dispute Resolution System adopted under Southern Common Market.

INTERNATIONAL JURISDICTION OVER CONTRACTUAL MATTERS

The rules on litigation jurisdiction over contractual matters will apply to disputes arising from civil or commercial international contracts between private-law legal entities or individuals provided that: They are domiciled or headquartered in different member states: At least one of the parties to the contract is domiciled or headquartered in any member state and, additionally, has made a choice of jurisdiction in favor of a court in one of the member states. In this case, there must be a reasonable connection between the jurisdiction chosen and the controversy. The scope of the application of the international jurisdiction guidelines over contractual matters excludes the following: legal relationships between bankrupt entities/individuals and their creditors and any other analogous proceedings (especially concordatas composition with creditors); matters under agreements involving family and succession law; social security contracts; administrative contracts; employment contracts; consumer sales contracts; transport contracts; insurance policies; and rights in rem.

Choice of Jurisdiction

Courts in member nations to whose jurisdiction the contracted parties have agreed to submit the matter in writing will have jurisdiction to settle controversies stemming from civil or commercial international contracts.

Agreement of choice

The jurisdiction can be agreed on at the time the contract is signed, during the life of the contract, or even when the dispute actually arises. The validity and effects of the choice of venue will be governed by the law of the member nations that normally have jurisdiction to hear the case, always resorting to the law most favorable to the validity of the contract. Whether or not jurisdiction is chosen, such jurisdiction will be prorogated in favor of the courts of the member state where the proceedings are in fact filed, provided the respondent voluntarily allows this in an affirmative and unfeigned way.

Subsidiary jurisdiction

Should the contracted parties not reach an agreement regarding the courts competent to settle disputes, the member state chosen by the plaintiff of the case in point will have jurisdiction: The court of the place where the contract is to be performed; or The court of the domicile of the respondent; or The court of the domicile or headquarters of the claimant when the latter can show that it has done its part. For purposes of item (i) above the place of performance of the contract will be the member state where the obligations on which the claim is based have been or should be performed, taking into consideration the following: For contracts involving certain specific items, the place where they existed at the time of contract signing; For contracts involving specific items according to their type, the place of domicile of the debtor at the time of contract signing; For contracts involving fungible items, the place of domicile of the debtor at the time of conclusion of the contract; and For service rendering contracts:

If in regard to items, the place where they were at the time of contract signing;

If effectiveness is related to any special place, the place where they were to produce effects;

In all other cases, the place of domicile of the debtor at the time of contract signing. For purposes of application of second item above for determination of the domicile of the respondent in a contractual dispute involving individuals, the following will be taken into consideration: The habitual residence: On a subsidiary basis, the central place of business; and In the absence of any such considerations, the place where found, meaning the actual residence. When dealing with a legal entity, the determination of the domicile will be based on where the administrative headquarters have been set up. The claim plaintiff can, as an alternative, file in any of the places where the legal entity has branches, establishments, agencies or any other type of representation. Legal entities headquartered in any member state that have concluded contracts with any other member state can be sued in the courts of this latter state should there be any dispute as to the construction and implementation of the obligations regulated by contract. In the event there is a codefendant, a suit on contractual matters can be adjudicated with the courts of jurisdiction in the territory of the domicile of any of the parties to the litigation. Additionally, any claims entailing personal collateral rights or intervention of nonmember states in contractual obligations can be filed with the court hearing the main proceeding.

Educational integration

University of São Paulo, located in the city of São Paulo, Brazil. Is one of the most highly esteemed university institutions in the region of Mercosur.

Based on the premise that education is a fundamental factor in the regional integration process, educational courses at the primary or junior high level, provided that they do not entail technical studies, will be recognized by member states as being on the same level for all member nations. Likewise, in order to permit continuing education, certificates proving course conclusion issued by an official institution accredited in one of the member states will be valid in all other member states. Nontechnical primary and junior high level studies that have not been completed will be accredited by any member state, thereby allowing course conclusion in another member nation. Studies will be completed using an equivalency table to determine the level achieved.

Regional Technical Commission

In order to harmonize the mechanisms favoring accreditation of studies undertaken in any member nation in any other member nation, and to resolve any situations that may not be covered by the equivalency table, a Regional Technical Commission will be created. This Commission will include delegations from the ministries of education of each member nation, and will meet whenever at least two member states think it necessary to convene. The meeting sites will be established on a rotating basis. Any disputes that arise among the member states as a result of application, construction or noncompliance regarding the provisions related to education will be initially resolved by direct diplomatic negotiations. Should the countries not reach an accord or should the dispute be only partially resolved, then the procedures set forth in the Dispute Resolution System will be resorted to. Should the member nations enter into a bilateral convention or accord whose provisions are more favorable to their students, the member states in question can apply whichever provisions they consider most advantageous.

FREE TRADE ZONES AND ECONOMIC INTEGRATION

The member nations can have commercial free-trade zones, industrial free-trade zones, export processing zones, and special customs areas, all of which target providing merchandise marketed or produced in these areas with treatment different from that afforded in their respective customs territories.

Tariffs

The member states can assess merchandise from these areas with the common external tariff used for Mercosur merchandise, or, in the case of certain special products, the domestic tariff prevailing in each individual state. In this way, the products from the free-trade zones can have the more favorable tax treatment established under Southern Common Market, given to the merchandise produced in the normal customs zones of each member state or, in the case of certain special products, can have the normal customs treatment prevailing in each nation.

Safeguards

Products produced or marketed in the free-trade zones of each member nation will be eligible for the safeguard system whenever this entails an increase not provided for in imports, but capable of causing damages or threatened damages to the importer country.

Incentives

In the event of the producing nation's granting special incentives for production from the free-trade zones that are not compatible with the corresponding guidelines established under the General Agreement on Tariffs and Trade (GATT), the member nation can make any adjustments needed to return the situation to equilibrium.

Creation

The member nations agreed that any free-trade zones that in August 1994 were already in operation could operate normally under Mercosur, along with any that are set up in light of legal guidelines prevailing or in course in Congress during this same time period. This means that a member nation can no longer create new free-trade zones that are more privileged.

Manaus and Tierra del Fuego FTZs

The actual implementation of Mercosur will not affect the special Manaus, Brazil, and Tierra del Fuego, Argentina, free-trade zones organized in light of their special geographic situations. These two free-trade zones may continue normal operations until 2013.

Reciprocal promotion and protection

The nations subscribing to the Asunci6n Treaty consider that the creation and maintenance of conditions favorable to individual or corporate investments for the jurisdiction of one of the member states in the territory of another state is essential to intensify the economic cooperation targeted so as to accelerate the integration process among all four member states. In this context, Argentina, Uruguay, Paraguay and Brazil signed on January 1, 1994 in the city of Colonia del Sacramento, Uruguay, the Colonia Protocol for the Reciprocal Promotion and Protection of Mercosur Investments (Colonia Protocol). It was established in this protocol that investments under Mercosur by investors resident or domiciled in the territory of any member state will be entitled to treatment no less favorable than that accorded by the other member state to national investors or nonmember states.

Investors

For purposes of construction of the Colonia Protocol, investors are considered to be: Individuals that are citizens of any of the member nations or that reside there on a permanent basis or are domiciled there, with due regard for legislation prevailing in such territory; Legal entities organized pursuant to the legislation of one of the member nations that are headquartered there; and Legal entities organized in the territory where the investment is made, actually and directly or indirectly controlled by the legal entities or individuals mentioned above.

Investments

The term investment includes all types of assets such as: movable or immovable property, such as rights in rem and guarantee in rem rights; Shares, corporate holdings and any other type of corporate participations; Credit instruments and rights that may have an economic value; Intellectual property rights or materials, Including copyrights and industrial property rights such as patents, industrial drawings, trademarks, commercial names, technical procedures, know-how and goodwill; Economic concessions involving public law, such as research, cultivation, extraction or natural resource exploration concessions.

INVESTMENT CLIMATE

Brazil-Uruguay International Border.

The nation receiving the investment cannot avail itself of unjustified or discriminatory means capable of restricting the investor's freedom to manage, maintain, use, enjoy and dispose of its investments.

Tax Issues

The member states are not however obligated to extend to investors in the other nations signatory to the Colonia Protocol the benefits of any treatment, preference or privilege resulting from international accords relating fully or partially to tax matters.

Exceptions

In addition, the member nations can temporarily establish a list of exceptions where the new treatment will not yet prevail. In this way, the various member nations decided to except the following economic sectors: Argentina: ownership of real estate on the frontier strip, air transportation, naval industry, nuclear plants, uranium mining, insurance and fishery; Brazil: mineral prospection and mining; use of hydraulic energy; health care; television and radio broadcasting and telecommunications in general, acquisition or leasing of rural properties; participation in the financial intermediation, insurance, social security and capitalization systems; chartering and cabotage as well as inland navigation; Paraguay: ownership of real property on the frontier strip; communications, including radio and television broadcasting; air, sea and land transportation; electricity, water and telephone services; prospecting for hydrocarbons and strategic minerals; import and refining of petroleum derivates and postal services; and Uruguay: electricity; hydrocarbons; basic petrochemicals, atomic energy; prospecting for strategic minerals; financial intermediation; railways, telecommunications; radio broadcasting; press and audiovisual means.

Expropriation and compensation

The member nations undertook to do nothing to nationalize or expropriate investments in their territories that pertain to investors from the signatory countries, unless such measures are taken based on public need. In such case, nothing discriminatory can be done, but everything must be implemented by due legal process. Compensation for the investment holder that is expropriated or nationalized should be both adequate and effective, and made in advance, based on the real investment value determined at the time the decision is publicly announced by the proper authorities. This payment will be updated until actual payment, and the affected investor will receive interest.

Transfers

The original member state investors will be ensured free transfer of their investments and any earnings thereon. These transfers can be made in freely convertible currency, using the exchange rate prevailing on the market pursuant to the procedures established by the member state receiving the investment. Member nations cannot adopt any exchange measures restricting free transfer of the funds invested or from activities exercised in their respective territories.

ROLE

Some South Americans see Mercosur as giving the capability to combine resources to balance the activities of other global economic powers, especially the North American Free Trade Agreement (NAFTA) and the European Union. The organization could also potentially pre-empt the Free Trade Area of the Americas (FTAA); however, over half of the current Mercosur member countries rejected the FTAA proposal at the IV Cumbre de las Américas (IV Summit of the Americas) in Argentina in 2005.

The development of Mercosur was arguably weakened by the collapse of the Argentine economy in 2001 and it has still seen internal conflicts over trade policy, between Brazil and Argentina, Argentina and Uruguay, Paraguay and Brazil, etc. In addition, many obstacles are to be addressed before the development of a common currency in Mercosur.

In 2004, Mercosur signed a cooperation agreement with the Andean Community of Nations trade bloc (CAN) and they published a joint letter of intent for future negotiations towards integrating all of South America. The prospect of increased political integration within the organization, as per the European Union and advocated by some, is still uncertain. Bolivia, also a member of CAN and an associate member of Mercosur before the UNASUR process started, plays a crucial part in relations, says Marion Hörmann, since Bolivia is traditionally seen as a mediator between the Andean countries and the rest of South America. Regional Integration: Key Role for Bolivia

The bloc comprises a population of more than 270 million people, and the combined Gross Domestic Product of the full-member nations is in excess of US$3.0 trillion a year (Purchasing power parity, PPP) according to International Monetary Fund (IMF) numbers, making Mercosur the fifth-largest economy in the World. It is the fourth-largest trading bloc after the European Union

The working of Mercosur has not met with universal approval within interested countries. Chile has to a certain extent preferred to pursue bilateral agreements with trading partners, and there have been calls from Uruguayan politicians for this example to be followed.

FTA WITH THIRD PARTIES

Recently, with the new cooperation agreement with Mercosur, the Andean Community gained four new associate members: Argentina, Brazil, Paraguay and Uruguay. These four Mercosur members were granted associate membership by the Andean Council of Foreign Ministers meeting in an enlarged session with the Commission (of the Andean Community) on 7 July 2005. This move reciprocates the actions of Mercosur which granted associate membership to all the Andean Community nations by virtue of the Economic Complementarity Agreements (Free Trade Agreements) signed between the CAN and individual Mercosur members.

Colombian president Álvaro Uribe signed a free trade agreement with Mercosur in December 2005, giving Colombian products preferential access to a market of 230 million people. Colombian entrepreneurs will also be able to import materials and capital goods from Mercosur at lower costs due to reduced tariffs resulting from the agreement.

The agreement's asymmetry clauses favor Colombia because it allows the gradual and progressive reduction of tariffs and likewise gives Colombia the opportunity to gradually reform its production system to adapt it to the requirements of the future negotiations within the scheme of Mercosur and the Union of South American Nations. Mercosur signed a free trade agreement with Israel in Uruguay in December 2007

BOLIVARIAN ALLIANCE FOR THE AMERICAS

Official languages	Spanish
Member states	8 Antigua and Barbuda Bolivia Cuba Dominica Ecuador Nicaragua Saint Vincent and the Grenadines Venezuela Haiti (Joining August 2012 as a full member)
Establishment	
- Cuba-Venezuela Agreement	14 December 2004
- People's Trade Agreement	29 April 2006

Area	
- Total	2,513,337 km^2 970,405 sq mi
Population	
- 2008 estimate	69,513,221
- Density	27.65/km^2 71.63/sq mi
GDP (PPP)	2008 estimate
- Total	$636.481 billion (21)
- Per capita	$9,156.25 (82)
Currency	6 Bolivian boliviano Cuban peso East Caribbean dollar Nicaraguan córdoba United States dollar Venezuelan bolívar
Time zone	(UTC-4 to -6)
Internet TLD	8 ag .bo .cu .dm .ec .ni .vc .ve
Website AlianzaBolivariana.org	

The **Bolivarian Alliance for the Peoples of Our America** (Spanish: *Alianza Bolivariana para los Pueblos de Nuestra América*, or ALBA) is an international cooperation organization based on the idea of social, political, and economic integration between the countries of Latin America and the Caribbean. It is associated with socialist and social democratic governments and is an attempt at regional economic integration based on a vision of social welfare, bartering and mutual economic aid, rather than trade liberalization as with free trade agreements. The member nations are Antigua and Barbuda, Bolivia, Cuba, Dominica,Ecuador, Nicaragua, Saint Vincent and the Grenadines and Venezuela. At the February 2012 summit, Suriname andSaint Lucia were admitted to ALBA as guest countries. ALBA nations are in the process of introducing a new regional currency, the SUCRE. It was intended to be the common virtual currency by 2010 and eventually a hard currency. On Tuesday, July 6, 2010, Venezuela and Ecuador conducted the first bilateral trade deal between two ALBA countries using the new trading currency, the Sucre, instead of the US dollar.

The name initially contained "Alternative" instead of "Alliance", but was changed on June 24, 2009.

The agreement was initially proposed by the government of Venezuela, led by Hugo Chávez, as an alternative to the Free Trade Area of the Americas (FTAA or ALCA in Spanish) proposed by theUnited States. The adjective *Bolivarian* refers to Simón Bolívar, after whom Bolivia is named and who is revered as a hero in Venezuelaand to a lesser extent in entire Spanish-speaking South America for his leadership of independence movements against Spanish colonial power.

The Cuba-Venezuela Agreement, which was signed on December 14, 2004, by Presidents Hugo Chávez and Fidel Castro, was aimed at the exchange of medical and educational resources andpetroleum between both nations. Venezuela delivers about 96,000 barrels of oil per day from its state-owned petroleum operations to Cuba at very favorable prices and Cuba in exchange sent 20,000 state-employed medical staff and thousands of teachers to Venezuela's poorest states. Venezuelans can also travel to Cuba for specialized medical care free of charge.

When it was launched in 2004, ALBA had two member states, Venezuela and Cuba.Subsequently a number of other Latin American and Caribbean nations have entered into this Peoples' Trade Agreement (Spanish: *Tratado de Comercio de los Pueblos*, or TCP) which aims to implement the principles of ALBA. Bolivia under Evo Morales joined in 2006, Nicaragua under Daniel Ortega in 2007, and Ecuador under Rafael Correa in 2009. Honduras, under Manuel Zelaya, joined in 2008, but withdrew in 2009 after the2009 Honduran coup d'état saw him replaced by Roberto Micheletti.

MONETARY UNION

In December 2008, ALBA member countries met again to approve the technical details of the introduction of the new currency that was named SUCRE.

In October 2009 leaders from ALBA agreed during a summit in Bolivia on the creation of the regional currency. "The document is approved," said Bolivian President Evo Morales, the summit host. President Hugo Chávez announced "The sucre - an autonomous and sovereign monetary system that will be agreed upon today so that it can be implemented in 2010." The three Caricom member states which are currently using the Eastern Caribbean Dollar have all agreed to use the new proposed SUCRE as a common currency for electronic transactions amongst ALBA members rather than the US dollar. These countries will not be issuing bills in SUCRE, it will instead be used for electronic payment, and each country can withdraw the equivalent in its own currency.

MEMBERSHIP

Common name	Official name	Date joined	Population	Area (km²)	GDP PPP (US$ bn)	Capital
Antigua and Barbuda	Antigua and Barbuda	2009-06-24	85,632	442	1.575	St. John's
Bolivia	Plurinational State of Bolivia	2006-04-29	9,119,152	1,098,581	50.904	La Paz
Cuba	Republic of Cuba	2004-12-14	11,451,652	110,861	114.1	Havana

Common name	Official name	Date joined	Population	Area (km²)	GDP PPP (US$ bn)	Capital
Dominica	Commonwealth of Dominica	2008-01-20	72,660	754	.977	Roseau
Ecuador	Republic of Ecuador	2009-06-24	14,573,101	256,370	127.426	Quito
Nicaragua	Republic of Nicaragua	2007-02-23	5,891,199	129,495	18.878	Managua
Saint Vincent and the Grenadines	Saint Vincent and the Grenadines	2009-06-24	120,000	389	1.259	Kingstown
Venezuela	Bolivarian Republic of Venezuela	2004-12-14	28,199,825	916,445	374.111	Caracas
ALBA Totals	8 Countries	–	69,513,221	2,513,337	636.481	

In addition, two states (Suriname and St Lucia) are "special guest members" which intend to become full members. Haiti, an observer member, also intends to join ALBA.

SUCRE

The **SUCRE** (Spanish: ***Sistema Único de Compensación Regional***, English: **Unified System for Regional Compensation**) is a proposed regional currency to be used in commercial exchanges between members of the regional trade bloc Bolivarian Alliance for the Americas (ALBA), which was created as an alternative to the Free Trade Agreement of the Americas (FTAA). The SUCRE is intended to replace the U.S. dollar as a medium of exchange, in order to decrease U.S. control of Latin American economies and to increase stability of regional markets.

The SUCRE was first used as a virtual currency in 2010, in at least two transactions between Ecuador and Venezuela. Eventually, the plan is for the SUCRE to become a hard currency.

The plan for the introduction of the SUCRE, initially as a virtual currency, parallels theEuropean Union's introduction of the euro in 1999, which was preceded by theEuropean Currency Unit in 1979. The SUCRE is the unit of account for all transactions in the clearinghouse. Its value derives from a basket of currencies from the member countries, weighted according to the relative size of the economies.

The treaty explicitly limits the backing assets of the basket of currencies to financial securities denominated in the respective currencies of the member states. Prohibition of alternative forms of currency backing (such as commodity backing) presents an inequity for Ecuador that, alone in the group, does not have its own national currency (it uses the US dollar)

In the case of ALBA members Dominica, Saint Vincent and the Grenadines and Antigua and Barbuda, the new currency poses a dilemma, as they are already a member of theEastern Caribbean Currency Union and use the East Caribbean dollar.

The SUCRE is named after Antonio José de Sucre, a leading figure in Latin America's independence struggle. Agreement in general terms for the currency was declared in Sucre's birthplace of Cumaná, capital of Venezuela's Sucre state, on April 16, 2009.The formal treaty establishing the regional payments clearinghouse was signed by the six presidents in Cochabamba, Bolivia, on October 17, 2009.

TREATY TERMS

The treaty constitutes a Regional Monetary Council, under Public international law, based in Caracas, Venezuela, charged with issuing and signing Sucres into circulation, and governing the payments clearinghouse. The two-tier council consists of an executive board and a secretariat; the former handling steering and strategy and the latter handling technical and administrative tasks. The Executive Director and the Executive Secretary each have three year terms. The Executive Director is appointed by the Board, which itself has twelve members; a Director and Deputy from each participating country.

The core operation of the SUCRE is a central payments clearinghouse handled by an Agent Bank selected by the Regional Monetary Council. Terms of payment operations through the clearinghouse are determined by bi-lateral and multi-lateral agreements between the Agent Bank and the Central Banks of the member six countries. Associated with the clearinghouse are reserve fund accounts of financial securities put forward by the member central banks, denominated in their respective currencies, to cover temporary payment shortfalls.

The "sucre" unit is distinct from existing national currencies and is created for the purpose of defending the monetary and financial sovereignty of the participating countries, towards a progressive decoupling from the U.S. dollar. The medium term objective is strengthening of economic and social cohesion by integrating regional economic complementarities. Member governments consider their productive sectors to have been damaged by premature exposure to stronger, more advanced and better funded competition from foreign corporations. The SUCRE is thus a monetary strategy of self-protection superior in many ways to tariffs, import controls or currency controls.

ANDEAN COMMUNITY OF NATIONS

Seat of Secretariat	Lima, Peru
Official Languages	Spanish (Community's working language),Quechua, Aymara, 34 other indigenous languages
Type	Trade bloc
Membership	4 South American states 2 North American 1 European 1 African observer states

	Leaders
- Secretary General	Adalid Contreras Baspineiro
	Establishment
- as the Andean Pact	1969
- as the CAN	1996
	Population
- 2010 estimate	101,119,783 (from combined census estimates of member states) (12th)
GDP (PPP)	estimate
- Total	$902.86 billion (16th)
- Per capita	$8,928.62
	Website
	http://www.comunidadandina.org/

The **Andean Community** (Spanish:***Comunidad Andina***, **CAN**) is a customs union comprising the South Americancountries of Bolivia, Colombia, Ecuadorand Peru. The trade bloc was called the**Andean Pact** until 1996 and came into existence with the signing of the**Cartagena Agreement** in 1969. Its headquarters are located in Lima, Peru.

The Andean Community has 98 million inhabitants living in an area of 4,700,000 square kilometers, whose Gross Domestic Product amounted to US$745.3 billion in 2005, including Venezuela, (who was a member at that time). It's estimated GDP PPP for 2011 amounts to US$902.86 billion, excluding Venezuela.

The original Andean Pact was founded in 1969 by Bolivia, Chile, Colombia, Ecuador and Peru. In 1973, the pact gained its sixth member, Venezuela. In 1976, however, its membership was again reduced to five when Chile withdrew. Venezuela announced its withdrawal in 2006, reducing the Andean Community to four member states.

Recently, with the new cooperation agreement with Mercosur, the Andean Community gained four new associate members: Argentina, Brazil, Paraguay and Uruguay. These four Mercosur members were granted associate membership by the Andean Council of Foreign Ministers meeting in an enlarged session with the Commission (of the Andean Community) on July 7, 2005. This moves reciprocates the actions of Mercosur which granted associate membership to all the Andean Community nations by virtue of the Economic Complementarity Agreements (Free Trade agreements) signed between the CAN and individual Mercosur members.

Current members:

Bolivia (1969)

Colombia (1969)

Ecuador (1969)

Peru (1969)

Associate members:

- Argentina (2005)
- Brazil (2005)
- Paraguay (2005)
- Uruguay (2005)
- Chile (2006)

Observer countries:

Mexico

Panama

Sahrawi Arab Democratic Republic

Spain

Former full members:

Venezuela (1973–2006), in the process of joining Mercosur

Chile (full member 1969-1976, observer 1976-2006, associate member since 2006)

RELATIONSHIP WITH OTHER ORGANIZATIONS

The Andean Community and Mercosur comprise the two main trading blocs of South America. In 1999, these organizations began negotiating a merger with a view to creating a "South American Free Trade Area" (SAFTA). On December 8, 2004 the Andean Community (CAN) signed a cooperation agreement with Mercosur and they published a joint letter of intention for future negotiations towards integrating all of South America in a Union of South American Nations (USAN), patterned after the European Union. It was formally established by the May 23, 2008, Constitutive Treaty of the USAN signed in Brasília.

During 2005, Venezuela decided to join Mercosur. Venezuela's official position first appeared to be that, by joining Mercosur, further steps could be taken towards integrating both trade blocs. CAN Secretary General Allan Wagner stated that the Venezuelan Foreign Minister Alí Rodríguez had declared that Venezuela did not intend to leave the CAN, and its simultaneous membership to both blocs marked the beginning of their integration.

However some analysts interpreted that Venezuela might eventually leave the CAN in the process. This prediction seems to have been finally verified in April 2006, with Venezuelan President Chávez's announcement of his country's withdrawal from the Andean Community after stating that, as Colombia and Peru have signed free trade agreements (FTAs) with the United States, the Community is "dead". Officials in Colombia and Peru have expressed their disagreement with this view, as did representatives from Venezuela's industrial sector (Conindustria).

Despite this announcement, Venezuela has yet to formally complete all the necessary withdrawal procedures. According to Venezuela's Commerce Minister María Cristina Iglesias, the entire process will take up to five years. Until then, Venezuela and its partners remain bound by the effects of the community's preexisting commercial agreements.

During a visit to Colombia in August 2007, President Hugo Chávez said that he has agreed to rejoin the Andean Community of Nations after the presidents of Ecuador and Bolivia asked him to do so. Recently, relations between Mercosur and Venezuela have weakened since Mercosur does not agree with some of his proposals.

In addition to CAN, Bolivia is also a member of the WTO, UNASUR and ALBA. Its attitude is considered crucial to relations between UNASUR and ALBA specifically, says Marion Hörmann, since Bolivia is traditionally seen as a mediator between the Andean countries and the rest of South America.

ORGANIZATION

- Andean Presidential Council
- Andean Foreign Relations Ministers Council
- Commission
- Headquarters (Lima, Peru)
- Andean Court of Justice
- Andean Parliament (Bogotá, Colombia)
- Latin American Reserve Fund
- Simón Bolívar Andean University

From January 1, 2005, the citizens of the member countries can enter the other Andean Community member states without the requirement of visa. The passengers should present the authorities their national ID cards.

Visitors to Venezuela will have to present their passports; they will then receive the Andean Migration Card (*Tarjeta Andina de Migración*), in which the time of temporary residence in the country is stated.

ANDEAN PASSPORT

The Andean passport was created in June 2001 pursuant to *Decisión 504*. This stipulates the issuing of a passport based on a standard model which contains harmonised features of nomenclature and security. The passport is effective in Ecuador, Peru, Venezuela, Bolivia, and Colombia (Bolivia and Colombia since early 2006).

THE UNION OF SOUTH AMERICAN NATIONS UNASUL

Administrative centers	Quito (Secretariat Headquarters) Cochabamba (Parliament seat)
Official languages	Spanish Portuguese Dutch English

Demonym	South American
Membership	12 members 2 observers
	Leaders
- President	Fernando Lugo
- Secretary General	Alí Rodríguez Araque
Legislature	South American Parliament
	Formation
- Cusco Declaration	8 December 2004
- Constitutive Treaty	23 May 2008
- Functioning entity	11 March 2011
	Area
- Total	17,731,457 km^2 6,846,154 sq mi
- Water (%)	8.91
	Population
- 2008 estimate	387.948 million
- Density	21.9/km^2 (192nd) 56.7/sq mi
GDP (PPP)	2010 estimate
- Total	$7.942 trillion (3rd)
- Per capita	$9,736 (77th)
GDP (nominal)	2010 estimate
- Total	$3.532 trillion (4th)
- Per capita	$7,421 (68th)
Time zone	(UTC-2 to -5)
	Website www.unasursg.org (Spanish)

The **Union of South American Nations UNASUL**, Spanish: *Unión de Naciones Suramericanas* - **UNASUR**) is an intergovernmental union integrating two existing customs unions: Mercosur and theAndean Community of Nations (CAN), as part of a continuing process of South American integration. It is modeled on theEuropean Union.

The UNASUR Constitutive Treaty was signed on May 23, 2008, at the Third Summit of Heads of State, held in Brasília, Brazil. According to the Constitutive Treaty, the Union's headquarters will be located in Quito, Ecuador. The South American Parliament will be located inCochabamba, Bolivia, while the headquarters of its bank, the Bank of the South are located in Caracas,Venezuela.

The combined population of the 12-member Union as at 1 July 2010 was estimated at 396,391,032.

On 4 May 2010, at an extraordinary heads of state summit held in Campana, 75 km (47 mi) north of Buenos Aires, former Argentine President Néstor Kirchner was unanimously elected the first Secretary-General of UNASUR for a two-year term. This new office was conceived as a first step towards the establishment of a permanent bureaucratic body for thesupranational union, eventually superseding Mercosur and CAN political bodies. On 1 December 2010, Uruguay became the ninth nation to ratify the UNASUR treaty, thus giving the union full legality.

As the Constitutive Treaty entered into force on 11 March 2011, UNASUR became a legal entity during a meeting of Foreign Ministers in Mitad del Mundo,Ecuador, where they had laid the foundation stone for the Secretariat Headquarters

At the Third South American Summit on 8 December 2004, presidents or representatives from 12 South American nations signed the *Cusco Declaration*, a two-page statement of intent announcing the foundation of the South American Community.Panama and Mexico attended the signing ceremony as observers.

The group announced their intention to model the new community after the European Union including a common currency, parliament, and passport. According to Allan Wagner Tizón, former Secretary General of the Andean Community, a complete union like that of the EU should be possible by 2019.

The mechanics of the new entity came out of the First South American Community of Nations Heads of State Summit, which was held in Brasília on 29–30 September 2005. An important operating condition of UNASUR is that no new institutions will be created in the first phase, so as not to increase bureaucracy, and the community will use the existing institutions belonging to the previous trade blocs.

The complete integration between the Andean Community and the Mercosur nations was formalized during the meeting of South American heads of state that took place on May 23, 2008 in Brasília.

In the 2004 South American Summit, representatives of twelve South American nations signed the Cuzco Declaration, a two-page letter of intent announcing the establishment of the then-named "South American Community of Nations". Panama and Mexico were present as observers. The leaders announced the intention of modeling the new community in the mold of the European Union, including a unified passport, a parliament and, eventually, a single currency. The then Secretary General of the Andean Community Allan Wagner speculated that an advanced union such as the EU should be possible within the next fifteen years.

STRUCTURE

At the moment, the provisional structure of the UNASUR is as follows:

A permanent Secretariat is to be established in Quito, Ecuador. The Secretary General, with a two-year mandate, is to be elected on a consensual basis among the Heads of State of the member states. Former Argentine President Néstor Kirchner was designated the first Secretary General on 4 May 2010.

The presidents of the member nations will have an annual meeting, which will have the superior political mandate. The first meeting was in Brasília (Brazil) on 29–30 September 2005. The second meeting was in Cochabamba (Bolivia) on 8–9 December 2006. The third meeting was held in Brasília on 23 May 2008.

The Presidency Pro Tempore, is exercised for a one-year period on a pro tempore basis by one of the heads of state of each UNASUR Member State, the succession following alphabetical order. The first leader to occupy this position was Chilean President Michelle Bachelet. According to Decisions Reached in the Political Dialogue which was signed during the I South American Energy Summit.

The ministers of foreign affairs of each country will meet once every six months. They will formulate concrete proposals of action and of executive decision. The President of the Mercosur's permanent representatives committee and the director of the Mercosur's department, the Andean Community's general secretary, ALADI's general secretary and the permanent secretaries of any institution for regional cooperation and integration, Amazon Cooperation Treaty Organization among others, will also be present at these meetings.

Sectorial Ministers' meeting will be called upon by the presidents. The meetings will be developed according to Mercosur's and CAN's mechanisms.

On 9 December 2005, a special commission was established in charge of advancing the process of South American Integration. It consists of 12 members, whose function is to elaborate proposals that will help the process of integration between the South American nations.

An Executive Commission, which was created by the II CSN meeting, was transformed in the Political Commission or Delegates Council, according to Decisions Reached in the Political Dialogue.

ORGANS OF THE UNASUR

The organs of UNASUR are

Council of Heads of State and of Government of Unasur

President Pro Tempore of UNASUR

Council of Minister of External Relationships of Unasur

Council of Delegates of Unasur

Secretary General of UNASUR

Ministerial Councils of the Unasur

They are eight Ministerial Councils of the Unasur

South American Council of Social Development

South American Council of fight against the drug traffic

South American Council of Health

South American Council of Education, Culture, Science, Technology and Innovation

South American Council of Defense

South American Council of Energy

South American Council of Economy and Finances

South American Council of Infrastructure and Planning

Other institutions of Unasur

South American Parliament

Bank of the South

SINGLE MARKET

One of the initiatives of UNASUR is the creation of asingle market, beginning with the elimination of tariffs for non-sensitive products by 2014, and for sensitive products by 2019. The process is to be developed upon the progressive convergence of the procedures of pre-existing Mercosur and CAN subregional economic blocks.

ECONOMIC DEVELOPMENT

Presidents of the seven founding countries (Argentina, Bolivia, Brazil, Ecuador, Paraguay, Venezuela and Uruguay) officially launched the South American Bank in Buenos Aires in December 2007. The heads of all the founding countries were at the ceremony, with the exception of President Tabaré Vázquez of Uruguay. The capital will be US$7b, with Venezuela responsible for US$3b and Brazil US$2b. The headquarters will be located in Caracas with offices in Buenos Aires and La Paz.

The Bank of the South will finance economic development projects to improve local competitiveness and to promote the scientific and technological development of the member states.

The founding chart affirms that the Bank will promote projects in "stable and equal" manner and priorities will be pointed to reinforce South American integration, to reduce asymmetries, and to promote egalitarian distribution of investments.

The Brazilian Minister, Guido Mantega, stated that the bank is not similar to theInternational Monetary Fund; it will be a credit institution similar to the World Bank.

INFRASTRUCTURE COOPERATION

There is an Initiative for Infrastructure Integration of South America (IIRSA) underway, which has received the support of the Inter-American Development Bank and the Andean Development Corporation.

UNASUR started plans of integration through infrastructure cooperation with the construction of the Interoceanic Highway, a road that intends to more firmly link the Pacific Coast countries, especially Chile and Peru with Brazil and Argentina by extending highways through the continent, allowing better connections to ports from Bolivia and the inner parts of Argentina, Peru, and

Brazil. The first corridor, between Peru and Brazil, began construction in September 2005, financed 60% by Brazil and 40% by Peru, was expected to be ready by the end of 2009.

The South American Energy Ring is intended to interconnect Argentina, Brazil, Chile, Paraguay, and Uruguay with natural gas from several sources, such as the Camisea Gas Project in Peru and Tarija Gas Deposits in Bolivia. Though this proposal has been signed and ratified, economic and political difficulties in Argentina and Bolivia have delayed this initiative, and to date, this agreement remains more like a protocol than an actual project, since Chile and Brazil are already building LNG terminals to import gas from overseas suppliers.

FREE MOVEMENT OF PEOPLES

Visits by South American citizens to any South American independent country of up to 90 days only require an identification document issued by the traveler's country. In November 24, 2006, Argentina, Bolivia, Brazil, Chile, Colombia, Ecuador, Guyana, Paraguay, Peru, Suriname, Uruguay and Venezuela abolished visa requirements for tourists between any of those nations.

Mercosur, Bolivia and Chile established that their territories together form an "area of free residence with the right to work" to all its citizens, with no additional requirements other than nationality. The Free Movement and Residence Agreement was established in the Brasília summit based in a previous document signed in December 6, 2002.

Citizens of any Mercosur countries will have a simplified process in temporary residence visa of up to 2 years in any other member countries, with the requirements of a valid passport, birth certificate, and no criminal record. Temporary residence can become permanent if a licit means of living can be verified.

Immigration

This section may stray from the topic of the article. Please help improve this section or discuss this issue on the talk page. (July 2011)

Brazil has introduced a new temporary residency program for citizens of Argentina, Bolivia, Chile, Paraguay, and Uruguay. Under the new program, eligible citizens of these countries will benefit from a simplified application process, which can be completed from within Brazil. If successful, they will receive a two-year residency status, after which they will be eligible for permanent residency.

Eligible citizens of the Mercosur member countries (Argentina, Paraguay, and Uruguay) and two Mercosur "associated countries" (Chile and Bolivia) can now apply for a special two-year temporary residency program in Brazil using a simplified application process. The new program was introduced by a government decree published on 8 October 2009, but administrative delays prevented the new program from being implemented until now.

Under the new program, natural-born citizens of these countries, or individuals who have held citizenship in these countries for at least five years, plus their legal dependents (regardless of nationality), may obtain temporary residency status in Brazil that will remain valid for two years. The temporary residency program is not linked to a specific employer, and from an immigration perspective, these residents are eligible to work for any employer in Brazil. After the first two years, the candidate is eligible for permanent residency.

Nationals of these five countries may apply for this residency program abroad at a Brazilian consular post or from within Brazil to the Brazilian Federal Police. Applicants must demonstrate their identity, citizenship and good character by presenting documents requested by immigration authorities, such as: passports, identity cards, or nationality certificates issued by their country of origin's consular post; birth certificates; marriage certificates (if applicable); declarations of criminal clearance or criminal clearance certificates; and registration fees.

According to Brazilian Labour Department, between 2005 and July, 2009: 3,083 Argentines, 1,303 Venezuelans, 1,168 Chileans, 476 Bolivians, 314 Uruguayans, 159 Paraguayans entered Brazil to work.

STRATEGIC AGREEMENTS AND MATERIALS

THE TREATY OF MONTEVIDEO

The Governments of the Argentine Republic, the Republic of Bolivia, the Federative Republic of Brazil, the Republic of Chile, the Republic of Colombia, the Republic of Ecuador, the United Mexican States, the Republic of Paraguay, the Republic of Peru, the Eastern Republic of Uruguay, and the Republic of Venezuela,

INSPIRED by the purpose of strengthening the friendship and solidarity links between their peoples.

PERSUADED that economic regional integration is one of the principal means for the Latin American countries to speed up their economic and social development process in order to ensure better standards of life for their peoples.

DECIDED to renew the Latin American integration process and establish objectives and mechanisms consistent with the region's real situation.

CERTAIN that the continuation of such process requires taking advantage of the positive experience obtained in the implementation of the Montevideo Treaty dated 18 February 1960.

AWARE that it is necessary to ensure a special treatment for countries at a relatively less advanced stage of economic development.

WILLING to encourage the development of solidarity and cooperation ties with other countries and integration areas of Latin America in order to promote a process converging towards the establishment of a regional common market.

CONVINCED of the need to contribute towards obtaining a new scheme of horizontal cooperation between developing countries and their integration areas, inspired by the principles of international law regarding development.

BEARING IN MIND the decision adopted by the Contracting Parties to the General Agreement on Tariffs and Trade whereby regional or general agreements may be drawn up between developing countries in order to mutually reduce or eliminate obstacles to their reciprocal trade.

THEY HEREBY AGREE to sign the present Treaty which, concurrent with the provisions herein contained, shall substitute the Treaty instituting the Latin American Free Trade Association.

CHAPTER I: OBJECTIVES, DUTIES AND PRINCIPLES

Article 1: By the present Treaty the Contracting Parties pursue the integration process leading to promote the harmonious and balanced socio-economic development of the region, and to that effect they hereby institute the Latin American Integration Association (hereafter referred to as the "Association"), with headquarters in the city of Montevideo, Eastern Republic of Uruguay.

The long-term objective of such process shall be the gradual and progressive establishment of a Latin American common market.

Article 2: The rules and mechanisms of the present Treaty, as well as those which may be established within its framework by member countries, shall have as their purpose the performance of the following basic duties of the Association: promotion and regulation of reciprocal trade, economic complementation, and development of economic cooperation actions encouraging market expansion.

Article 3: In the implementation of the present Treaty and the evolution towards its final objective, member countries shall bear in mind the following principles:

a. Pluralism, sustained by the will of member countries to integrate themselves, over and above the diversity which might exist in political and economic matters in the region;

b. Convergence, meaning progressive multilateralization of partial scope agreements by means of periodical negotiations between member countries, with a view to establish the Latin American common market;

c. Flexibility, characterized by the capacity to allow the conclusion of partial scope agreements, ruled in a form consistent with the progressive attainment of their convergence and the strengthening of integration ties;

d. Differential treatments, as determined in each case, both in regional and partial scope mechanisms, on the basis of three categories of countries, which will be set up taking into account their economic-structural characteristics. Such treatments shall be applied in a determined scale to intermediate developed countries, and in a more favourable manner to countries at a relatively less advanced stage of economic development; and

e. Multiple, to make possible various forms of agreements between member countries, following the objectives and duties of the integration process, using all instruments capable of activating and expanding markets at regional level.

CHAPTER II: MECHANISMS

Article 4: In order to fulfill the basic duties of the Association set forth in article 2 of the present Treaty, member countries hereby establish an area of economic preferences, comprising a regional tariff preference, regional scope agreements, and partial scope agreements.

First section - Regional tariff preference

Article 5: Member countries shall reciprocally grant a regional tariff preference to be applied with reference to the level in force for third countries and be subject to the corresponding regulation.

Second section - Regional scope agreements

Article 6: Regional scope agreements are those in which all member countries participate. They shall be drawn up within in framework of the objectives and provisions of the present Treaty, and may refer to the same matters and include those instruments foreseen for the partial scope agreements provided for in the third section of the present chapter.

Third section - Partial scope agreements

Article 7: Partial scope agreements are those wherein all member countries do not participate. These agreements shall tend to create the conditions necessary to deepen the regional integration process by means of their progressive multilateralization.

Rights and obligations to be established in partial scope agreements shall exclusively bind the signatory member countries or those adhered thereto.

Article 8: Partial scope agreements may refer to trade, economic complementation, agriculture, trade promotion, or adopt other modalities concurring with article 14 of the present Treaty.

Article 9: Partial scope agreements shall be governed by the following general rules:

a. They shall be open for accession to the other member countries, prior negotiation;

b. They shall contain clauses promoting convergence in order that their benefits reach all member countries;

c. They may contain clauses promoting convergence with other Latin American countries, in concurrence with the mechanisms established in the present Treaty;

d. They shall include differential treatments depending on the three categories of countries recognized by the present Treaty. The implementation of such treatments as well as negotiation procedures for their periodical revision at the request of any member country which may consider itself at a disadvantage shall be determined in each agreement;

e. Tariff reductions may be applied to the same products or tariff sub-items and on the basis of a percentage rebate regarding the tariffs applied to imports originating from non-participating countries;

f. They shall be in force for a minimum term of one year; and

g. They may include, among others, specific rules regarding origin, safeguard clauses, non-tariff restrictions, withdrawal of concessions, renegotiation of concessions, denouncement, coordination and harmonization of policies. Should these specific rules not have been adopted, the general provisions to be established by member countries on the respective matters shall be taken into account.

Article 10: Trade agreements are exclusively aimed towards trade promotion among member countries, and shall be subject to the specific rules to be established for that purpose.

Article 11: Economic complementation agreements are aimed, among other objectives, to promote maximum utilization of production factors, stimulate economic complementation, ensure equitable conditions for competition, facilitate entry of products into the international market, and encourage the balanced and harmonious development of member countries.

These agreements shall be subject to the specific rules to be established for that purpose.

Article 12: Agricultural agreements are aimed to promote and regulate intraregional trade of agricultural and livestock products. They shall contemplate flexibility elements bearing in mind the participating countries' socio-economic characteristics of production. These agreements may refer to specific products or groups of products, and may be based on temporary, seasonal, per quota or mixed concessions, or on contracts between State or para-State organizations. They shall be subject to the specific rules to be established for that purpose.

Article 13: Trade promotion agreements shall refer to non-tariff matters and tend to promote intrarregional trade flows.

They shall be subject to the specific rules to be established for that purpose.

Article 14: Member countries may establish, through the corresponding regulations, specific rules to conclude other modalities of partial scope agreements.

For this purpose, they shall take into consideration, among other matters, scientific and technological cooperation, tourism promotion and preservation of the environment.

CHAPTER III: SYSTEM IN FAVOUR OF COUNTRIES AT A RELATIVELY LESS ADVANCED STAGE OF ECONOMIC DEVELOPMENT

Article 15: Member countries shall establish conditions favouring participation of countries at a relatively less advanced stage of economic development in the economic integration process, based on the principles of non-reciprocity and community cooperation.

Article 16: For the purpose of ensuring them an effective preferential treatment, member countries shall establish market opening as well as set up programs and other specific forms of cooperation.

Article 17: Actions favouring relatively less developed countries shall be concluded through regional scope and partial scope agreements.

In order to ensure the effectiveness of such agreements, member countries shall execute negotiated rules concerning preservation of preferences, elimination of non-tariff restrictions and application of safeguard clauses in justified cases.

First section - Regional scope agreements

Article 18: For each relatively less developed country, member countries shall approve negotiated lists of preferably industrial products originating from each relatively less developed country, for which total elimination of customs duties and other restrictions shall be accorded, without reciprocity, by all other member countries of the Association.

Member countries shall set up the necessary procedures to achieve progressive extension of the respective liberalization lists. Corresponding negotiations may be carried out when deemed convenient.

At the same time, member countries shall endeavour to set up effective compensation mechanisms to take care of negative effects which might influence intraregional trade of the relatively less developed land-locked countries.

Second section - Partial scope agreements

Article 19: Partial scope agreements negotiated by the relatively less developed countries with other member countries shall conform, wherever pertinent, with the provisions contained in articles 8 and 9 of the present Treaty.

Article 20: In order to encourage effective and collective cooperation in favour of relatively less developed countries, member countries shall negotiate Special Cooperation Programs with each one of them.

Article 21: In order to facilitate utilization of tariff cuts, member countries may set up cooperation programs and actions in the fields of preinvestment, financing and technology, mainly directed towards supporting the relatively less developed countries, with special regard, among them, to land-locked countries.

Article 22: Notwithstanding the proceeding articles, treatments in favour of relatively less developed countries may include collective and partial cooperation actions calling for effective mechanisms meant to compensate the disadvantageous situation faced by Bolivia and Paraguay due to their land-locked location.

Provided that criteria referred to gradual timing are adopted within the regional tariff preference referred to in article 5 of the present Treaty, attempts shall be made to preserve the margins granted in favour of land-locked countries by means of cumulative tarlff cuts.

At the same time, attempts shall be made to establish compensation formulae, both as regards the regional tariff preference when deepened, and regional and partial scope agreements.

Article 23: Member countries shall endeavour to grant land-locked countries facilities to establish free zones, warehouses or ports and other administrative international transit facilities in their territories.

CHAPTER IV: CONVERGENCE AND COOPERATION WITH OTHER LATIN AMERICAN COUNTRIES AND AREAS OF ECONOMIC INTEGRATION

Article 24: Member countries may establish multilateral association or relationship systems encouraging convergence with other countries and areas of economic integration of Latin America, including the possibility of agreeing with these countries or areas the establishment of a Latin American tariff preference.

Member countries shall in due course regulate the characteristics of these systems.

Article 25: Likewise, member countries may draw up partial scope agreements with other Latin American countries and areas of economic integration, in accordance with the various modalities foreseen in the third section of chapter II of the present Treaty, and under the terms of the respective regulative provisions.

Notwithstanding the above, these agreements shall be subject to the following rules:

a. Concessions granted by participating member countries shall not be extensive to the others, excepting the relatively less developed countries;

b. When a member country includes products already negotiated in partial agreements with other member countries, concessions granted may be higher than those agreed with the former; in this case, consultation with the affected member countries shall be carried out in order to find mutually satisfactory solutions, unless the respective partial agreements include clauses concerning automatic extension or waiver of preferences contained in the partial agreements referred to in the present article; and

c. They shall be multilaterally assessed by the member countries within the Committee in order to acknowledge the scope of the agreements drawn up and facilitate participation of other member countries in same.

CHAPTER V: COOPERATION WITH OTHER AREAS OF ECONOMIC INTEGRATION

Article 26: Member countries shall undertake the actions necessary to establish and develop solidarity and cooperation links with other integration areas outside Latin America, through the Association's participation in horizontal cooperation programs carried out at international level, thus implementing the basic principles and commitments adopted within the context of the

Declaration and Action Program on the establishment of a New International Economic Order and of the Charter of Economic Rights and Duties of States.

The Committee shall adopt adequate measures to facilitate compliance with the objectives set forth.

Article 27: At the same time, member countries may draw up partial scope agreements with other developing countries or respective economic integration areas outside Latin America, following the various modalities foreseen in the third section of chapter II of the present Treaty, and under the terms of the pertinent regulative provisions.

Notwithstanding the above, these agreements shall be subject to the following rules:

a. Concessions granted by member countries participating in them shall not be extended to other members, with the exception of the relatively less developed countries;

b. When products already negotiated with other member countries in partial scope agreements are included, concessions granted may not be higher than those agreed with the former, and in such case they shall be automatically extended to those countries; and

c. They shall be declared consistent with the commitments undertaken by member countries within the frame of the present Treaty, in accordance with captions a) and b) of the present article.

CHAPTER VI: INSTITUTIONAL ORGANIZATION

Article 28: The political bodies of the Association are:

a. The Council of Ministers of Foreign Affairs (referred to as the "Council" in this Treaty);

b. The Evaluation and Convergence Conference (referred to as the "Conference" in this Treaty); and

c. The Committee of Representatives (referred to as the "Committee" in this Treaty).

Article 29: The technical body of the Association is the General Secretariat (referred to as the "Secretariat" in this Treaty).

Article 30: The Council is the supreme body of the Association and shall adopt whatever decisions may correspond to the higher governing policy of the economic integration process.

The Council shall have the following powers:

a. To issue general rules aimed at a better compliance with the objectives of the Association, as well as at the harmonious development of the integration process;

b. To examine the results of the tasks carried out by the Association;

c. To adopt corrective measures of multilateral scope, following the recommendations adopted by the Conference as per terms of article 33, caption a) of the present Treaty;

d. To establish the guide-lines to be followed by the other bodies of the Association in their tasks;

e. To set the basic rules to govern the relations of the Association with other regional associations, international organizations or agencies;

f. To review and update basic rules governing convergence and cooperation agreements with other developing countries and the respective areas of economic integration;

g. To take cognizance of questions submitted by the other political bodies and decide upon them;

h. To delegate upon the other political bodies the power to decide on specific matters aimed at a better compliance with the Association objectives;

y. To accept accession of new member countries;

j. To adopt amendments and additions to the Treaty as per precepts of article 61;

k. To appoint the Secretary-General; and

l. To adopt its own Rules of Procedure.

Article 31: The Council shall be composed of the Ministers of Foreign Affairs of the member countries. However, when in some countries the competence of integration matters is assigned to a Minister or Secretary of State other than the Minister of Foreign Affairs, member countries may be represented at the Council, with full powers, by the respective Minister or Secretary.

Article 32: The Council shall meet and take decisions with the presence of all member countries.

The Council shall meet when convened by the Committee.

Article 33: The Conference shall have the following powers:

a. To examine the operation of the integration process in all its aspects and the convergence of partial scope agreements through their progressive multilateralization, as well as to recommend the Council the adoption of multilateral scope corrective measures;

b. To promote actions of broader scope regarding economic integration;

c. To periodically review the implementation of differential treatments, taking into account not only the evolution of the economic structure of the countries and consequently their degree of development, but also the effective use made by beneficiary countries of the applied differential treatment, as well as of the procedures aimed to improve the implementation of such treatments;

d. To evaluate the results of the system in favour of countries at a relatively less advanced stage of economic development and adopt measures for its more effective application;

e. To carry out multilateral negotiations to determine and deepen the regional tariff preference;

f. To foster negotiation and conclusion of regional scope agreements, wherein all member countries participate, which refer to any matter pertaining to the present Treaty, as per precepts of article 6;

g. To comply with all the tasks entrusted to it by the Council;

h. To commend the Secretariat such studies as it deems convenient; and

y. To adopt its own Rules of Procedure.

Article 34: The Conference shall be composed of Plenipotentiaries of member countries.

The Conference shall hold regular sessions every three years at the request of the Committee. It shall also meet at any other time in extraordinary session, when convened by the latter to deal with questions of its specific competence.

The Conference shall meet and take decisions with the presence of all member countries.

Article 35: The Committee is the permanent body of the Association and shall have the following powers and duties:

a. To promote the conclusion of regional scope agreements, under the terms of article 6 of the present Treaty and, for that purpose, to convene governmental meetings at least once a year with the following aims:

    i. Give continuity to the activities of the new integration process;

    ii. Evaluate and guide the operation of the process;

    iii. Analyze and promote measures to attain more advanced mechanisms of integration; and

    iv. Undertake sectoral and multisectoral negotiations with the participation of all member countries in order to reach regional scope agreements basically referred to tariff cuts;

b. To adopt the measures necessary to implement the present Treaty and all its supplementary rules;

c. To regulate the present Treaty;

d. To perform the tasks entrusted to it by the Council and the Conference;

e. To adopt the annual work program of the Association and its annual budget;

f. To fix the contributions of member countries to the Association budget;

g. To adopt, as proposed by the Secretary-General, the structure of the Secretariat;

h. To convene the Council and the Conference;

y. To represent the Association before third parties;

j. To commend studies to the Secretariat;

k. To submit recommendations to the Council and the Conference;

l. To present reports on its activities to the Council;

m. To propose formulae to solve issues brought forth by member countries claiming non-observance of some of the rules or principles of the present Treaty;

n. To multilaterally assess partial agreements as may be drawn up by the countries under the terms of article 25 of the present Treaty;

ñ. To declare the compatibility of partial agreements to be drawn up by member countries under the terms of article 27 of the present Treaty;

o. To create auxiliary bodies;

p. To adopts its own Rules of Procedure; and

q. To take care of business of common interest not falling within the competence of the other bodies of the Association.

Article 36: The Committee shall be composed of a Permanent Representative of each member country with the right to one vote.

Each Permanent Representative shall have a Deputy.

Article 37: The Committee shall meet and adopt resolutions with the presence of two thirds of the member countries' Representatives.

Article 38: The Secretariat shall be headed by a Secretary-General and composed of technical and administrative staff.

The Secretary-General shall hold office for a period of three years and may be re-elected for an equal term.

The Secretary-General shall act in such capacity with respect to all the political bodies of the Association.

The Secretariat shall have the following powers and duties:

a. To submit proposals to the corresponding Association bodies, through, the Committee, leading towards a better accomplishment of the objectives and duties of the Association;

b. To carry out the necessary studies to fulfill its technical duties and those entrusted to it by the Council, the Conference and the Committee, and to perform the other activities provided for in the annual work program;

c. To carry out studies and actions leading to proposals to member countries, through their Permanent Representatives, regarding conclusion of the agreements foreseen by the present Treaty, within the guide-lines established by the Council and the Conference;

d. To represent the Association before international economic organization and institutions in order to deal with questions of common interest;

e. To administer the Association assets and represent it for such purposes in public and private law acts and contracts;

f. To request technical advice and cooperation of individuals and national and international organizations;

g. To propose the creation of auxiliary bodies to the Committee;

h. To process and furnish member countries, in a systematic and updated manner, statistical information and data on foreign trade regulation systems of member countries in order to facilitate the preparation and carrying out of negotiations within the various Association mechanisms, as well as the further utilization of the respective concessions;

y. To analyze on its own initiative, for all countries, or at the request of the Committee, compliance of agreed commitments, and evaluate legal provisions of member countries which directly or indirectly alter concessions granted;

j. To call meetings of non-governmental auxiliary bodies and coordinate their operation;

k. To periodically evaluate the progress of the integration process and permanently follow up the activities undertaken by the Association and the commitments resulting from the agreements achieved within in framework of same;

l. To organize and put into operation an Economic Promotion Unit for relatively less developed countries and carry out actions to obtain technical and financial resources, as well as studies and projects to comply with the promotion program. At the same time, to draw up an annual report on the advantages obtained from the system in favour of the relatively less developed countries;

m. To prepare the Association's expenditure budget, for approval by the Committee, as well as such subsequent reforms which might be necessary;

n. To prepare and present to the Committee the draft annual work programs;

m. To engage, admit and dismiss technical and administrative staff, in accordance with the regulations ruling its structure;

o. To comply with requests received from any of the political bodies of the Association; and

p. To present an annual report to the Committee on the results of the application of the present Treaty and the legal provisions derived therefrom.

Article 39: The Secretary-General shall be appointed by the Council.

Article 40: In the performance of their duties, the head of the technical body, as well as the technical and administrative staff, shall not seed or receive instructions from any Government or national or international organizations. They shall refrain from any attitude not consistent with their character as international officers.

Article 41: Member countries pledge themselves to respect the international nature of the duties of the Secretary-General and Secretariat staff or of its engaged experts and consultants, and to abstain from influencing them in the performance of their duties.

Article 42: Auxiliary bodies shall be established for consultation, assessment and technical support. In particular, one body shall be set up composed of officers responsible for the integration policy of member countries.

At the same time, consultative auxiliary bodies shall be set up composed of representatives of the various sectors of economic activity of each one of the member countries.

Article 43: The Council, the Conference and the Committee shall adopt their decisions by the affirmative vote of two thirds of the member countries.

Decisions on the following matters excepted from this general rule shall be adopted by a two-thirds affirmative vote, provided there is no negative vote:

a. Amendments or additions to the present Treaty;

b. Adoption of decisions corresponding to the higher governing policy of the integration process;

c. Adoption of decisions executing the results of multilateral negotiations to determine and deepen the regional tariff preference;

d. Adoption of decisions leading to give partial scope agreements a multilateral regional level;

e. Acceptance of accession of new member countries;

f. Regulation of the Treaty provisions;

g. Establishment of the percentages of member countries' contributions to the budget of the Association;

h. Adoption of corrective measures arising from the evaluations of the progress achieved within the integration process;

y. Authorization of a term of less than five years regarding obligations, in case of Treaty denouncement;

j. Adoption of guide-lines to be followed by the Association bodies in their tasks; and

k. Establishment of basic rules governing the relations of the Association with other regional associations, international organizations or agencies.

Abstention shall not mean a negative vote. Absence at the time of voting shall be interpreted as abstention.

The Council may eliminate subjects from this list of exceptions by the affirmative vote of two thirds of the member countries, provided there is no negative vote.

CHAPTER VII: GENERAL PROVISIONS

Article 44: Any advantages, favourable treatments, franchises, immunities and privileges which member countries apply to products originating from or bound to any other member country or non-member country, pursuant to decisions or agreements not foreseen in the present Treaty or the Cartagena Agreement, shall be immediately and unconditionally extended to the other member countries.

Article 45: Any advantages, favourable treatments, franchises, immunities and privileges already granted or to be granted under agreements between member countries or between these and third countries to facilitate border traffic shall be exclusively applicable to the countries which sign or may have signed them.

Article 46: As regards taxes, charges and other internal duties, products originating from the territory of a member country shall be entitled within the territory of the other member countries to a treatment not less favourable than that applied to similar national products.

Member countries shall adopt such steps as may be required to comply with the preceding provision, in accordance with their respective National Constitutions.

Article 47: In the case of products included in the regional tariff preference or in regional or partial scope agreements which are not produced or will not be produced in substantial quantities in its territory, each member country shall endeavour to avoid that taxes or other internal measures applied result in annulment or reduction of any concession or advantage obtained by any member country as a result of the respective negotiations.

If a member country considers itself at a disadvantage by the measures contained in the preceding paragraph, it may resort to the Committee so that the situation raised may be examined and pertinent recommendations issued.

Article 48: Within the territory of other member countries, capitals originating from member countries shall have the right to a treatment not less favourable than that granted to capitals coming from any other non-member country, notwithstanding the provisions set out in agreements which might be concluded on this matter by member countries under the terms of the present Treaty.

Article 49: Member countries may establish supplementary rules on trade policy regulating, among other matters, the application of non-tariff restrictions, a system of origin, the adoption of safeguard clauses, export promotion systems and border traffic.

Article 50: No provision under the present Treaty shall be interpreted as precluding the adoption and observance of measures regarding:

a. Protection of public morality;

b. Implementation of security laws and regulations;

c. Regulation of imports and exports of arms, munitions, and other war materials and, under exceptional circumstances, all other military equipment;

d. Protection of human, animal and plant life and health;

e. Imports and exports of gold and silver in bullion form;

f. Protection of national treasures of artistic, historical or archeological value; and

g. Exportation, use and consumption of nuclear materials, radioactive products or any other material used for the development and exploitation of nuclear energy.

Article 51: Products imported and exported by any member country shall have the right to free transit throughout the territory of the other member countries, and be exclusively subject to payment of charges normally applicable for services rendered.

CHAPTER VIII: LEGAL STATUS, IMMUNITIES AND PRIVILEGES

Article 52: The Association shall be endowed of complete legal status and specially of the capacity:

a. To contract;

b. To acquire such movable and immovable property indispensable to carry out its objectives and to dispose of it;

c. To file suits; and

d. To keep funds in any currency and effect the necessary transfers.

Article 53: Representatives and other diplomatic officers of member countries accredited before the Association, as well as international officers and advisers of the Association, shall be endowed of diplomatic immunities and privileges and such other rights necessary for exercising their duties within the territory of member countries.

Member countries hereby pledge themselves to draw up within the shortest possible term an agreement aimed at regulating the contents of the proceeding paragraph, wherein such privileges and immunities shall be defined.

The Association shall draw up an agreement with the Government of the Eastern Republic of Uruguay in order to determine the privileges and immunities to which the Association, its bodies and its international officers and advisers shall be entitled.

Article 54: The legal status of the Latin American Free Trade Association established by the Montevideo Treaty signed on 18 February 1960 shall continue, in all its effects, within the Latin American Integration Association. Therefore, from the date when the present Treaty enters into force, the rights and obligations of the Latin American Free Trade Association shall correspond to the Latin American Integration Association.

CHAPTER IX: FINAL PROVISIONS

Article 55: The present Treaty may not be signed with reservations, neither may these be received on the occasion of its ratification or accession.

Article 56: The present Treaty shall be ratified by the signatory countries at the earliest possible term.

Article 57: The present Treaty shall enter into force thirty days after the deposit of the third instrument of ratification as regards the first three countries to ratify it. Concerning the other signatories, it shall enter into force on the thirtieth day following the deposit of the respective instrument of ratification and in the order in which such ratifications are deposited.

Instruments of ratification shall be deposited with the Government of the Eastern Republic of Uruguay, which shall report the date of deposit to the Governments of the signatory States of the present Treaty, as well as to those which have adhered thereto.

The Government of the Eastern Republic of Uruguay shall notify the date of enforcement of the present Treaty to the Government of each one of the signatory States.

Article 58: Upon its entry into force, the present Treaty shall remain open for accession to those Latin American countries which may so request. Acceptance of such accessions shall be adopted by the Council.

The Treaty shall enter into force for the adherent country thirty days after the date of its admission.

Adherent countries shall on that date put in force the commitments resulting from the regional tariff preference as well as the regional scope agreements concluded prior to the date of their accession.

Article 59: The present Treaty provisions shall not affect the rights and obligations resulting from agreements signed by any of the signatory countries prior to the date of their enforcement.

Article 60: The present Treaty provisions shall not affect the rights and obligations resulting from agreements signed by any of the signatory countries in the term between its signature and the date of its ratification. For countries which later become members of the Association, the provisions of this article refer to agreements signed prior to their incorporation.

However, each member country shall take the measures necessary to harmonize the provisions of the agreements in force with the objectives of the present Treaty.

Article 61: Member countries may introduce amendments or additions to the present Treaty. These shall be executed in protocols to enter into force upon ratification by all member countries and deposit of the respective instruments, subject to other criteria established thereof.

Article 62: The present Treaty shall have an indefinite duration.

Article 63: Any member country wishing to with draw from the present Treaty shall report such intention to the other member countries during one of the Committee sessions, formally delivering the denouncement document to the Committee one year after the date of advice referred to above. Once such denouncement has been executed, all rights and obligations corresponding to its condition as a member country shall automatically cease for the denouncing Government.

Notwithstanding the above, rights and obligations resulting from the regional tariff preference shall continue to be effective for a period of five more years, except if, at the time of denouncement, the member countries agree to the contrary. The above term shall start as from the date the denouncement is executed.

With reference to rights and obligations resulting from regional and partial scope agreements, the situation of the denouncing member country shall adjust to the specific rules which may have been established in each agreement. Should these rules not exist, the general provision contained in the previous paragraph of the present article shall apply.

Article 64: The present Treaty shall be known as the 1980 Montevideo Treaty.

CHAPTER X: TRANSITIONAL PROVISIONAL

Article 65: Pending ratification of the present Treaty by all signatory countries, as from the date of its enforcement by ratification of the first three countries, signatory countries which have not yet ratified shall be subject, both as regards their reciprocal relations and their relations with ratifying signatory countries, to the provisions of the legal structure of the Montevideo Treaty dated 18 February 1960, where appropriate, and specially to the resolutions adopted at the Meeting of the Council of Ministers of the Latin American Free Trade Association held on 12 August 1980.

These provisions shall no longer be applied to relations between signatory countries which have ratified the present Treaty and those which have not done so, as from one year following the date of its enforcement.

Article 66: The bodies of the Latin American Free Trade Association established by the Montevideo Treaty dated 18 February 1960 shall cease to exist as from the date of enforcement of the present Treaty.

Article 67: Non-ratifying signatory countries may participate in the Association bodies with the right to speak and vote whenever possible or of interest to them as long as ratification is pending, or until expire of the term established in the second paragraph of article 65.

Article 68: Signatory countries ratifying the present Treaty after its enforcement shall be subject to all provisions adopted prior to that moment by the Association bodies.

Article 69: The resolutions adopted by the Council of Ministers of the Latin American Free Trade Association at its Meeting of 12 August 1980 shall be incorporated to the legal framework of the present Treaty upon its entry into force.

DONE at the city of Montevideo, on the twelfth day of the month of August of the year nineteen hundred and eighty, in an original in the Spanish and Portuguese languages, both texts being equally valid. The Government of the Eastern Republic of Uruguay shall act as depositary of the present Treaty and forward duly authenticated copy of same to the Governments of the other signatory and adherent countries.

SOUTHERN COMMON MARKET (MERCOSUR) AGREEMENT (ALSO KNOWN AS THE TREATY OF ASUNCIÓN)

(Original: Spanish)

Treaty Establishing a Common Market between the Argentine Republic. the Federal Republic of Brazil. the Republic of Paraguay and the Eastern Republic of Uruguay

The Argentine Republic, the Federative Republic of Brazil, the Republic of Paraguay and the Eastern Republic of Uruguay, hereinafter referred to as the "States Parties",

CONSIDERING that the expansion of their domestic markets, through integration, is a vital prerequisite for accelerating their processes of economic development with social justice,

BELIEVING that this objective must be achieved by making optimum use of available resources, preserving the environment, improving physical links, coordinating macroeconomic policies and ensuring complementarily between the different sectors of the economy, based on the principles of gradualism, flexibility and balance,

BEARING IN MIND international trends, particularly the integration of large economic areas. and the importance of securing their countries a proper place in the international economy.

BELIEVING that this integration process is an appropriate response to such trends,

AWARE that this Treaty must be viewed as a further step in efforts gradually to bring about Latin American integration, in keeping with the objectives of the Montevideo Treaty in 1980,

CONVINCED of the need to promote the scientific and technological development of the States Parties and to modernize their economies in order to expand the supply and improve the quality of available goods and services, with a view to enhancing the living conditions of their populations,

REAFFIRMING their political will to lay the bases for increasingly close ties between their peoples, with a view to achieving the above-mentioned objectives,

HEREBY AGREE AS FOLLOWS:

CHAPTER I: PURPOSES, PRINCIPLES AND INSTRUMENTS

Article I

The States Parties hereby decide to establish a common market, which shall be in place by 31 December 1994 and shall be called the "common market of the southern cone" (MERCOSUR).

This common market shall involve:

The free movement of goods, services and factors of production between countries through, inter alia, the elimination of customs duties and non-tariff restrictions on the movement of goods, and any other equivalent measures;

The establishment of a common external tariff and the adoption of a common trade policy in relation to third States or groups of States, and the co-ordination of positions in regional and international economic and commercial forums;

The co-ordination of macroeconomic and sectoral policies between the States Parties in the areas of foreign trade, agriculture, industry, fiscal and monetary matters, foreign exchange and capital, services, customs, transport and communications and any other areas that may be agreed upon, in order to ensure proper competition between the States Parties;

The commitment by States Parties to harmonize their legislation in the relevant areas in order to strengthen the integration process.

Article 2

The common market shall be based on reciprocity of rights and obligations between the States Parties .

Article 3

During the transition period, which shall last from the entry into force of this Treaty until 31 December 1994, and in order to facilitate the formation of the common market, the States Parties shall adopt general rules of origin, a system for the settlement of disputes and safeguard clauses, as contained in Annexes 11. III and IV respectively to this Treaty.

Article 4

The States Parties shall ensure equitable trade terms in their relations with third countries. To that end, they shall apply their domestic legislation to restrict imports whose prices are influenced by subsidies, dumping or any other unfair practice. At the same time, States Parties shall co-ordinate their respective domestic policies with a view to drafting common rules for trade competition.

Article 5

During the transition period, the main instruments for putting in place the common market shall be:

(a) A trade liberalization programma, which shall consist of progressive, linear and automatic tariff reductions accompanied by the elimination of non-tariff restrictions or equivalent measures, as well as any other restrictions on trade between the States Parties, with a view to arriving at a zero tariff and no non-tariff restrictions for the entire tariff area by 31 December 1994 (Annex I);

(b) The co-ordination of macroeconomic policies, which shall be carried out gradually and in parallel with the programmes for the reduction of tariffs and the elimination of non-tariff restrictions referred to in the preceding paragraph;

(c) A common external tariff which encourages the foreign competitiveness of the States Parties;

(d) The adoption of sectoral agreements in order to optimize the use and mobility of factors of production and to achieve efficient scales of operation.

Article 6

The States parties recognize certain differentials in the rate at which the Republic of Paraguay and the Eastern Republic of Uruguay will make the transition. These differentials are indicated in the trade liberalization programme (Annex 1).

Article 7

In the area of taxes, charges and other internal duties, products originating in the territory of one State Party shall enjoy, in the other States Parties, the same treatment as domestically produced products .

Article 8

The States Parties undertake to abide by commitments made prior to the date of signing of this Treaty, including agreements signed in the framework of the Latin American Integration Association (ALADI), and to co-ordinate their positions in any external trade negotiations they may undertake during the transitional period. To that end:

(a) They shall avoid affecting the interests of the States Parties in any trade negotiations they may conduct among themselves up to 31 December 1994;

(b) They shall avoid affecting the interests of the other States Parties or the aims of the common market in any agreements they may conclude with other countries members of the Latin American Integration Association during the transition period;

(c) They shall consult among themselves whenever negotiating comprehensive tariff reduction schemes for the formation of free trade areas with other countries members of the Latin American Integration Association;

(d) They shall extend automatically to the other States Parties any advantage, favour, exemption, immunity or privilege granted to a product originating in or destined for third countries which are not members of the Latin American Integration Association.

CHAPTER II: ORGANIZATIONAL STRUCTURE

Article 9

The administration and implementation of this Treaty, and of any specific agreements or decisions adopted during the transition period within the legal framework established thereby, shall be entrusted to the following organs:

(a) The Council of the common market

(b) The Common Market Group

Article 10

The Council shall be the highest organ of the common market, with responsibility for its political leadership and for decision-making to ensure compliance with the objectives and time-limits set for the final establishment of the common market.

Article 11

The council shall consist of the Ministers for Foreign Affairs and the Ministers of the Economy of the States Parties.

It shall meet whenever its members deem appropriate, and at least once a year with the participation of the Presidents of the States Parties.

Article 12

The presidency of the Council shall rotate among the States Parties, in alphabetical order, for periods of six months.

Meetings of the Council shall be co-ordinated by the Minister for Foreign Affairs, and other ministers or ministerial authorities may be invited to participate in them.

Article 13

The Common Market Group shall be the executive organ of the common market and shall be co-ordinated by the Ministries of Foreign Affairs.

The Common Market Group shall have powers of initiative. Its duties shall be the following:

- to monitor compliance with the Treaty;

- to take the necessary steps to enforce decisions adopted by the Council;

- to propose specific measures for applying the trade liberalization programme, co-ordinating macroeconomic policies and negotiating agreements with third parties;

- to draw up programmes of work to ensure progress towards the formation of the common market.

The Common Market Group may set up whatever working groups are needed for it to perform its duties. To start with, it shall have the working groups mentioned in Annex V.

The Common Market Group shall draw up its own rules of procedure within 60 days of its establishment .

Article 14

The Common Market Group shall consist of four members and four alternates for each country, representing the following public bodies:

- Ministry of Foreign Affairs;

- Ministry of Economy or its equivalent (areas of industry, foreign trade and/or economic co-ordination);

- Central Bank.

In drafting and proposing specific measures as part of its work up to 31 December 1994, the Common Market Group may, whenever it deems appropriate, call on representatives of other government agencies or the private sector.

Article 15

The Common Market Group shall have an administrative secretariat whose main functions shall be to keep the Group's documents and report on its activities. It shall be headquartered in the city of Montevideo.

Article 16

During the transition period, decisions of the Council of the common market and the Common Market Group shall be taken by consensus, with all States Parties present.

Article 17

The official languages of the common market shall be Spanish and Portuguese, and the official version of its working documents shall be that drafted in the language of the country in which each meeting takes place.

Article 18

Prior to the establishment of the common market on 31 December 1994, the States Parties shall convene a special meeting to determine the final institutional structure of the administrative organs of the common market, as well as the specific powers of each organ and its decision-making procedures.

CHAPTER III: PERIOD OF APPLICATION

Article 19

This Treaty shall be of unlimited duration and shall enter into force 30 days after the date of deposit of the third instrument of ratification. The instruments of ratification shall be deposited with the Government of the Republic of Paraguay, which shall notify the Governments of the other States Parties of the date of deposit.

The Government of the Republic of Paraguay shall notify the Governments of each of the other States Parties of the date of entry into force of this Treaty.

CHAPTER IV: ACCESSION

Article 20

This Treaty shall be open to accession, through negotiation, by other countries members of the Latin American Integration Association; their applications may be considered by the States Parties once this Treaty has been in force for five years.

Notwithstanding the above, applications made by countries members of the Latin American Integration Association who do not belong to subregional integration schemes or an extraregional association may be considered before the date specified.

Approval of applications shall require the unanimous decision of the States Parties.

CHAPTER V: DENUNCIATION

Article 21

Any State Party wishing to withdraw from this Treaty shall inform the other States Parties of its intention expressly and formally and shall submit the document of denunciation within 60 days to the Ministry of Foreign Affairs of the Republic of Paraguay, which shall distribute it to the other States Parties.

Article 22

Once the denunciation has been formalized, those rights and obligations of the denouncing State deriving from its status as a State Party shall cease, while those relating to the liberalization programme under this Treaty and any other aspect to which the States Parties, together with the denouncing State, may agree within the 60 days following the formalization of the denunciation shall continue. The latter rights and obligations of the denouncing Party shall remain in force for a period of two years from the date of the above-mentioned formalization.

CHAPTER VI: GENERAL PROVISIONS

Article 23

This Treaty shall be called the "Treaty of Asuncion".

Article 24

In order to facilitate progress towards the formation of the common market, a Joint Parliamentary Commission of MERCOSUR shall be established. The executive branches of the States Parties shall keep their respective legislative branches informed of the progress of the common market established by this Treaty.

DONE at the city of Asuncion, on 26 March 1991, in one original in the Spanish and Portuguese languages, both texts being equally authentic. The Government of the Republic of Paraguay shall be the depositary of this Treaty and shall send a duly authenticated copy thereof to the Governments of signatory and acceding States Parties.

For the Government of the Argentine Republic:

Carlos Saul Menem

Guido di Tella

For the Government of the Federative Republic of Brazil:

Fernando Collor

Francisco Rezek

For the Government of the Republic of Paraguay:

Andres Rodriguez

Alexis Frutos Vaesken

For the Governrnent of the Eastern Republic of Uruguay:

Luis Alberto Lacalle Herrera

Hector Gros Espiell

ANNEX I: Trade Liberalization Programme

Article I

The States Parties hereby agree to eliminate, by: 31 December 1994 at the latest, any duties, charges and other restrictions applied in their reciprocal trade.

With regard to the schedules of exceptions submitted by the Republic of Paraguay and the Eastern Republic of Uruguay, the period for their elimination shall extend to 31 December 1995, on the terms of article 7 of this annex.

Article 2

For the purposes of the preceding article:

(a) "Duties and charges" shall mean customs duties and any other charges of equivalent effect, whether related to fiscal, monetary, foreign exchange or other matters, levied on foreign trade. This concept does not cover fees and similar charges corresponding to the approximate cost of services rendered; and

(b) "Restrictions" shall mean any administrative, financial, foreign exchange or other measures by which a State Party unilaterally prevents or impedes reciprocal trade. This concept does not cover measures taken in the situations envisaged in article 50 of the Montevideo Treaty of 1980.

Article 3

As of the date of entry into force of the Treaty, the States Parties shall begin a programme of gradual, linear and automatic tariff reductions, which shall benefit products classified according to the tariff nomenclature used by the Latin American Integration Association, observing the following timetable:

DATE	30 June	31 Dec.	30 June	31 Dec.	30 June	31 Dec.	30 June	31 Dec.

	1991	1991	1992	1992	1993	1993	1994	1994
PERCENTAGE TARIFF REDUCTION	47	54	61	68	75	82	89	100

Preferences shall apply to the tariff in force at the time of their application and shall consist of a percentage reduction in the most favourable duties and charges applied to imports of products coming from third countries not members of the Latin American Integration Association.

If one of the States Parties increases this tariff for imports from third countries, the established timetable shall continue to apply at the tariff level in force on 1 January 1991.

If tariffs are reduced, the corresponding preference shall apply automatically to the new tariff on the date on which that new tariff enters into force.

For the above purposes, the States Parties shall exchange among themselves and shall transmit to the Latin American Integration Association, within 30 days of the entry into force of the Treaty, updated copies of their customs tariffs and of those in force on I January 1991.

Article 4

Preferences agreed to in partial scope agreements concluded by the States Parties among themselves in the framework of the Latin American Integration Association shall be expanded, under the present tariff reduction programme, according to the following timetable:

DATE / PERCENTAGE TARIFF REDUCTION								
31 Dec. 1990	30 June 1991	31 Dec. 1991	30 June 1992	31 Dec. 1992	30 June 1993	31 Dec. 1993	30 June 1994	31 Dec. 1994
00 to 40	47	54	61	68	75	82	89	100
41 to 45	52	59	66	73	80	87	94	100
46 to 50	57	64	71	78	85	92	100	
51 to 55	61	67	73	79	86	93	100	
56 to 60	67	74	81	88	95	100		

61 to 65	71	77	83	89	96	100		
66 to 70	75	80	85	90	95	100		
71 to 75	80	85	90	95	100			
76 to 80	85	90	95	100				
81 to 85	89	93	97	100				
86 to 90	95	100						
91 to 95	100							
96 to 100								

These reductions shall apply only in the context of the corresponding partial scope agreements and shall not benefit other members of the common market; nor shall they apply to products included in the respective schedules of exceptions.

Article 5

Without prejudice to the mechanism described in articles 3 and 4, States Parties may also expand preferences by means of negotiations conducted in the framework of the agreements envisaged in the Montevideo Treaty of 1980.

Article 6

The tariff reduction timetable referred to in articles 3 and 4 of this annex shall not apply to products included in the schedules of exceptions submitted by each of the States Parties with the following quantifies of ALADI nomenclature items:

Argentine Republic: 394
Federative Republic of Brazil: 324
Republic of Paraguay: 439
Eastern Republic of Uruguay: 960

Article 7

The schedules of exceptions shall be reduced at the end of each calendar year in accordance with the following timetable:

(a) For the Argentine Republic and the Federative Republic of Brazil, by 20 per cent per year of the component items; this reduction applies from 31 December 1990;

(b) For the Republic of Paraguay and the Eastern Republic of Uruguay, the reduction shall be at the following rates:

10 per cent on the date of entry into force of the Treaty
10 per cent on 31 December 1991
20 per cent on 31 December 1992
20 per cent on 31 December 1993
20 per cent on 31 December 1994
20 per cent on 31 December 1995

Article 8

The schedules of exceptions contained in appendices I, II, III and IV include the first reduction envisaged in the preceding article.

Article 9

Products which are removed from schedules of exceptions on the terms set forth in Article 7 shall automatically benefit from the preferences resulting from the tariff reduction programme established in Article 3 of this annex. They shall benefit, at the least, from the minimum percentage reduction provided on the date on which they are removed from the schedules.

Article 10

States Parties may apply up to 31 December 1994, to products included in the tariff reduction programme, only the non-tariff restrictions expressly mentioned in the notes supplementing the complementarity agreement to be concluded by the States Parties in the framework of the Montevideo Treaty of 1980.

As of 31 December 1994, all non-tariff restrictions shall be eliminated from the common market area.

Article 11

In order to ensure observance of the tariff reduction timetable established in Articles 3 and 4, and also the formation of the common market, the States Parties shall co-ordinate any rnacroeconomic and sectoral policies which may be agreed upon and to which the Treaty establishing the common market refers, beginning with those connected with trade flows and the composition of the States Parties' productive sectors.

Article 12

The provisions of this Annex shall not apply to the partial scope agreements, economic complementarity agreements Nos. 1, 2, 13 and 14 or trade and agricultural agreements signed in the framework of the Montevideo Treaty of 1980, such agreements being governed exclusively by their own provisions.

(The Spanish and Portuguese read: THIS IS A TRUE COPY OF THE ORIGINAL WHICH IS IN THE POSSESSION OF THE TREATY DEPARTMENT OF THE MINISTRY OF FOREIGN AFFAIRS)

(Signed) Bernardino H. Saguier Caballero
Under-Secretary for Foreign Affairs

ANNEX II: GENERAL RULES OF ORIGIN

Chapter I: General Rules for Classification of Origin

Article 1

The following shall be classified as originating in the States Parties:

(a) Products manufactured wholly in the territory of any of the Parties, when only materials originating in the States Parties are used in their manufacture;

(b) Products included in the chapters or headings of the tariff nomenclature of the Latin Arnerican Integration Association referred to in Annex 1 of resolution 78 of the Committee of Representatives of that Association, simply by virtue of the fact that they are produced in their respective territories.

The following shall be classified as produced in the territory of a State Party:

(i) Mineral, plant and animal products, including hunting and fishing products, extracted, harvested or gathered, born and raised in its territory or in its territorial waters or exclusive economic zone;

(ii) Marine products extracted outside its territorial waters and exclusive economic zone by vessels flying its flag or leased by companies established in its territory; and

(iii) Products resulting from operations or processes carried out in its territory by which they acquire the final form in which they will be marketed, except when such processes or operations simply involve assembly, packaging, division into lots or volumes, selection and classification, marking, the putting together of assortments of goods or other equivalent operations or processes;

(c) Products in whose manufacture materials not originating in the States Parties are used, when such products are changed by a process carried out in the territory of one of the States Parties which results in their reclassification in the tariff nomenclature of the Latin American Integration Association under a heading different from that of such materials, except in cases where the States Parties determine that the requirement of Article 2 of this Annex must also be met.

However, products resulting from operations or processes carried out in the territory of a State Party, by which they acquire the final form in which they will be marketed, shall not be classified as originating in the States Parties when such operations or processes use only materials or inputs not originating in their respective countries and simply involve assembly, division into lots or volumes, selection, classification, marking, the putting together of assortments of goods or other similar operations or processes;

(d) Until 31 December 1994, products resulting from assembly operations carried out in the territory of a State Party using materials originating in the States Parties and third countries, when the value of those materials is not less than 40 per cent of the f.o.b. export value of the final product; and

(e) Products which, in addition to being produced in their territory, meet the specific requirements established in Annex 2 of Resolution 78 of the Committee of Representatives of the Latin American Integration Association.

Article 2

In cases where the requirement of Article 1 (c) cannot be met because the process carried out does not involve a change in nomenclature heading, it shall suffice that the c.i.f. value of the third country materials at the port of destination or the maritime port does not exceed 50 per cent of the f.o.b. export value of the goods in question.

In considering materials originating in third countries for States Parties with no outlet to the sea, warehouses and free zones granted by the other States Parties when the rnaterials arrive by sea shall be treated as the port of destination.

Article 3

The States Parties may establish, by mutual consent, specific requirements of origin which shall prevail over general classification criteria.

Article 4

In determining the specific requirements of origin referred to in Article 3 and in reviewing those already established, State Parties shall take the following elements, individually or jointly, as a basis:

I. Materials and other inputs used in production:

(a) Raw materials:

(i) Preponderant raw material or that which essentially characterizes the product; and

(ii) Main raw materials.

(b) Parts or components:

(i) Part or component which essentially characterizes the product;

(ii) Main parts or components; and

(iii) Percentage of parts or components in relation to total weight.

(c) Other inputs.

II. Type of processing used.

III. Maximum proportion of the value of materials imported from third countries in relation to the total value of the product arrived at using the valuation procedure agreed to in each case.

Article 5

In exceptional cases, where specific requirements cannot be met because of circumstantial supply problems: availability, technical specifications, delivery date and price, taking into account the provisions of Article 4 of the Treaty, materials not originating in the States Parties may be used.

In the situation envisaged in the preceding paragraph, the exporting country shall issue the corresponding certificate informing the importing State Party and the Common Market Group, together with any background information and evidence justifying the issue of that document.

If such cases occur repeatedly, the exporting State Party or the importing State Party shall inform the Common Market Group of the situation so that the specific requirement can be reviewed.

This article does not cover products resulting from assembly operations and shall apply pending the entry into force of the common external tariff for products subject to specific requirements of origin and their materials or inputs.

Article 6

Any State Party may request that requirements of origin established pursuant to Article 1 above be reviewed. Such requests shall propose and justify the requirements applicable to the product or products in question.

Article 7

For the purpose of meeting requirements of origin, materials and other inputs originating in the territory of any State Party and used by a State Party in the manufacture of a given product shall be classified as originating in the territory of this latter State Party.

Article 8

The criterion of maximum use of materials or other inputs originating in States Parties may not be taken into account in establishing requirements which involve the imposition of materials or other inputs of those States Parties when, in their view, such materials or inputs do not meet adequate supply, quality or price standards or are not adapted to the industrial processes or technologies used.

Article 9

In order for originating goods to benefit from preferential treatment, they must have been shipped directly from the exporting country to the importing country. For these purposes, the following shall be deemed direct shipment:

(a) Goods not shipped through the territory of a country that is not a party to the Treaty;

(b) Goods shipped in transit through one or more countries that are not parties to the Treaty, with or without transshipment or temporary storage, under the supervision of the competent customs authority in such countries, provided that:

(i) Transit is justified by geographical reasons or transport considerations;

(ii) The goods are not intended for trade or use in the country of transit; and

iii) The goods are not subjected, during shipment and storage, to any operation other than loading, unloading or handling to keep them in good condition or ensure their conservation.

Article 10

For the purposes of these general rules, it shall be understood that:

(a) Products coming from free zones located within the geographical boundaries of any of the States Parties shall meet the requirements envisaged in these general rules;

(b) The term "materials" shall include raw materials, intermediate products and parts and components used in the manufacture of goods.

CHAPTER II: Declaration, Certification and Verification

Article 11

In order for imports of products originating in the States Parties to benefit from the reductions in duties, charges and restrictions they have granted each other, the export documentation for such products must include a declaration certifying that they meet the requirements of origin established in accordance with the preceding chapter.

Article 12

The declaration referred to in the preceding article shall be issued by the final producer or the exporter of the goods and certified by an official department or professional association with legal personality, authorized by the Government of the exporting State Party.

In authorizing professional associations, States Parties shall make sure that they are organizations which have national jurisdiction and can delegate authority to regional or local associations while remaining directly responsible for the veracity of the certifications issued.

The States Parties undertake to establish, within a period of 90 days from the entry into force of the Treaty, a harmonized regime of administrative penalties for cases of false certification, without prejudice to the corresponding criminal proceedings.

Article 13

Certificates of origin issued for the purposes of this Treaty shall be valid for 180 days from the date of their issue.

Article 14

In all cases, the standard form annexed to agreement No .25 of the Committee of Representatives of the Latin American Integration Association shall be used until such time as another form approved by the States Parties comes into effect.

Article 15

States Parties shall transmit to the Latin American Integration Association the list of official departments and professional associations authorized to issue the certification referred to in the preceding article. with a record and exact copy of the authorized signatures.

Article 16

If a State Party considers that the certificates issued by an official department or professional association authorized by another State Party are not in compliance with the provisions of these general rules, it shall inform that State Party accordingly so that the latter can take whatever steps it deems necessary to solve the problems that have arisen.

In no case may the importing country hold up import procedures for products covered by the certificates referred to in the preceding paragraph. It may, however, in addition to requesting the corresponding additional information from the governmental authorities of the exporting country, take whatever measures it deems necessary to safeguard fiscal interests.

Article 17

For the purposes of subsequent verification, copies of certificates and the corresponding documents shall be kept for two years from the date of their issue.

Article 18

The provisions of these general rules and any amendments thereto shall not affect goods already loaded for shipment on the date of their adoption.

Article 19

The provisions of this Annex shall not apply to the partial scope agreements, economic complementarity agreements Nos. 1, 2, 13 and 14 or trade and agricultural agreements signed in the framework of the Montevideo Treaty of 1980, such agreements being governed exclusively by their own provisions.

(The Spanish and Portuguese versions read: THIS IS A TRUE COPY OF THE ORIGINAL WHICH IS IN THE POSSESSION OF THE TREATY DEPARTMENT OF THE MINISTRY OF FOREIGN AFFAIRS.)

(Signed) Bernardino H. Saguier Caballero
Under-Secretary for Foreign Affairs

ANNEX III: SETTLEMENT OF DISPUTES

1. Any dispute arising between the States Parties as a result of the application of the Treaty shall be settled by means of direct negotiations.

   If no solution can be found, the States Parties shall refer the dispute to the Common Market Group which, after evaluating the situation, shall within a period of 60 days make the relevant recommendations to the Parties for settling the dispute. To that end, the Common Market Group may establish or convene panels of experts or groups of specialists in order to obtain the necessary technical advice.

   If the Common Market Group also fails to find a solution, the dispute shall be referred to the Council of the common market to adopt the relevant recommendations.

2. Within 120 days of the entry into force of the Treaty, the Common Market Group shall propose to the Governments of States Parties a system for the settlement of disputes which shall apply during the transition period.

3. Before 31 December 1994, the States Parties shall adopt a permanent disputes settlement system for the common market.

(The Spanish and Portuguese read: THIS IS A TRUE COPY OF THE ORIGINAL WHICH IS IN THE POSSESSION OF THE TREATY DEPARTMENT OF THE MINISTRY OF FOREIGN AFFAIRS.)

(Signed) Bernardino H. Saguier Caballero
Under-Secretary for Foreign Affairs

ANNEX IV: SAFEGUARD CLAUSES

Article I

Each State Party may, up to 31 December 1994, apply safeguard clauses to imports of products benefiting from the trade liberalization programme established under the Treaty.

The States Parties hereby agree that they shall use these rules only in exceptional cases.

Article 2

If imports of a given product damage or threaten serious damage to its market as a result of a significant increase in imports of that product from the other States Parties over a short period of time, the importing country shall request the Common Market Group to hold consultations with a view to ending such a situation.

The importing country shall accompany its request with a detailed statement of the supporting facts, reasons and justifications.

The Common Market Group shall begin consultations within a maximum of 10 calendar days from the submission of the request by the importing country and shall conclude them, having taken a decision thereon, within 20 calendar days from the start of consultations.

Article 3

The existence or otherwise of damage or the threat of serious damage within the meaning of these rules shall be determined by each country, taking into account trends, inter alia, in the following aspects related to the product in question.

(a) Production level and capacity used;

(b) Employment level;

(c) Share of the market;

(d) Level of trade between the parties concerned or participating in the consultations;

(e) Performance of imports and exports in relation to third countries.

None of the above-mentioned factors shall, on its own, be decisive for determining the existence of damage or the threat of serious damage.

In determining the existence of damage or the threat of serious damage, factors such as technological changes or shifts in consumer preferences towards similar and/or directly competitive products in the same sector shall not be taken into account.

Application of the safeguard clause shall be subject, in each country, to the final approval of the national section of the Common Market Group.

Article 4

In order not to interrupt any trade flows which may have been generated, the importing country shall negotiate a quota for imports of the product in respect of which the safeguard clause has been invoked. This quota shall be governed by the same preferences and other conditions established in the trade liberalization programme.

The above-mentioned quota shall be negotiated with the State Party in which the imports originate, during the period of consultation referred to in Article 2. If the period of consultation ends without an agreement being reached, the importing country which considers itself affected may fix a quota which shall be maintained for one year.

In no event may a quota fixed unilaterally by the importing country be less than the average physical volume imported in the last three calendar years.

Article 5

Safeguard clauses shall apply for a year and may be extended for a further consecutive year on the terms established in this Annex. Such measures may be adopted only once for each product.

In no event may the application of safeguard clauses extend beyond 31 December 1994.

Article 6

The application of safeguard clauses shall not affect goods already loaded for shipment on the date of their adoption. Such goods shall be computed into the quota provided for in article 4.

Article 7

During the transition period, any State Party which considers itself affected by serious difficulties in its economic activities shall request the Common Market Group to hold consultations so that the necessary corrective measures can be taken.

Within the periods established in Article 2 of this Annex, the Common Market Group shall evaluate the situation and decide on the measures to be taken, according to the circumstances.

(The Spanish and Portuguese versions read: THIS IS A TRUE COPY OF THE ORIGINAL WHICH IS IN THE POSSESSION OF THE TREATY DEPARTMENT OF THE MINISTRY OF FOREIGN AFFAIRS.)

(Signed) Bernardino H. Saguier Caballero
Under-Secretary for Foreign Affairs

ANNEX V: WORKING GROUPS OF THE COMMON MARKET GROUP

For the purposes of co-ordinating macroeconomic and sectoral policies, the Common Market Group shall establish. within 30 days of its formation, the following working groups:

Sub-Group 1: Commercial issues

Sub-Group 2: Customs issues

Sub-Group 3: Technical standards

Sub-Group 4: Fiscal and monetary policies relating to trade

Sub-Group 5: Inland transport

Sub-Group 6: Maritime transport

Sub-Group 7: Industrial and technological policy

Sub-Group 8: Agricultural policy

Sub-Group 9: Energy policy

Sub-Group 10: Co-ordination of rnacroeconomic policies

(The Spanish and Portuguese versions read: THIS IS A TRUE COPY OF THE ORIGINAL WHICH IS IN THE POSSESSION OF THE TREATY DEPARTMENT OF THE MINISTRY OF FOREIGN AFFAIRS.)

PROTOCOL OF OURO PRETO

(**Ouro Preto - December 17, 1994**)

The Argentine Republic, the Federative Republic of Brazil, the Republic of Paraguay and the Eastern Republic of Uruguay, hereinafter referred to as the "States Parties",

In compliance with the provisions of Article 18 of the Treaty of Asuncion of 26 March 1991,

Aware of the importance of the progress made and of the introduction of the customs union as a stage in the establishment of a common market,

Reaffirming the principles and objectives of the Treaty of Asuncion and mindful of the need to give special consideration to the less developed countries and regions of Mercosul,

Mindful of the forces for change inherent in any integration process and the consequent need to adapt the institutional structure of Mercosul to the transformations that have taken place,

Recognising the outstanding achievements of the existing bodies during the transition period,

Hereby agree as follows:

CHAPTER I: STRUCTURE OF MERCOSUL

Article 1

The institutional structure of Mercosul shall comprise the following organs:

I.The Council of the Common Market (CCM);

II. The Common Market Group (CMG);

III. The Mercosul Trade Commission (MTC);

IV. The Joint Parliamentary Commission (JPC);

V. The Economic-Social Consultative Forum (ESCF);

VI. The Mercosul Administrative Secretariat (MAS).

Sole paragraph - Auxiliary organs necessary to attain the objectives of the integration process may be established, under the terms of this Protocol.

Article 2

The following are inter-governmental organs with decision-making powers: the Council of the Common Market, the Common Market Group and the Mercosul Trade Commission.

Section I: Council of the Common Market

Article 3

The Council of the Common Market is the highest organ of Mercosul, with responsibility for the political leadership of the integration process and for making the decisions necessary to ensure the achievement of the objectives defined by the Treaty of Asuncion and the final establishment of the common market.

Article 4

The Council of the Common Market shall consist of the Ministers for Foreign Affairs and the Ministers of the Economy of the States Parties, or their equivalents.

Article 5

The Presidency of the Council of the Common Market shall be rotated among the States Parties, in alphabetical order, for periods of six months.

Article 6

The Council of the Common Market shall meet whenever it deems appropriate, and at least once every six months, with the participation of the Presidents of the States Parties.

Article 7

The meetings of the Council of the Common Market shall be co-ordinated by the Ministers for Foreign Affairs, and other ministers or ministerial authorities may be invited to participate.

Article 8

The following are duties and functions of the Council of the Common Market:

I. To supervise the implementation of the Treaty of Asuncion, its protocols, and agreements signed within its context;

II. To formulate policies and promote the measures necessary to build the common market;

III. To assume the legal personality of Mercosul;

IV. To negotiate and sign agreements, on behalf of Mercosul, with third countries, groups of countries and international organisations. These functions may be delegated, by express mandate, to the Common Market Group under the conditions laid down in paragraph VII of Article 14;

V. To rule on proposals submitted to it by the Common Market Group;

VI. To arrange meetings of ministers and rule on agreements which those meetings refer to it;

VII. To establish the organs it considers appropriate, and to modify or abolish them;

VIII. To clarify, when it considers necessary, the substance and scope of its decisions;

IX. To appoint the Director of the Mercosul Administrative Secretariat;

X. To adopt financial and budgetary decisions;

XI. To approve the rules of procedure of the Common Market Group.

Article 9

The rulings of the Council of the Common Market shall take the form of Decisions which shall be binding upon the States Parties.

Section II: The Common Market Group

Article 10

The Common Market Group is the executive organ of Mercosul.

Article 11

The Common Market Group shall consist of four members and four alternates for each country, appointed by their respective governments, who must include representatives of the Ministries of Foreign Affairs, the Ministries of the Economy (or their equivalents) and the Central Banks. The Common Market Group shall be co-ordinated by the Ministries of Foreign Affairs.

Article 12

When drafting and proposing specific measures in the course of doing its work, the Common Market Group may, whenever it deems appropriate, call on representatives of other organs of government or of the institutional structure of Mercosul.

Article 13

The Common Market Group shall hold ordinary or extraordinary meetings, as often as necessary, in accordance with the terms of its rules of procedure.

Article 14

The following are duties and functions of the Common Market Group:

I. To monitor, within the limits of its competence, compliance with the Treaty of Asuncion, its Protocols, and agreements signed within its framework;

II. To propose draft Decisions to the Council of the Common Market;

III. To take the measures necessary to enforce the Decisions adopted by the Council of the Common Market;

IV. To draw up programmes of work to ensure progress towards the establishment of the common market;

V. To establish, modify or abolish organs such as working groups and special meetings for the purpose of achieving its objectives;

VI. To express its views on any proposals or recommendations submitted to it by other Mercosul organs within their sphere of competence;

VII. To negotiate, with the participation of representatives of all the States Parties, when expressly so delegated by the Council of the Common Market and within the limits laid down in special mandates granted for that purpose, agreements on behalf of Mercosul with third countries, groups of countries and international organisations. When so mandated, the Common Market Group shall sign the aforementioned agreements. When so authorised by the Council of the Common Market, the Common Market Group may delegate these powers to the Mercosul Trade Commission;

VIII. To approve the budget and the annual statement of accounts presented by the Mercosul Administrative Secretariat;

IX. To adopt financial and budgetary Resolutions based on the guidelines laid down by the Council;

X. To submit its rules of procedure to the Council of the Common Market;

XI. To organise the meetings of the Council of the Common Market and to prepare the reports and studies requested by the latter;

XII. To choose the Director of the Mercosul Administrative Secretariat;

XIII. To supervise the activities of the Mercosul Administrative Secretariat;

XIV. To approve the rules of procedure of the Trade Commission and the Economic-Social Consultative Forum.

Article 15

The decisions of the Common Market Group shall take the form of Resolutions which shall be binding upon the States Parties.

Section III: The Mercosul Trade Commission

Article 16

It shall be the task of the Mercosul Trade Commission, a body responsible for assisting the Common Market Group, to monitor the application of the common trade policy instruments agreed by the States Parties in connection with the operation of the customs union, as well as to follow up and review questions and issues relating to common trade policies, intra-Mercosul trade and third countries.

Article 17

The Mercosul Trade Commission shall consist of four members and four alternates for each State Party and shall be co-ordinated by the Ministries of Foreign Affairs.

Article 18

The Mercosul Trade Commission shall meet at least once a month, or whenever requested to do so by the Common Market Group or any of the States Parties.

Article 19

The following are duties and functions of the Mercosul Trade Commission:

I. To monitor the application of the common trade policy instruments both within Mercosul and with respect to third countries, international organisations and trade agreements;

II. To consider and rule upon the requests submitted by the States Parties in connection with the application of and compliance with the common external tariff and other instruments of common trade policy;

III. To follow up the application of the common trade policy instruments in the States Parties;

IV. To analyse the development of the common trade policy instruments relating to the operation of the customs union and to submit Proposals in this respect to the Common Market Group;

V. To take decisions connected with the administration and application of the common external tariff and the common trade policy instruments agreed by the States Parties;

VI. To report to the Common Market Group on the development and application of the common trade policy instruments, on the consideration of requests received and on the decisions taken with respect to such requests;

VII. To propose to the Common Market Group new Mercosul trade and customs regulations or changes in the existing regulations;

VIII. To propose the revision of the tariff rates for specific items of the common external tariff, inter alia, in order to deal with cases relating to new production activities within Mercosul;

IX. To set up the technical committees needed for it to perform its duties properly, and to direct and supervise their activities;

X. To perform tasks connected with the common trade policy requested by the Common Market Group;

XI. To adopt rules of procedure to be submitted to the Common Market Group for approval.

Article 20

The decisions of the Mercosul Trade Commission shall take the form of Directives or Proposals. The Directives shall be binding upon the States Parties.

Article 21

In addition to the duties and functions described in Articles 16 and 19 of this Protocol, the Mercosul Trade Commission shall be responsible for considering complaints referred to it by the National Sections of the Mercosul Trade Commission and originated by States Parties or individuals, whether natural or legal persons, relating to the situations provided for in Article 1 or 25 of the Brasilia Protocol, when they fall within its sphere of competence.

Paragraph 1. The examination of the aforesaid complaints within the Mercosul Trade Commission shall not prevent the complainant State Party taking action under the Brasilia Protocol for the Settlement of Disputes.

Paragraph 2. Complaints arising in the circumstances described in this Article shall be dealt with in accordance with the procedure laid down in the Annex to this Protocol.

Section IV: The Joint Parliamentary Commission

Article 22

The Joint Parliamentary Commission is the organ representing the parliaments of the States Parties within Mercosul.

Article 23

The Joint Parliamentary Commission shall consist of equal numbers of members of parliament representing the States Parties.

Article 24

The members of the Joint Parliamentary Commission shall be appointed by the respective national parliaments, in accordance with their internal procedures.

Article 25

The Joint Parliamentary Commission shall endeavour to speed up the corresponding internal procedures in the States Parties in order to ensure the prompt entry into force of the decisions taken by the Mercosul organs provided for in Article 2 of this Protocol. Similarly, it shall assist with the harmonisation of legislations, as required to advance the integration process. When necessary, the Council shall request the Joint Parliamentary Commission to examine priority issues.

Article 26

The Joint Parliamentary Commission shall submit Recommendations to the Council of the Common Market through the Common Market Group.

Article 27

The Joint Parliamentary Commission shall adopt its rules of procedure.

Section V: The Economic-Social Consultative Forum

Article 28

The Economic-Social Consultative Forum is the organ representing the economic and social sectors and shall consist of equal numbers of representatives from each State Party.

Article 29

The Economic-Social Consultative Forum shall have a consultative function and shall express its views in the form of Recommendations to the Common Market Group.

Article 30

The Economic-Social Consultative Forum shall submit its rules of procedure to the Common Market Group, for approval.

Section VI: The Mercosul Administrative Secretariat

Article 31

Mercosul shall have an Administrative Secretariat to provide operational support. The Mercosul Administrative Secretariat shall be responsible for providing services to the other Mercosul organs and shall be headquartered in the city of Montevideo.

Article 32

The Mercosul Administrative Secretariat shall carry out the following activities:

I. Serve as the official archive for Mercosul documentation;

II. Publish and circulate the decisions adopted within the framework of Mercosul. In this context, it shall;

Make, in co-ordination with the States Parties, authentic translations in Spanish and Portuguese of all the decisions adopted by the organs of the Mercosul institutional structure, in accordance with the provisions of Article 39;

Publish the Mercosul official journal.

III. Organise the logistical aspects of the meetings of the Council of the Common Market, the Common Market Group and the Mercosul Trade Commission and, as far as possible, the other Mercosul organs, when those meetings are held at its headquarters. In the case of meetings held outside its headquarters, the Mercosul Administrative Secretariat shall provide support for the State in which the meeting is held;

IV. Regularly inform the States Parties about the measures taken by each country to incorporate in its legal system the decisions adopted by the Mercosul organs provided for in Article 2 of this Protocol;

V. Compile national lists of arbitrators and experts, and perform other tasks defined in the Brasilia Protocol of 17 December 1991;

VI. Perform tasks requested by the Council of the Common Market, the Common Market Group and the Mercosul Trade Commission;

VII. Draw up its draft budget and, once this has been approved by the Common Market Group, do everything necessary to ensure its proper implementation;

VIII. Submit its statement of accounts annually to the Common Market Group, together with a report on its activities.

Article 33

The Mercosul Administrative Secretariat shall be headed by a Director who shall be a national of one of the States Parties. He shall be chosen by the Common Market Group, on a rotating basis, after consultation with the States Parties and shall be appointed by the Council of the Common Market. His term of office shall be two years and he may not be re-elected.

CHAPTER II: LEGAL PERSONALITY

Article 34

Mercosul shall possess legal personality of international law.

Article 35

In the exercise of its functions, Mercosul may take whatever action may be necessary to achieve its objectives, in particular sign contracts, buy and sell personal and real property, appear in court, hold funds and make transfers.

Article 36

Mercosul shall make headquarters agreements.

CHAPTER III: DECISION-MAKING SYSTEM

Article 37

The decisions of the Mercosul organs shall be taken by consensus and in the presence of all the States Parties.

Chapter IV: Internal Applications of the Decisions Adopted by Mercosul Organs

Article 38

The States Parties undertake to take all the measures necessary to ensure, in their respective territories, compliance with the decisions adopted by the Mercosul organs provided for in Article 2 of this Protocol. Sole paragraph. The States Parties shall inform the Mercosul Administrative Secretariat of the measures taken to this end.

Article 39

The content of the Decisions of the Council of the Common Market, the Resolutions of the Common Market Group, the Directives of the Mercosul Trade Commission and the Dispute Settlement Arbitration Rulings shall be published in full, in Spanish and Portuguese, in the Mercosul official journal, together with any instrument which, in the view of the Council of the Common Market or the Common Market Group requires official publicity.

Article 40

In order to ensure the simultaneous entry into force in the States Parties of the decisions adopted by the Mercosul organs provided for in Article 2 of this Protocol, the following procedure must be followed:

> **I.** Once the decision has been adopted, the States Parties shall take the necessary measures to incorporate it in their domestic legal system and inform the Mercosul Administrative Secretariat.
>
> **II.** When all the States Parties have reported incorporation in their respective domestic legal systems, the Mercosul Administrative Secretariat shall inform each State Party accordingly.
>
> **III.** The decisions shall enter into force simultaneously in the States Parties 30 days after the date of the communication made by the Mercosul Administrative Secretariat, under the terms of the preceding subparagraph. To this end, the States Parties shall, within the time-limit mentioned, publish the entry into force of the decisions in question in their respective official journals.

CHAPTER V: LEGAL SOURCES OF MERCOSUL

Article 41

The legal sources of Mercosul are:

I. The Treaty of Asuncion, its protocols and the additional or supplementary instruments;

II. The agreements concluded within the framework of the Treaty of Asuncion and its protocols;

III. The Decisions of the Council of the Common Market, the Resolutions of the Common Market Group and the Directives of the Mercosul Trade Commission adopted since the entry into force of the Treaty of Asuncion.

Article 42

The decisions adopted by the Mercosul organs provided for in Article 2 of this Protocol shall be binding and, when necessary, must be incorporated in the domestic legal systems in accordance with the procedures provided for in each country's legislation.

CHAPTER VI: DISPUTE SETTLEMENT SYSTEM

Article 43

Disputes which arise between the States Parties concerning the interpretation, application or non-fulfilment of the provisions of the Treaty of Asuncion and the agreements concluded within its framework or of Decisions of the Council of the Common Market, Resolutions of the Common Market Group and Directives of the Mercosul Trade Commission shall be subject to the settlement procedures laid down in the Brasilia Protocol of 17 December 1991.

Sole paragraph. The Directives of the Mercosul Trade Commission are also incorporated in Articles 19 and 25 of the Brasilia Protocol.

Article 44

Before the Common External Tariff convergence process is complete, the States Parties shall review the present Mercosul dispute settlement system with a view to adopting the permanent system referred to in paragraph 3 of Annex III to the Treaty of Asuncion and Article 34 of the Brasilia Protocol.

CHAPTER VII: BUDGET

Article 45

The Mercosul Administrative Secretariat shall have a budget to cover its operating expenses and the expenses authorised by the Common Market Group. This budget shall be funded by equal contributions from the State Parties.

Chapter VIII: Languages

Article 46

The official languages of Mercosul are Spanish and Portuguese. The official version of the working documents shall be that in the language of the country hosting the meeting.

Chapter IX: Review

Article 47

When they consider it opportune, the States Parties shall convene a diplomatic conference for the purpose of reviewing the institutional structure of Mercosul established by the present Protocol and the specific functions of each of its organs.

Chapter X: Entry Into Force

Article 48

This Protocol, which forms an integral part of the Treaty of Asuncion, shall be of unlimited duration and shall enter into force 30 days after the date of deposit of the third instrument of ratification. The Protocol and its instruments of ratification shall be deposited with the Government of the Republic of Paraguay.

Article 49

The Government of the Republic of Paraguay shall notify the Governments of the other States Parties of the date of deposit of the instruments of ratification and of entry into force of this Protocol.

Article 50

With regard to accession and denunciation, the rules established by the Treaty of Asuncion shall apply to this Protocol in their entirety. Accession to or denunciation of the Treaty of Asuncion or this Protocol shall imply, ipso jure, accession to or denunciation of this Protocol and the Treaty of Asuncion.

CHAPTER XI: TRANSITIONAL PROVISION

Article 51

The institutional structure provided for in the Treaty of Asuncion of 26 March 1991 and the organs it created shall be maintained until this Protocol enters into force.

CHAPTER XII: GENERAL PROVISIONS

Article 52

This Protocol shall be called the "Ouro Preto Protocol".

Article 53

All the provisions of the Treaty of Asuncion of 26 March 1991 which conflict with the terms of this Protocol or with the content of the Decisions adopted by the Council of the Common Market during the transition period are hereby repealed.

Done at the city of Ouro Preto, Federative Republic of Brazil, on 17 December 1994, in one original in the Portuguese and Spanish languages, both texts being equally authentic. The Government of Paraguay shall send an authenticated copy of this Protocol to the Governments of the other States Parties.

Argentine Republic	Carlos Saul Menem Guido Di Tella
Federative Republic of Brazil	Itamar Franco Celso L. N. Amorin
Republic of Paraguay	Juan Carlos Wasmosy Luis Ramirez

Eastern Republic of Uruguay Boettner
Luis Alberto Lacalle Herrera Sergio Abreu

ANNEX TO THE PROTOCOL OF OURO PRETO GENERAL PROCEDURE FOR COMPLAINTS TO THE MERCOSUL TRADE COMMISSION

Article 1

Complaints submitted by the National Sections of the Mercosul Trade Commission and originated by States Parties or individuals, whether natural or legal persons, in accordance with the provisions of Article 21 of the Protocol of Ouro Preto shall be subject to the procedure laid down in this Annex.

Article 2

The complainant State Party shall submit its complaint to the Pro-Tempore Chairman of the Mercosul Trade Commission who shall take the necessary steps to include the question on the Agenda of the next meeting of the Mercosul Trade Commission at least one week beforehand. If no decision is taken at that meeting, the Mercosul Trade Commission shall, without taking further action, pass on the dossier to a Technical Committee.

Article 3

Within a maximum of thirty (30) calendar days, the Technical Committee shall prepare and submit to the Mercosul Trade Commission a joint opinion on the question. This opinion or the conclusions of the experts making up the Technical Committee, if there is no joint opinion, shall be taken into consideration by the Mercosul Trade Commission when it rules on the complaint.

Article 4

The Mercosul Trade Commission shall rule on the complaint at its first ordinary meeting following receipt of the joint opinion or, should there be none, the conclusions of the experts, although an extraordinary meeting may also be convened for the purpose.

Article 5

If a consensus cannot be reached at the first meeting mentioned in Article 4, the Mercosul Trade Commission shall submit to the Common Market Group the various alternatives proposed, together with the joint opinion or the conclusions of the experts on the Technical Committee, in order that an appropriate decision may be taken. The Common Market Group shall give a ruling within thirty (30) calendar days of the receipt by the Pro-Tempore Chairman of the proposals submitted by the Mercosul Trade Commission.

Article 6

If there is agreement that the complaint is justified, the State Party against which it is made shall adopt the measures approved in the Mercosul Trade Commission or the Common Market Group. In each case, the Mercosul Trade Commission or, subsequently, the Common Market Group shall fix a reasonable period for the implementation of these measures. If this period expires without the State against which the complaint is made having complied with the provisions of the decision adopted, whether by the Mercosul Trade Commission or the Common Market Group, the complainant State may resort directly to the procedure provided for in Chapter IV of the Brasilia Protocol.

Article 7

If a consensus cannot be reached in the Mercosul Trade Commission, or subsequently, in the Common Market Group or if the State against which the complaint is made does not comply within the period provided for in Article 6 with the provisions of the decision adopted, the complainant State may resort directly to the procedure established in Chapter IV of the Brasilia Protocol and shall inform the Mercosul Administrative Secretariat accordingly.

Before giving a ruling, within fifteen (15) days of its being set up, the Arbitration Tribunal must announce the interim measures it considers appropriate under the conditions laid down in Article 18 of the Brasilia Protocol.

PROTOCOL ON PROMOTION AND PROTECTION OF INVESTMENTS COMING FROM NON-MERCOSUR STATE PARTIES

MERCOSUR/CMC/DEC. Nº 11/94:

IN VIEW OF: Art. 10 of the Treaty of Asuncion, Resolution No 39/94 of the Common Market Group, and Recommendation No 9/94 of SGT No 4, on "Fiscal and Monetary Policies Related to Trade."

WHEREAS:

The creation of favorable conditions for (extra-zonal) investments in the territory of the MERCOSUR State Parties will intensify economic cooperation.

The promotion and protection of such investments will help to stimulate individual economic initiative and to heighten development in the four State Parties.

For these purposes, it is fitting to establish a common legal framework for the treatment to be accorded third states pertaining to promotion and protection of investments.

THE COMMON MARKET COUNCIL DECIDES:

Article 1

To approve the "PROTOCOL ON PROMOTION AND PROTECTION OF INVESTMENTS COMING FROM NON-MERCOSUR STATE PARTIES," on treatment to be accorded third states pertaining to promotion and protection of investments, included as an Annex to this Decision.

ANNEX

PROTOCOL ON PROMOTION AND PROTECTION OF INVESTMENTS COMING FROM NON-MERCOSUR STATE PARTIES

The Argentine Republic, the Federative Republic of Brazil, the Republic of Paraguay, and the Oriental Republic of Uruguay, hereinafter designated "State Parties"

Taking into account the Treaty of Asuncion signed on March 26, 1991, whereby the State Parties decide to create the Common Market of the South (MERCOSUR);

Considering the Colonia Protocol on Reciprocal Promotion and Protection of Investments within MERCOSUR, approved by the Common Market Council Decision No 11/93, the purpose of which is to promote investments by investors from the MERCOSUR State Parties, within the scope of territorial application of the Treaty of Asuncion;

Underscoring the need for reconciling the general legal principles to be applied by each of the State Parties to investments coming from non- MERCOSUR states (hereinafter designated "Third States")so as not to create differentiated conditions that would distort the flow of investments;

Acknowledging that the promotion and protection of investments based on agreements with Third States will help to stimulate individual economic initiative and will increase the prosperity of the four States Parties;

Have agreed on the following:

Article 1

The State Parties are committed to grant the investments made by investors from Third States a treatment no more favorable than that stipulated in this Protocol.

Article 2

For the purpose indicated in the preceding, the general treatment to be agreed upon by each State Party toward Third States shall not recognize for the latter benefits and rights exceeding those recognized for the investor upon the following regulatory bases:

A) DEFINITIONS

1) The term "investment", according to the laws and regulations of the State Party in whose territory the investment is made, shall designate all types of assets invested directly or indirectly by investors from a Third State in the territory of the State Party, according to the latter's legislation. It shall include in particular, but not exclusively:

a) personal and real property, as well as the other rights in rem, such as mortages, surety, and collateral rights;

b) stock shares, partnerships shares, and any other type of share in business firms;

c) credit instruments and rights to benefits having an economic value; loans shall be included only when they are directly linked to a specific investment;

d) intellectual or intangible property rights, including, especially, copyrights, patents, industrial designs, trademarks, commercial names, technical procedures, know-how, and good will value;

e) economic concessions conferred by law or by contract, including concessions for prospecting, cultivation, extraction, or exploitation of natural resources.

2) The term "investor" shall designate:

a) any natural person who is a national of a State Party or Third State, according to their respective legislations. The provisions of the agreements to be entered into shall not apply to investments made in the territory of a State Party by natural persons who are nationals of Third States if such persons, on the date of the investment, reside or are domiciled permanently in said territory, according to the legislation in effect, unless it is proven that the funds relating to these investments come from abroad.

b) any juridical person established in accordance with the laws and regulations of a State Party or Third State that has its headquarters in the territory where it is established.

c) any juridical person established in accordance with the legislation of any country that is effectively controlled by natural or juridical persons defined in a) and b) of this number.

3) The term "profits" shall designate all the sums produced by an investment, such as earnings, rents, dividends, interest, royalties, and other current income.

4) The term "territory" shall designate the national territory of each State Party or Third State, including the maritime zones adjacent to the external boundary of the national territorial sea over which the State Party involved or the Third State may, according to international law, exercise sovereign rights or jurisdiction.

B) PROMOTION OF INVESTMENTS

1) Each State Party shall promote in its territory the investments of investors from Third States, and shall accept said investments according to its laws and regulations.

2)When one of the State Parties has accepted an investment in its territory, it shall grant the necessary authorization for its best implementation, including the execution of contracts on licenses, commercial or administrative assistance, and entry of the necessary personnel.

C) PROTECTION OF INVESTMENTS

1) Each State Party shall ensure a fair and equitable treatment for the investments of investors from Third States, and shall not damage their management, maintenance, use, benefit, or disposition through unjustified or discriminatory measures.

2) Each State Parties shall grant full protection for such investments, and may not accord them a treatment less favorable than that granted to the investments of its own national investors, or the investments made by investors from other states.

3) The State Parties shall not extend to investors from Third States the benefits of any treatment, preference, or privilege resulting from:

a) their participation or association in a free trade area, customs union, common market, or similar regional agreement;

b) an international agreement totally or partially related to tax matters.

D) EXPROPRIATIONS AND COMPENSATIONS

1) None of the State Parties shall adopt nationalization or expropriation measures, nor any other measure that may have the same effect against investments located in their territory belonging to investors from Third States, unless said measures are adopted for reasons of public utility or social benefit, on a non-discriminatory basis, and subject to due legal process. The measures

shall be accompanied by provisions for the payment of a fair, adequate, and prompt or timely compensation.

The amount of said compensation shall correspond to the value of the expropriated investment.

2) Investors from a Third State who suffer losses in their investments in the territory of the State Party, owing to war or other armed conflict, national state of emergency, rebellion, insurrection, or rioting, shall receive, insofar as restitution, indemnification, compensation, or other reparation is concerned, a treatment no less favorable than that accorded its own investors or the investors from other states.

E) TRANSFERS

1)Each State Party shall grant the investors from a Third State the free transfer of investments and profits, and particularly, although not exclusively, of:

a) the capital and additional sums necessary for the maintenance and development of the investments;

b) the benefits, earnings, rents, interest, dividends, and other current income;

c) the funds for reimbursement of loans, as defined in Article 2, letter a), paragraph (1), (c);

d) the royalties and fees, and any other payment relating to the rights specified in Article 2, letter a), paragraph (1), d) and e);

e) the proceeds from a total or partial sale or liquidation of an investment;

f) the compensation, indemnification, or other payments specified in Article 2, letter d);

g) the salaries of the nationals of a Third State who have obtained authorization to work in connection with an investment.

2)The transfers shall be made without delay, in freely convertible currency.

F) SUBSTITUTION

1) If a Third State or an agency designated by it makes a payment to an investor by virtue of a guaranty or insurance to cover non-commercial risks that it has contracted in connection with an investment, the State Party in whose territory the investment was made shall recognize the validity of the substitution in favor of the Third State or of one of its agencies, with respect to any right or entitlement of the investor, for purposes of obtaining the pertinent pecuniary compensation.

G) RESOLUTION OF CONTROVERSIES BETWEEN A STATE PARTY AND A THIRD STATE

1) Controversies that may arise between a State Party and a Third State relating to the interpretation or application of the agreement that they enter into shall be resolved through diplomatic channels insofar as possible.

2) If said controversy cannot be settled in this manner within a reasonable period of time, to be determined, it shall be subjected to international arbitration.

H) RESOLUTION OF CONTROVERSIES BETWEEN AN INVESTOR FROM A THIRD STATE AND A PARTY STATE RECEIVING THE INVESTMENT

1) Any controversy relating to the interpretation or application of an agreement on reciprocal promotion and protection of investments that may arise between an investor from a Third State and a Party State shall be resolved through friendly consultations insofar as possible.

2) If the controversy cannot be resolved within a reasonable period of time after it has been posed by either of the parties, at the investor's request it may be submitted:

a) either to the competent courts of the State Party in whose territory the investment was made, or

b) to international arbitration under the conditions described in section 3.

Once an investor has submitted the controversy to the jurisdiction of the State Party involved, or to international arbitration, the selection of either of these procedures shall be final.

3) In the event of an appeal for international arbitration, the controversy may, at the discretion of the investor, be subjected to an "ad hoc" court of arbitration or to an international arbitration.

4) The arbitration body shall decide, based on the provisions of the agreement entered into, the right of the State Party involved in the controversy, including the rules relating to conflicts of laws, and the terms of possible private agreements concluded in connection with the investment, as well as based on the principles of international law pertaining to the subject.

5) The arbitrator's decisions shall be definitive and binding on the parties to the controversy. The State Party shall execute them in accordance with its legislation.

I) INVESTMENTS AND CONTROVERSIES COVERED IN THE AGREEMENT

The rules of the agreements to be entered into may be applied to all the investments made before or after the date that they took effect, but shall not apply to any controversy, claim, or dispute that may have arisen before they took effect.

J) DURATION AND TERMINATION

The minimum period of validity of the agreements shall be ten years. In the case of those investments made before the expiration date of the agreement's effective period, the State Party may decide that its provisions shall remain in effect for a maximum period of 15 years beginning from that date forward.

Article 3

The State Parties are obliged to exchange information on the future negotiations and those in progress on agreements for reciprocal promotion and protection of investments with Third States, and prior consultations shall be held regarding any substantial amendment to the general treatment agreed upon in Article 2 of this Protocol. For this purpose, the Commission on the Promotion and Reciprocal Protection of Investments of the Common Market Group, and any body which may eventually replace it, shall concern itself with the consultations and the exchange of information pertaining to the subject.

Article 4

This Protocol is an integral part of the Treaty of Asuncion.

Accession of a State to the Treaty of Asuncion shall imply, ipso jure, accession to this Protocol.

This Protocol shall go into effect 30 days after the date of deposit of the fourth ratification instrument.

The Government of the Republic of Paraguay shall be the depositary of this Protocol and of the ratification instruments, and shall send a duly authenticated copy thereof to the Governments of the other State Parties.

PROTOCOL HARMONIZATION OF INTELLECTUAL PROPERTY IN THE MERCOSUR, TRADEMARK, INDICATIONS OF SOURCE AND APPELLATIONS OF ORIGIN

DECISIONS COUNCIL COMMON MARKET **MERCOSUR / CMC / DEC. No. 08/95**

SEEN: The Article 13 of the Treaty of Asunción, Decision No. 4/91 of the Common Market Council, Resolution No. 39/94 of the Common Market Group and Recommendation No. 7/94 SWG No. 7.

WHEREAS:

The need to promote effective and adequate protection of intellectual property rights relating to trade marks, indications of provenance and designations of origin.

To be established for such purposes and principles that serve rules for the application of intellectual property rights relating to trade marks, indications of provenance and designations of origin.

THE COMMON MARKET COUNCIL
DECIDES:

Article 1 - To approve the Protocol Harmonization of Intellectual Property in MERCOSUR on trade marks, indications of source and appellations of origin which appears as Annex to this Decision.

CMC VIII - ASUNCION 5/VIII/95

ANNEX

PROTOCOL Harmonization of INTELLECTUAL PROPERTY IN MERCOSUR, trade-mark, INDICATIONS OF SOURCE AND DESIGNATIONS OF ORIGIN.

The Governments of Argentina, the Federative Republic of Brazil, the Republic of Paraguay and the Eastern Republic of Uruguay;

DESIRING TO reduce distortions and impediments to trade and movement of goods and services in the territory of States Parties to the Treaty of Asuncion;

RECOGNIZING the need to promote effective and adequate protection of intellectual property rights relating to trade marks, indications of source and appellations of origin and ensure that the exercise of such rights does not in itself constitute a barrier to legitimate trade;

RECOGNIZING the need to establish for such purpose, rules and principles that serve to guide administrative action, legislative and judicial branches of each State Party to the recognition and enforcement of intellectual property rights relating to trade marks, indications of source and appellations of origin ;

AGREEING to such rules and principles must conform to the standards set in existing multilateral instruments internationally, including the Paris Convention for the Protection of Industrial Property (Stockholm Act 1967) and the Agreement on Trade-Related Intellectual Property Trade Related, signed on 15 April 1994 as an annex to the Agreement establishing the World Trade Organization, negotiated under the Uruguay Round of GATT

GENERAL PROVISIONS

Article 1
Nature and Scope of Obligations

States Parties shall ensure effective protection of intellectual property on trade marks, indications of source and appellations of origin, ensuring at least the protection afforded by the principles and rules set out in this Protocol.
They may, however, grant more extensive protection, provided it is not inconsistent with the rules and principles of the Treaties referred to in this Protocol.

Article 2
Effective international obligations

1) States Parties undertake to respect the rules and principles of the Paris Convention for the Protection of Industrial Property (Stockholm Act 1967) and the Agreement on Trade-Related Aspects of Intellectual Property Trade (1994), Annex the Agreement establishing the World Trade Organization (1994).

2) Nothing in this Protocol shall affect the obligations of States Parties arising out of the Paris Convention for the Protection of Industrial Property (Stockholm Act 1967) or the Agreement on Trade Related Aspects of Intellectual Property Trade-Related (1994).

Article 3
National Treatment

Each State Party shall accord to nationals of other States Parties treatment no less favorable than that it accords to its own nationals with regard to the protection and enforcement of intellectual property rights relating to trade marks, indications of source and appellations of origin
.

Article 4
Waiver of legalization

1) States Parties shall, to the extent possible, dispense the legalization of documents and signatures in proceedings relating to intellectual property rights regarding trademarks, indications of source and appellations of origin.

2) States Parties shall, to the extent possible, waive the submission of sworn or legalized translation in proceedings relating to intellectual property relating to trade marks, indications of source and appellations of origin, when the originals were in language Spanish or Portuguese.

3) States Parties may require a sworn or legalized translation when this is necessary in case of litigation in administrative or judicial.

BRANDS
Article 5
Definition of brand

1) States Parties shall recognize as a mark for registration for any sign capable of distinguishing the goods or services trade.

2) Any State Party may require, as a condition of registration, that signs be visually perceptible.

3) States Parties shall protect service marks and collective marks and may also, provide for protection of certification marks.

4) The nature of the product or service to which the mark is to be applied shall, in any case, an obstacle to registration of the mark.

Article 6
Signs Considered Brands

1) The markings may include, among others, invented words, names, nicknames, slogans, letters, figures, monograms, figures, portraits, labels, badges, stamps, borders, lines and bands, combinations, arrangements of colors, and shape of the products, their packaging or fittings, or local media or sale of products or services.

2) The markings may include domestic or foreign geographical indications, provided they are not indications of source or appellation of origin in accordance with the definition given in Articles 19 and 20 of this Protocol.

Article 7
of the provisions of the Registration

May apply for registration of a mark natural or legal persons under public or private law which have a legitimate interest.

Article 8
Priority for registration of a mark

Have priority in obtaining the registration of a mark who first requested it, unless that right is claimed by a third party who has used publicly, peacefully and in good faith, in any State Party, for at least six months, provided that in making its objection requesting registration of the mark.

Article 9
Marks unregistrable

1) States Parties shall prohibit the registration, among others, of descriptive signs or generically used to designate the goods or services or types of products or services that the mark distinguishes, or constitute an indication of source or appellation.

2) also prohibit the registration, among others, misleading signs, contrary to morality or public order, offensive to persons living or dead or faiths; constituted by national symbols of any country that can falsely suggest links with people living or dead or national symbols of any country, or prejudicial to its value or respectability.

3) States Parties reject applications for registration of trademarks that demonstrably affect third party rights and declare invalid the requested trademark registrations in bad faith proven affecting rights.

4) States Parties shall prohibit in particular the registration of a sign that imitates or reproduces, in whole or in part, a mark that the applicant clearly could not ignore as belonging to an owner established or domiciled in any of the States Parties and susceptible cause confusion or association.

5) Article 6 bis of the Paris Convention for the Protection of Industrial Property shall apply *mutatis mutandis* , to services. To determine the reputation of the mark within the meaning of that provision shall take into account the knowledge of the sign in the relevant market sector, including knowledge in State Party where protection is claimed, acquired by the effect of a advertising sign.

6) States Parties shall in its territory trademark protection of nationals of States Parties have reached an exceptional level of knowledge against reproduction or imitation, in any line of business, provided that there is a possibility of injury.

Article 10
Deadline for Registration and Renewal

1) The term of a trademark registration will expire 10 years from the date of authorization in the respective State Party.
2) The term of registration may be renewed for equal and successive periods of ten years from the previous expiration date.
3) States Parties undertake to comply at least with the provisions of Article 5 bis of the Paris Convention for the Protection of Industrial Property (Stockholm 1967).
4) On the occasion of the extension can not make any adjustments to the mark, nor the expansion of the list of goods or services covered by the registration.
5) For the purposes of renewing a trademark registration, any State Party may:
a) conduct a substantive examination of the record,
b) call or admit oppositions,
c) require that the mark is in use,
d) require that the mark has been registered or renewed in some other country or regional office.

Article 11

Rights conferred by registration

The registration of a mark shall confer on its holder the exclusive right to use and to prevent any third party to perform without their consent, in others, the following acts: use in commerce of an identical or similar mark for any goods or services where such use would create a likelihood of confusion or association with the owner of record, or an unjust economic or commercial injury because of a dilution of the distinctiveness or the market value of the brand, or take unfair advantage of the reputation of the trademark or its owner.

Article 12

Use of Certain Third Party Directions

Registration of a trademark does not confer the right to prohibit a third party from using, among others, the following information, provided that such use is made in good faith and is not liable to cause confusion about the commercial origin of the goods or services:
a) your name or address, or those of their business establishments;
b) statements or information concerning the availability, use, application or compatibility of their products or services, in particular regarding replacement parts or accessories.

Article 13

Exhaustion of rights

The registration of a trademark shall not impede the free movement of products bearing legitimately introduced in the market by the owner or with his authorization. States Parties undertake to make provision in their legislation measures providing for exhaustion of the rights conferred by registration.

Article 14

Invalidity of Registration and Prohibition of Use

1) At the request of any interested person, and provided that the owner of the trademark registration, the competent authority of the State Party shall declare the nullity of that record if it was made in contravention of any of the prohibitions set forth in Articles 8 and 9.

2) Where the grounds of invalidity shall give with respect to one or more of the products or services for which the mark was registered, declared invalid only for those products or services, and are removed from the respective list in the registry the brand.

3) States Parties may establish a limitation period for an action for nullity.

4) The nullity not prescribe when the registration was obtained in bad faith.

Article 15

Cancellation of registration for non-use of the mark

1) The States Parties which there exists an obligation to use the mark, at the request of any interested person, and provided that the owner of the trademark registration, the national authority may cancel the registration of a trademark when it does not been used in any of the States Parties during the five years preceding the date of commencement of the cancellation action. The request for cancellation shall not later than five years from the date of registration of the mark. No registration will be canceled if there are grounds qu the national competent authority considers justified the lack of use.

2) States Parties where there exists an obligation to use the trademark may provide partial revocation of registration when disuse only affect one or more of the goods or services identified by the mark.

Article 16

Use of marks

1) States Parties, where there exists an obligation to use the brand, establish the criteria for the required use of the sea shall be determined by agreement between the competent national authorities.

2) The use of the mark in any of the States Parties will be enough to avoid cancellation of registration to any request in any of them.

3) The burden of proof of use of the mark for the proprietor of the mark.

Article 17

Challenge to request registration and records

States Parties undertake to provide an administrative procedure to object to applications for trademark registration. They also undertake to establish an administrative procedure for revocation of registration.

Article 18

Classification of Goods and Services

States Parties that do not use the International Classification of Goods and Services for the Registration of Marks, established by the Nice Agreement of 1957, and their current revisions and updates, undertake to adopt the necessary measures for the purposes of its application.

INDICATIONS AND ORIGIN AND DESIGNATIONS OF ORIGIN

Article 19

Obligation of protection and definitions

1) States Parties undertake to protect each other's indications of source and appellations of origin.

2) indication of source is the geographical name of the country, city, region or locality in its territory, to be known as centr extraction, production or manufacture of a particular product or a particular service delivery.

3) designation of origin is considered the geographical name of country, city, region or locality in its territory, product or service designated by the qualities or characteristics are due exclusively or essentially to the geographical environment, including natural and human factors.

Article 20

Prohibition of trade mark registration

The indications of source and appellations of origin provided for in paragraphs 2 and 3 above shall not be registered as trademarks.

FINAL PROVISIONS

Article 21

States Parties shall provide for the protection of plant varieties and other varieties either by patents or a sui generis system or any other system resulting from the combination of both.

Article 22

The States Parties to implement effective measures to curb production in the trade in pirated or counterfeit.

Article 23

States Parties shall establish cooperation in the sense of examining and resolving difficulties inherent in the movement of goods and services in MERCOSUR, issues arising from intellectual property.

Article 24

States Parties undertake to make efforts in order to conclude, at the earliest, additional agreements on patents, utility models, industrial designs, copyright and related rights, and other matters relating to intellectual property.

Article 25

Disputes between States Parties concerning the application, interpretation or breach of the provisions of this Protocol shall be settled by direct diplomatic negotiations. If by such negotiations failed to produce an agreement, or if the dispute is settled only in part, the procedures provided in the dispute settlement system in force in the MERCOSUR.

Article 26

This Protocol, part of the Treaty of Asunci6n, shall enter into force for the first two states to ratify it, thirty days after the deposit of the second instrument of ratification. For the other signatories shall enter into force on the thirtieth day after the deposit of instruments of ratification in the order they were received.

Article 27

The accession of a State to the Treaty of Asuncion entail ipso jure accession to this Protocol.

Article 28

The Government of the Republic of Paraguay shall be the depositary of this Protocol, and the instruments of ratification and transmit certified true copies thereof to the Governments of the other States Parties. The Government of the Republic of Paraguay shall notify the Governments of the other States Parties of the date of entry into force of this Protocol and the deposit of instruments of ratification.

Done at the city of Asunci6n, Republic of Paraguay on the fifth day of the month of August 1995, in an original, in Spanish and Portuguese languages, both texts being equally authentic.

PROTOCOL OF BRASILIA FOR THE SOLUTION OF CONTROVERSIES

PREAMBLE

The Argentine Republic, the Federal Republic of Brazil, the Republic of Paraguay, and the Eastern Republic of Uruguay, hereinafter referred to as the "State Parties":

In compliance with the dispositions found in Article 3 and in Annex III of the Treaty of Asuncion signed on the 26th day of March of 1991, by virtue of which the State Parties have obligated themselves to adopt a System for the Solution of Controversies which shall be in effect during the period of transition;

IN RECOGNITION of the importance of having an efficient instrument to ensure compliance of the aforesaid Treaty and of the dispositions which are derived therefrom;

CONVINCED that the System for the Solution of Controversies contained in the present Protocol will contribute to the strengthening of relations between the State Parties on a foundation of justice and equity;

THEY HAVE AGREED on the following:

CHAPTER I SCOPE OF APPLICATION

Article 1

The controversies which arise between the State Parties regarding the interpretation, application or non?compliance of the dispositions contained in the Treaty of Asuncion, of the agreements celebrated within its framework, as well as any decisions of the Common Market Council and the resolutions of the Common Market Group, will be submitted to the procedure for resolution established in the present Protocol.

CHAPTER II DIRECT NEGOTIATIONS

Article 2

The State Parties to any controversy will first attempt to resolve it through direct negotiations.

Article 3

1. In any controversy, the State Parties will inform the Common Market Group, through the Administrative Secretariat, regarding the actions that are undertaken during the negotiations and their results.

2. The direct negotiations cannot, except pursuant to an agreement between the parties, exceed a time limit of fifteen (15) days from the date one of the State Parties originally raised the controversy.

CHAPTER III PARTICIPATION OF THE COMMON MARKET GROUP

Article 4

1. If during the direct negotiations an agreement cannot be reached or if the controversy can only be resolved in part, any of the State Parties to the controversy can submit it for consideration by the Common Market Group.

2. The Common Market Group will evaluate the situation, giving an opportunity to the parties to the controversy to state their respective positions and requiring, whenever it considers it necessary, the advice of experts selected from a list which is referred to in Article 30 of the present Protocol.

3. The costs which arise as a result of this advice will be borne in equal parts by the State Parties to the controversy or in a proportion as determined by the Common Market Group.

Article 5

At the conclusion of this procedure the Common Market Group will formulate its recommendations to the State Parties involved in the controversy suggesting a solution to the dispute.

Article 6

The procedure described in the present chapter cannot be extended for a period greater than thirty (30) days, beginning with the date on which the controversy was submitted for consideration to the Common Market Group.

CHAPTER IV ARBITRAL PROCEDURE

Article 7

1. When a controversy cannot be resolved through the application of the procedures referred to in Chapters II and III, any of the State Parties to the controversy can communicate to the Administrative Secretariat its intention to resort to the arbitral procedure which is established in the present Protocol.

2. The Administrative Secretariat will immediately notify the other State Party or Parties involved in the controversy and the Common Market Group of this communication and will be entrusted with the means required for the development of the procedures.

Article 8

The State Parties declare that they recognize as obligatory, ipso facto and without need of a special agreement, the jurisdiction of the Arbitral Tribunal which in each case is established in order to hear and resolve all controversies which are referred to in the present Protocol.

Article 9

1. The arbitral procedure will be tried before an ad hoc Tribunal composed of three (3) arbitrators contained in a list which is referred to in Article 10.

2. The arbitrators will be chosen in the following manner:

i. Each State Party to the controversy will designate one (1) arbitrator. The third arbitrator, who cannot be a national of the State Parties to the controversy, will be designated upon common agreement and he or she will preside over the Arbitral Tribunal. The arbitrators should be named at the end of fifteen (15) days from the date on which the Administrative Secretariat communicated to the other State Parties to the controversy the intention of one of them to resort to arbitration;

ii. Each State Party to the controversy will also nominate an alternate arbitrator, who should meet the same requirements, in order to replace the nominal arbitrator in the event of his or her incapacity or withdrawal from the Arbitral Tribunal, whether it be at the moment of its formation or during the course of the proceedings.

Article 10

Each State Party will designate ten (10) arbitrators, which will be included in a list which will be registered with the Administrative Secretariat. The List, as well as any successive modifications, will be made known to the State Parties.

Article 11

If one of the State Parties to the controversy should not nominate its arbitrator within the time limit indicated in Article 9, than [sic] he or she shall be chosen by the Administrative Secretariat from among the arbitrators of this State, pursuant to the order established in its respective list.

Article 12

1. If no agreement can be reached between the State Parties to the controversy concerning the selection of a third arbitrator within the time limit established in Article 9, the Administrative Secretariat, at the request of either, will proceed to designate the arbitrator by lottery from among a list of sixteen (16) arbitrators put together by the Common Market Group.

2. The aforesaid list, which should also be registered with the Administrative Secretariat, will be made up in equal parts of nationals from the State Parties and of nationals from third countries.

Article 13

The arbitrators that make up the lists which are referred to in Articles 10 and 12 should consist of jurists of recognized competence in those matters which can be the subject matter of a controversy.

Article 14

If two or more State Parties maintain the same position in a controversy, they will unify their representation before the Arbitral Tribunal and will designate one arbitrator upon common agreement within the time limit established in Article 9(2)(i).

Article 15

In each case, the Arbitral Tribunal shall establish its seat in one of the State Parties and will adopt its own rules of procedure. These rules should guarantee that each party to the controversy shall have the fullest opportunity to be heard and to present its proof and arguments and it shall also be guaranteed that the proceedings occur in an expeditious manner.

Article 16

The State Parties to a controversy shall inform the Arbitral Tribunal of any requests that have been satisfied prior to the arbitral proceeding and will make a brief presentation of the principles of fact or law as per their respective positions.

Article 17

The State Parties to the controversy will chose who will represent them before the Arbitral Tribunal and they can designate advisors to defend their rights.

Article 18

1. The Arbitral Tribunal can, at the request of an interested party and to the extent that there exist well?founded presumptions that a continuation of the current situation will cause severe and irreparable damage to one of the State Parties, issue provisional measures which it considers appropriate, according to the circumstances and pursuant to the conditions that the Tribunal itself establishes, in order to prevent such damages.

2. The parties to the controversy shall immediately or within the time limit determined by the Arbitral Tribunal, comply with whatever provisional measure, until such time as the decision that is referred to in Article 20 is issued.

Article 19

1. The Arbitral Tribunal will decide the controversy based on the dispositions of the Treaty of Asuncion, of the agreements celebrated within its framework, on the decisions of the Common Market Council, the resolutions of the Common Market Group, as well as on the principles and dispositions of international law which are applicable to the matter.

2. The present disposition does not restrict the ability of the Tribunal to decide any controversy ex aequo et bono [on equity], if the parties so agree.

Article 20

1. The Arbitral Tribunal shall issue its decision in writing within sixty (60) days, extendible for an additional time limit of thirty (30) days, from the time its President is designated.

2. The decision of the Arbitral Tribunal shall be adopted by majority vote, and it should be supported and signed by the President and the other arbitrators. The members of the Arbitral Tribunal will not be allowed to explain their dissenting votes and they must maintain the confidentiality of the vote.

Article 21

1. The decisions of the Arbitral Tribunal cannot be appealed, and are binding on the State Parties to the controversies from the moment the respective notification is received and will be deemed by them to have the effect of res judicata.

2. The decisions should be complied with within a time limit of fifteen (15) days, unless the Arbitral Tribunal fixes a different time limit.

Article 22

1. Any of the State Parties to the controversy can, within fifteen (15) days following notification of the decision, request a clarification of the same or an interpretation as to how it should be complied with.

2. The Arbitral Tribunal will issue a pronouncement within the next fifteen (15) days.

3. If the Arbitral Tribunal considers that the circumstances require it, it can suspend compliance with the decision until such time as it decides the proffered request.

Article 23

If a State Party does not comply with a decision of the Arbitral Tribunal within a time limit of thirty (30) days, the other State Parties to the controversy can adopt temporary compensatory measures, such as the suspension of concessions or their equivalent, which should tend to lead to compliance.

Article 24

1. Each State Party to a controversy shall defray the costs arising from the performance of duties by its designated arbitrator.

2. The President of the Arbitral Tribunal shall receive pecuniary compensation, which, along with the other costs of the Arbitral Tribunal, should be defrayed in equal amounts by the State Parties to the controversy, unless the Tribunal decides to distribute them in different proportions.

CHAPTER V PRIVATE PARTY COMPLAINTS

Article 25

The procedure established in the present chapter shall apply to all complaints made by private parties (whether physical persons or juridical entities) as a result of the sanction or application, by any of the State Parties, of legal or administrative measures which have a restrictive, discriminatory or unfairly competitive effect, in violation of the Treaty of Asuncion, of the agreements celebrated within its framework, the decisions of the Common Market Council or the resolutions of the Common Market Group.

Article 26

1. The private parties that are affected will file their complaints with the National Section of the Common Market Group of the State Party wherein they maintain their usual residency or which is the headquarters of their business.

2. Private parties should provide all the elements which will allow the aforesaid National Section to determine the truth of the violation and the existence or threat of prejudice.

Article 27

Unless a complaint refers to a question which has already led to the initiation of proceedings for the Solution of Controversies pursuant to Chapters II, III or IV of this Protocol, the National Section of the Common Market Group which accepted the complaint in conformity with Article 26 of this chapter can, in consultation with the affected private party:

a. Initiate direct contacts with the National Section of the Common Market Group of the State Party to which is attributed the violation with the goal of finding, as a result of these consultations, an immediate solution to the question that has been put forth; or

b. Can refer the complaint without further ado to the Common Market Group.

Article 28

If the question cannot be resolved within a time limit of fifteen (15) days from the date the communication of the complaint was made pursuant to Article 27(a), the National Section which made the communication can, upon the request of the affected private party, refer the matter without further ado to the Common Market Group.

Article 29

1. Upon receipt of the complaint, the Common Market Group, in its first meeting following receipt, will evaluate the reasons upon which the National Section accepted it. If it concludes that the necessary requirements are not present to sustain it, it will reject the complaint without further ado.

2. If the Common Market Group does not reject the complaint, it will immediately convene a group of experts who should then issue a report with their conclusions within a non?extendible time period of thirty (30) days following their designation.

3. Within this time limit, the group of experts will give the affected private party and the State against which a complaint has been filed the opportunity to be heard and to present their arguments.

Article 30

1. The group of experts which is referred to by Article 29 will be composed of three (3) members chosen by the Common Market Group or, in the absence of an agreement with respect to one or more of the experts, these shall be selected by a vote the State Parties shall carry out from among a list of twenty four (24) experts. The Administrative Secretariat shall communicate to the Common Market Group the name of the expert or experts which received the largest number of votes. In this last case, and unless the Common Market Group decides otherwise, one of the designated experts cannot be a national of a State against which a complaint has been made nor of the State in which the private party filed its complaint, pursuant to the provisions of Article 26.

2. With the goal of establishing a list of experts, each of the State Parties shall designate six (6) persons of recognized competence in matters which can be the subject matter of a controversy. This list shall remain recorded with the Administrative Secretariat.

Article 31

The costs arising from the experts' performance of their duties will be defrayed in a proportion to be determined by the Common Market Group or, in the event of a lack of agreement, in equal parts by the parties directly involved.

Article 32

The experts will forward their conclusions to the Common Market Group. If this report verifies the legal basis of the complaint made against a State Party, any other State Party can then demand that corrective measures be adopted or that the disputed measure be annulled. If this demand is not met within a time limit of fifteen (15) days, the State Party that made it can then proceed directly to the arbitral procedure pursuant to the conditions established in Chapter IV of the Present Protocol.

CHAPTER VI FINAL DISPOSITIONS

Article 33

The present Protocol, an integral part of the Treaty of Asuncion, will enter into force once all four State Parties deposit the respective instruments of ratification. These instruments should be deposited with the Government of the Republic of Paraguay which will then inform the Governments of the other State Parties of the date of deposit.

Article 34

The present Protocol shall remain in effect until a Permanent System for the Solution of Controversies for the Common Market, as referred to in Number 3 of Annex III to the Treaty of Asuncion, shall enter into force.

Article 35

The accession on the part of any State to the Treaty of Asuncion shall, ipso jure, mean its accession to the present Protocol.

Article 36

Spanish and Portuguese shall, whenever applicable, be the official languages for any of the proceedings contemplated in the present Protocol.

Done in the city of Brasilia on the seventeenth day of the month of December of the year nineteen hundred and ninety one in one original in the Spanish and Portuguese languages, both texts being equally authentic. The Government of the Republic of Paraguay shall be the depository of the present Protocol and will forward a duly authenticated copy of the same to the Governments of the other State Parties.

AGREEMENT BETWEEN INTERNATIONAL FREIGHT STATES OF MERCOSUR

MONTEVIDEO PROTOCOL ON TRADE IN SERVICES IN MERCOSUR

PREAMBLE

The Republic of Argentina, the Federative Republic of Brazil, the Republic of Paraguay and the Eastern Republic of Uruguay, Parties Southern Common Market (MERCOSUR);

Reaffirming

that according to the Treaty of Asunci6n Common Market requires, among other commitments, the free service circulaarte expanded market;

Recognizing

the importance of liberalization of trade in services for the development of the economies of the Member States of MERCOSUR, for deepening the Customs Union and the gradual establishment of the Common Market;

Considering

the need for less developed countries and regions of the MERCOSUR to increasing participation in the services market and promote trade in services on the basis of reciprocal rights and obligations;

Wishing

enshrine a common instrument rules and principles for trade in services between the Member States of MERCOSUR, with a view to the expansion of trade under conditions of transparency and progressive liberalization balance;

Taking

account of the General Agreement on Trade in Services (GATS) of the World Trade Organization (WTO), in particular Article V, and the commitments made by States Parties to the GATS;

Have agreed as follows:

PART I

Purpose and Scope

Articlel. Purpose

1. , this Protocol is to promote free trade in services in MERCOSUR.

Article II. Scope

1. This Protocol shall apply to measures taken by States Parties affecting trade in services in MERCOSUR, including those relating to:

i. the provision of a service;

ii. the purchase, payment or use of a service;

iii. access to services offered to the general public required by those States parties, and use thereof, in connection with the provision of a service;

iv. the presence, including commercial presence, of persons of a State Party in the territory of another State Party to provide a service;

2. For the purposes of this Protocol, defines trade in services as the provision of a service:

a. the territory of a State Party to the territory of any other State;

b. in the territory of a State Party to the service consumer of any other Member State;

c. by a service provider of a State Party, through commercial presence in the territory of any other State;

d. by a service provider of a State Party, through presence of natural persons of a State Party in the territory of any other State Party.

3. For the purposes of this Protocol:

a. the term "measures taken by States Parties" measures taken by:

i. governments and central, state, provincial, departmental, municipal or local and

ii. non-governmental bodies in the exercise of powers delegated by the governments or authorities referred to in subparagraph i).

In fulfilling its obligations and commitments under this Protocol, each State Party shall take appropriate measures within its power to ensure compliance by governments and state, provincial, departmental, and municipal or local governmental bodies within their territories;

b. "services" includes any service in any sector except services supplied in the exercise of governmental authority;

c. a "service in the exercise of governmental authority" means any service which is not supplied on a commercial basis nor in competition with one or more service providers.

PART II

General Obligations and Disciplines

ArticleIII. Deal of the most favored nation

1. With respect to measures covered by this Protocol, each State Party shall accord immediately and unconditionally to services and service providers of any other State Party treatment no less favorable than that accorded to like services and providers similar services to any other State Party or third countries.

2. The provisions of this Protocol shall be construed as preventing a State Party from conferring or according advantages to adjacent countries, whether or not Member States, in order to facilitate exchanges limited to contiguous frontier zones of services produced and consumed locally.

ArticleIV. market access

1. In regard to market access through the modes of supply identified in Article II, each State Party shall accord to services and service providers of the other States Parties treatment no less favorable than that provided for as specified in its Schedule of specific commitments. States Parties undertake to allow cross-border movement of capital is an essential part of a commitment to market access content in its schedule of specific commitments on cross-border trade and capital transfers to their territory in the case of commitments access to markets undertaken regarding commercial presence.

2. States Parties can not maintain or adopt either on the basis of a regional subdivision or on its entire territory, measures regarding:

a. the number of service providers, either in the form of numerical quotas, monopolies, exclusive service suppliers or the requirement of an economic needs test;

b. the total value of service transactions or assets in the form of numerical quotas or the requirement of an economic needs test;

c. the total number of service operations or on the total quantity of service output expressed in terms of designated numerical units in the form of quotas or the requirement of an economic needs test, excluding measures which limit inputs for the supply of services.

d. the total number of natural persons that may be employed in a particular service sector or that a service supplier may employ and who are necessary for the provision of a specific service and are directly related to it, in the form of numerical quotas or the requirement of an economic needs test;

e. specific types of legal entity or joint venture through which a service provider can provide a service, and

f. participation of foreign capital in terms of maximum percentage limit on foreign shareholding or the total value of individual or aggregate foreign investment.

ArticleV. National Treatment

1. A State Party shall accord to services and service suppliers of any other Member State, in respect of all measures affecting the supply of services, treatment no less favorable than that it accords to its own like services or providers similar services.

2. Specific commitments assumed under this Article shall not oblige States Parties to compensate for any inherent competitive disadvantages which result from the foreign character of the services or relevant service providers.

3. A State Party may meet the requirement of paragraph 1 by according to services and service suppliers of the other States Parties formally identical treatment or formally different treatment to that it accords to its own like services and service related.

4. shall be considered formally identical treatment or formally different less favorable if it modifies the conditions of competition in favor of services or service providers to the State Party compared to like services or similar service providers of another Party.

ArticleVI. Additional Commitments

States Parties may negotiate commitments with respect to measures affecting trade in services, but they are not subject to scheduling, under Articles IV and V, including those relating to qualifications, standards or issues with the licenses. These commitments are inscribed in schedules of specific commitments of States Parties.

Article VII. schedules of specific commitments

1. A State shall specify in a schedule of specific commitments sectors, sub-sectors and activities with respect to which assume commitments and, for each mode corresponding provision, indicate the terms, limitations and conditions on market access and national treatment. Each State Party may also specify additional commitments under Article VI. Where applicable, each State Party shall specify deadlines for the implementation of commitments and the date of entry into force of such commitments.

2. Articles IV and V shall not apply to:

a. sectors, sub-sectors, activities or measures that are not specified in the schedule of specific commitments;

b. measures specified in its Schedule of specific commitments that are inconsistent with Article IV or Article V.

3. measures that do not conform simultaneously with Article IV and Article V should be listed in the column relating to Article IV. In this case, the entry will be deemed as a condition or restriction of Article V.

4. Schedules of specific commitments shall be annexed to this Protocol and be an integral part thereof.

Article VIII. Transparency

1. A State shall promptly publish before the date of its entry into force, except in cases of force majeure, all relevant measures of general application relating to this Protocol or affect its operation. Also each State Party shall publish international agreements signed with any country and relating to, or affect, to trade in services.

2. Where it is not feasible to publish the information referred to above, it will be publicly available otherwise.

3. A State Party shall promptly, and at least annually, to the MERCOSUR Trade Commission, the establishment of new laws, regulations or administrative guidelines or introducing amendments to existing deemed significantly affect trade in services.

4. A State Party shall respond promptly to all requests for specific information made by other States Parties on any of its measures of general application or international agreements referred to in paragraph 1. Each State Party shall provide specific information to States Parties upon request, through service or services established under paragraph 4 of Article III of the GATS, on all these issues or those who are subject to notification under paragraph 3 .

5. A State Party may notify the MERCOSUR Trade Commission, any action taken by another State Party, in its opinion, affects the operation of this Protocol.

ArticleIX. Disclosure of confidential information

Nothing in this Protocol shall require any Member State the obligation to provide confidential information the disclosure of which may constitute an obstacle to the enforcement or otherwise be contrary to the public interest or would prejudice the legitimate commercial interests of public or private .

Article X. Domestic Regulation

1. Each State Party shall ensure that all measures of general application affecting trade in services are administered in a reasonable, objective and impartial.

2. A State Party shall maintain or establish courts or legal proceedings, arbitration or administrative permit, at the request of an affected service, prompt review of administrative decisions affecting trade in services and, where justified, the application of appropriate solutions. When such procedures are not independent of the agency entrusted with the administrative decision concerned, the State Party shall ensure that the procedures in fact an objective and impartial.

The provisions of this paragraph shall be construed to require a State party to institute such tribunals or procedures where this would be inconsistent with its constitutional structure or the nature of its legal system.

3. When a license, registration, certificate or other authorization for the provision of a service, the competent authorities of the State Party concerned, within a reasonable time after the filing of an application:

> i. when the petition is complete, a decision on the same informing the concerned person, or
>
> ii. if the application is not complete, inform the applicant without unnecessary delay regarding the status of the application as well as additional information that may be required according to the law of the State Party.

4. With a view to ensuring that measures relating to technical standards, requirements and procedures, qualification, and licensing requirements do not constitute unnecessary barriers to trade in services, States Parties shall ensure that these requirements and methods, inter alia:

i. based on objective and transparent criteria, such as competence and the ability to provide the service;

ii. not more burdensome than necessary to ensure the quality of service, and

iii. in the case of licensing procedures, not in themselves a restriction on the service.

5. A State Party shall establish appropriate procedures to verify the competence of professionals of other States Parties.

Article XI. Recognition

1. A State Party recognizes, unilaterally or by agreement, education, experience, licenses, registrations or certifications obtained in the territory of another State Party or of any country which is not part of MERCOSUR:

a. Nothing in this Protocol shall be construed as requiring the State party recognize that education, experience, licenses, registrations or certifications obtained in the territory of another State Party;

b. the State Party shall provide to any other State Party adequate opportunity to:

i. demonstrate that education, experience, licenses, registrations and certifications obtained in the territory should also be recognized, or,

ii. so you can enter into an agreement or arrangement having equivalent effect.

2. Each State Party undertakes to encourage relevant entities within their territories, among others, the nature of government and professional associations, in cooperation with competent institutions of other States Parties, to develop standards and criteria mutually acceptable to the exercise of the relevant professions and activities in the field of services, through licensing, registration and certification service providers and to propose recommendations to the Common Market Group on Mutual Recognition.

3. rules and criteria referred to in paragraph 2 may be developed, among others, based on the following elements: education, examination, experience and ethical behavior, professional development and recertification, scope, local knowledge , consumer protection and requirements of citizenship, residence or domicile.

4. Upon receipt of the recommendation referred to in paragraph 2, the Common Market Group shall examine it within a reasonable time to determine their consistency with this Protocol. Based on this review, each State Party undertakes to instruct the competent authorities, where necessary, to implement the provisions of the relevant bodies of MERCOSUR within a mutually agreed period.

5. The Common Market Group shall periodically, and at least once every three years, the implementation of this Article.

Article XII. Antitrust

With regard to the acts performed in the provision of services by service providers or public or private entities, aimed at producing or produce effects on competition in MERCOSUR and affecting trade in services between the States Parties shall apply the provisions of Protocol Antitrust MERCOSUR.

Article XIII. general Exceptions

Subject to the measures listed below are not applied in a manner which would constitute a means of arbitrary or unjustifiable discrimination between countries where prevailing conditions prevail, or a disguised restriction on trade in services, nothing in this Protocol shall be construed as preventing a State Party from adopting or enforcing measures:

a. necessary to protect public morals or maintain public order and can only invoke the public policy exception is raised when an imminent and sufficiently serious threat to one of the fundamental interests of society;

b. necessary to protect the life and health of people and animals or plant life;

c. necessary to secure compliance with laws or regulations which are not inconsistent with the provisions of this Protocol, including those relating to:

i. the prevention of deceptive practices and fraudulent practices, or the means to deal with the effects of a default on services contracts;

ii. protecting the privacy of individuals in relation to the processing and dissemination of personal data and the protection of confidentiality of individual records and accounts;

iii. security;

d. inconsistent with Article V, as expressed in this Protocol, provided that the difference in treatment is aimed at ensuring the equitable taxation or collection of direct taxes, effective for services or providers of other States Parties , comprising the steps taken by a State Party under its taxation system, as stipulated in Article XIV, letter d) of the GATS.

e. inconsistent with Article III, as expressed in this Protocol, provided that the difference in treatment is the result of an agreement to avoid double taxation or provisions to avoid double taxation in any other international agreement or arrangement that is binding to the State Party applying the measure.

ArticleXIV. Exceptions security

1. Nothing in this Protocol shall be interpreted as meaning that:

a. impose a State Party to furnish any information the disclosure of which it considers contrary to its essential security interests, or

b. prevent a State Party from taking any measures it considers necessary for the protection of its essential security interests:

i. concerning the provision of services directly or indirectly for the supply of the armed forces;

ii. relating to fissionable materials or fusible or those used for their manufacture;

iii. taken in time of war or other emergency in international relations; or

c. prevent a State Party from taking any measures which fulfill the obligations assumed by it under the United Nations Charter for the maintenance of peace and security.

2. He informed the MERCOSUR Trade Commission of the measures taken under subparagraphs b) and c) of paragraph 1 and its termination.

ArticleXV. Procurement

1. Articles III, IV and V shall not apply to laws, regulations or requirements governing the procurement by governmental agencies of services purchased for governmental purposes and not for commercial resale or use in the provision of services for sale trade.

2. Notwithstanding paragraph 1, and recognizing that such laws, regulations or requirements may have distortive effects on trade in services, the States Parties agree to apply common disciplines on government procurement in general be established in MERCOSUR.

Article XVI. Grants

1. States Parties recognize that under certain circumstances, subsidies may have distortive effects on trade in services. The States Parties agree to apply common disciplines on subsidies in general will be established in MERCOSUR.

2. shall apply the mechanism provided for in paragraph 2 of Article XV of the GATS.

Article XVII. Denial of Benefits

A State Party may deny the benefits of this protocol to a service provider of another State Party, upon notification and consultation, when that State Party demonstrates that the service is being provided by a person from a country that is not a party MERCOSUR.

Article XVIII. Definitions

1. the purposes of this Protocol:

a. "Measure" means any measure by a State Party, whether in the form of law, regulation, rule, procedure, decision, administrative action, or any other form;

b. "Providing a service" includes the production, distribution, marketing, sale and delivery of a service;

c. "Commercial presence" means any type of business or professional establishment, through, inter alia, of the constitution, acquisition or maintenance of a juridical person, as well as branches and representative offices located in the territory of a State Party In order to provide a service.

d. "Sector" of a service means:

i. with reference to a specific commitment, one or more subsectors of that service, or all of them, as specified in the Schedule of Specific Commitments of a State Party.

ii. otherwise, the whole of that service sector, including all sub-sectors;

e. "Service of another Member State" means a service:

i. from or in the territory of that State Party;

ii. in the case of the provision of a service through commercial presence or through the presence of natural persons, by a service supplier of that other State Party;

f. "Service provider" means a person who provides a service. When the service is not provided by a juridical person but through other forms of commercial presence such as a branch or a representative office, however will be awarded to the service provider (ie, a legal person) through that presence, the treatment given to service providers under the Protocol. Such treatment shall be extended to the presence through which the service is provided, without requiring extended to any other part of the supplier located outside the territory in which the service is provided.

g. "Service consumer" means any person who receives or uses a service;

h. "Person" means a natural person or a legal person;

i. "Natural person of another Member State" means a natural person who resides in the territory of that other State Party or of any other State Party, in accordance with the laws of that other State Party, a national of that State Party or have the right of permanent residence in that other Member State;

j. "Legal person" means any legal entity duly constituted or organized under the law applicable to the child, whether or not for profit, whether public, private or mixed and is organized under any type of company or association.

k. "Juridical person of another Member State" means a body corporate that is incorporated or organized under the laws of that other State Party which has his headquarters and developing or plans to develop substantive business operations in the territory of that State Party or of any other State Party.

PART III

Liberalization Program

Article XIX. Negotiation of Specific Commitments

1. In compliance with the objectives of this Protocol, States Parties shall successive rounds of negotiations in order to complete within a period of ten years from the date of entry into force of this Protocol, the program of liberalization of trade in MERCOSUR services. The rounds of negotiations will be held annually and will have as its main objective the progressive incorporation of sectors, subsectors, activities and modes of supply of services liberalization Program Protocol and the reduction or elimination of the adverse effects of the measures on trade in services, as a way to ensure effective market access. This process will aim to promote the interests of all participants on a mutually advantageous basis and to securing an overall balance of rights and obligations.

2. progressive liberalization process in each round will be routed through negotiations directed at increasing the level of specific commitments undertaken by States Parties in their schedules of specific commitments.

3. In the development of the liberalization program is allowed differences in the level of commitments made in response to the specific needs of different sectors and with the objectives outlined in the following paragraph.

4. liberalization process shall respect the right of each State to regulate and to introduce new regulations within their territory to achieve the objectives of national policies in the service sector. Such regulations may include, among others, national treatment and market access, since it does not nullify or impair the obligations arising from this Protocol and specific commitments.

Article XX. Amendment or suspension of commitments

1. A State Party may, during the implementation of the liberalization program referred to in Part III of this Protocol, modify or suspend specific commitments included in its schedule of specific commitments.

This modification or suspension shall apply only as of the date it is established and the principle of non-retroactivity to preserve acquired rights.

2. A State shall utilize the present regime only in exceptional cases, provided that when it does, notify the Common Market Group and places before it the facts, reasons and justifications for such an amendment or withdrawal of commitments. In such cases, the State Party concerned or consult with the States Parties concerned are considered to reach a consensus on specific measures to be applied and the period of its validity.

PART IV

Institutional Provisions

ArticleXXI. Council of the Common Market

The Common Market Council adopt the outcome of negotiations on specific commitments and any changes and / or suspension thereof.

ArticleXXII. Common Market Group

1. Negotiations on services is competition in MERCOSUR Common Market Group With respect to this Protocol, the Common Market Group shall have the following functions:

a. convene and oversee negotiations under Article XIX of this Protocol. To this end, the Common Market Group will establish the scope, criteria and instruments for holding negotiations on specific commitments;

b. receive notices and results of consultations on modification and / or discontinuation of specific commitments as provided by Article XX;

c. to carry out the functions set out in Article XI;

d. periodically assess the development of trade in services in MERCOSUR and

e. perform such other duties as may be assigned by the Council of the Common Market in services trade.

2. For the purposes of the functions stated above, the Common Market Group will be a subsidiary body and regulate its composition and method of operation.

Article XXIII. MERCOSUR Trade Commission

1. Notwithstanding the functions referred to previous articles the application of this Protocol shall be borne by the MERCOSUR Trade Commission, which has the following functions:

a. receive, in accordance with Article VIII of this Protocol, to be presented by the States Parties;

b. receive information from the States Parties regarding the exceptions in Article XIV.

c. receive information from States Parties with regard to actions that may constitute abuse of a dominant position or practices that distort competition and make it known to the national enforcement bodies Protocol Competition;

d. understand queries and complaints submitted by States Parties concerning the application, interpretation or breach of this Protocol and the commitments undertaken in Schedules of specific commitments, applying the mechanisms and procedures in MERCOSUR and

e. perform such other duties as may be assigned by the Common Market Group in services.

Article XXIV. Dispute

Any disputes which may arise between States Parties concerning the application, interpretation or breach of the commitments set out in this Protocol shall be resolved in accordance with the procedures and mechanisms existing solution in MERCOSUR.

PART V

Final Provisions

Article XXV. Annexes

The Annexes to this Protocol shall form an integral part thereof.

Article XXVI. Review

1. In order to achieve the object and purpose of this Protocol, it may be revised, taking into account the development and regulation of trade in services in MERCOSUR and progress in services in the World Trade Organization and other specialized forums.

2. In particular, based on the evolution of the functioning of the institutional provisions of this Protocol and the institutional structure of MERCOSUR, Part IV may be amended with a view to their improvement.

Article XXVII. Effective

1. This Protocol, part of the Treaty of Asunción, shall be indefinite and shall enter into force thirty days after the date of deposit of the third instrument of ratification.

2. This Protocol and its instruments of ratification shall be deposited with the Government of the Republic of Paraguay, who will send certified copy of this Protocol to the Governments of the other States Parties.

3. Schedules of specific commitments will be incorporated into national law in accordance with the procedures of each State Party.

ArticleXXVIII. Notifications

The Government of the Republic of Paraguay shall notify the Governments of the other States Parties of the date of the deposit of instruments of ratification and entry into force of this Protocol.

Article XXIX. Accession or complaint

On accession or denunciation, governed as a whole, to this Protocol, the rules established by the Treaty of Asunci6n. The accession or denunciation of the Treaty of Asuncion or this Protocol mean, *ipso jure* , accession or denunciation of this Protocol and the Treaty of Asunci6n.

Article XXX. Designation

This Protocol shall be called Montevideo Protocol on Trade in Services of the Southern Common Market.

Done at the city of Montevideo, Republic of Uruguay, on the fifteenth day of December in the year 1997, in one original in the Spanish and Portuguese languages, both texts being equally authentic.

REGULATORY FRAMEWORK OF THE COMMON REGULATIONS ON PROTECTION AGAINST IMPORTS DUMPED FROM NON MEMBERS OF THE SOUTHERN COMMON MARKET (MERCOSUR).

Southern Common Market (MERCOSUR) Decisions of the Council of the Common Market MERCOSUR / CMC / DEC. No. 11/97:

SEEN : The Arts. 1 and 4 of the Treaty of Asunci6n , the Arts. 16 and 19 of the Protocol of Ouro Preto , Decision No. 7/93 and N 9/95 of the Common Market Council, Resolution No. 80/97 of the Common Market Group and Directives N 1/95 and N 9/97 MERCOSUR Trade Commission.

WHEREAS :

The continued consolidation of MERCOSUR Customs Union and the need to adopt measures to give sufficient strength to the common commercial policy;

In that sense, it is necessary to establish a harmonized treatment of imports from third countries, trade protection;

They also need to adapt TDI, in light of the commitments made by the States Parties of MERCOSUR in the Uruguay Round of GATT in the matter;

The Technical Committee No. 6 Unfair Trade Practices and Safeguard of the MERCOSUR Trade Commission is responsible for the development of common trade policy instruments in the areas of trade protection and safeguards, and

The Technical Committee No. 6 concluded the negotiations on the draft "Common Regulatory Framework Regulation on protection against dumped Imports from non-member Southern Common Market (MERCOSUR)."

THE COMMON MARKET COUNCIL DECIDES:

Section 1 - Passing the "Common Regulatory Framework Regulation on protection against dumped Imports from non-members of the Southern Common Market (MERCOSUR)," in its Spanish and Portuguese, identical and equally valid, consisting as Annex to this Decision and are an integral part of it. Art 2 - Instruct the MERCOSUR Trade Commission (CCM) to develop, from the regulatory framework, the rules it may consider necessary for the development and implementation of the Common Regulations AD. Art. 3 - Pending the approval of the Common Regulations AD, States Parties shall apply antidumping measures in accordance with their national legislation, in accordance with the provisions of the regulatory framework of the Common Regulations on protection against dumped Imports from countries not members MERCOSUR. States Parties made adjustments in their national legislation, if need be, in order of their alignment with the Framework. Art. 4 - The State party undertake research for the application of anti-dumping action against imports from countries not members of MERCOSUR, send the other States Parties, to his knowledge, the acts published in compliance with the provisions of Article 12 of the Agreement on Implementation of Article VI of the General Agreement on Tariffs and Trade 1994, the Agreement Establishing the World Trade Organization (WTO Agreement), and copies of the reports to the Committee on Anti-WTO , pursuant to Article 16 paragraph 4 of that agreement. These communications shall be made through the Committee on Trade Remedies and Safeguards (CDCS).Art 5. - When a State Party considers that another State Party is making imports from third markets at dumping prices, which are affecting their exports, may request, through the CCM, the consultations with the aim of meeting the terms of entry of these products, which will be held within thirty (30) days from the date of such request. Art 6. - When a State party to another State Party, through the CCM, a duly justified request, the application of anti-dumping measures in their favor, the treatment of the request and the decision whether or not to the same course is conform to the provisions of Article 14 of the Agreement on Implementation of Article VI of the General Agreement on Tariffs and Trade 1994 WTO Agreement. Where a State Party decides not to proceed with an application for anti-dumping measures in favor of another State Party, shall state the reasons for the decision, through the CCM. Art. 7. - Imports from MERCOSUR States Parties of products subject to anti-dumping measures will be subject to compliance with the MERCOSUR Origin Regime established by the Eighth Additional Protocol to ECA 18 or other relevant rules of origin. States Parties shall apply to such imports for customs procedures to avoid any actions of medidasantidumping elusive, as provided in these rules. Art 8. - The CCM shall establish a program of cooperation among States Parties in order to reconcile operating procedures, technical and statistical data relating to the conduct deinvestigaciones for antidumping measures. Art 9. - Regarding anti-dumping investigations intrazone applies the provisions of the Decision of the Common Market Council No. 18/96, in accordance with the provisions of the preceding article. Art 10. - With the approval of this regulatory framework is not effective Decision No. 7/93.

TRADE AND INVESTMENT COOPERATION ARRANGEMENT AND ACTION PLAN BETWEEN CANADA AND THE MERCOSUR

Canada and the Southern Common Market (**MERCOSUR**), hereinafter referred to as "the Parties";

Desiring to enhance the long-standing bonds of friendship and cooperation between Canada and MERCOSUR;

Noting the importance they attach to the strengthening of trade and economic relations in the Western Hemisphere;

Reaffirming their resolution to conclude the negotiation of Free Trade Area of the Americas no later than 2005;

Building on their mutual commitment to the World Trade Organization and their cooperation in the Cairns Group;

Declaring their intention to establish a bilateral framework for the expansion and diversification of Canada-MERCOSUR trade and investment;

Wishing to explore opportunities to strengthen bilateral cooperation in other areas and activities;

;**HAVE REACHED** the following understanding:

1. **Objectives**

   The Parties will seek to:

   a. enhance economic relations between Canada and the MERCOSUR, in particular concerning trade in goods and services, as well as investment;

   b. strengthen their cooperation with a view to liberalizing trade and investment between them by identifying those measures that impede or distort trade and investment flows between Canada and the MERCOSUR;

   c. facilitate the increased involvement of the private sector, in particular of the smaller and medium-sized enterprises, in trade and commercial cooperation between Canada and the MERCOSUR;

   d. increase mutual understanding of their respective positions in the negotiations of the Free Trade Area of the Americas; and,

   e. develop greater co-ordination and consultation in the World Trade Organization and in the Cairns Group.

2. **Expansion of trade and investment**

   1. The Parties will endeavour to create the most favourable conditions for expanding trade in goods and services, and the expansion of investment between them in accordance with the annexed Action Plan.

   2. The Parties will examine all questions set out in the Action Plan influencing bilateral economic relations or their respective interests in respect of trade and

investment in third countries, including multilateral and plurilateral questions of common interest arising in appropriate fora.

3. In enhancing the expansion of trade and investment between the private sectors in Canada and the MERCOSUR, the Parties will, in particular, foster regular exchanges of information on opportunities for trade and investment and for other promotional initiatives, including contacts at the business level, in accordance with the annexed Action Plan.

1. **Consultative Group and Advisory Council**

   1. The Parties establish the Consultative Group on Trade and Investment Cooperation (hereinafter referred to as the Consultative Group) chaired by high-level officials of the Parties responsible for international trade, or their designated alternate. In the case of the MERCOSUR, the responsible representatives are the Coordinators of the Common Market Group. The Consultative Group may comprise other high-level officials or their designated alternate as may be mutually decided from time to time.

   2. The Consultative Group will convene periodically, ordinarily once every twelve months, to review and direct progress on the Action Plan. Special meetings will be held at the request of either Party. The meetings of the Consultative Group will alternate between Canada and MERCOSUR or another agreed location at the request of either Party. Sessions of the Consultative Group will be chaired by the host Party.

   3. The Parties will establish an Advisory Council of business representatives to advise them on areas of particular concern to the private sector.

2. **Final Clauses**

   1. Nothing in this Arrangement affects the respective rights and obligations of either Party to the other Party under Agreements, Conventions or other instruments to which they are both Parties, either individually or collectively.

   2. This Arrangement may be amended by the written concurrence of both Parties.

   3. The Arrangement comes into effect on signature and will remain in effect unless terminated by either Party on 180 days notice to the other Party.

Done at Buenos Aires, on June 16, 1998, in two originals in the English, French, Portuguese and Spanish languages, being all equally valid.

FOR CANADA & FOR MERCOSUR
THE ARGENTINE REPUBLIC
THE FEDERATIVE REPUBLIC OF BRAZIL
THE REPUBLIC OF PARAGUAY
THE EASTERN REPUBLIC OF URUGUAY

TRADE AND INVESTMENT COOPERATION ARRANGEMENT BETWEEN CANADA AND THE MERCOSUR ACTION PLAN

1. This Action Plan constitutes an integral part of the Trade and Investment Cooperation Arrangement between Canada and the MERCOSUR signed at Buenos Aires on June 16, 1998.

2. The Action Plan, in conformity with the objectives of the said Arrangement, will include the following areas of priority interest:

   a. Expansion of trade and strengthening of economic cooperation

      - identification and analysis of factors and measures, including those of third countries, influencing bilateral trade and investment;
      - definition of options and appropriate actions in order to promote market access for goods and services;
      - negotiation of Foreign Investment Protection Agreements between Canada and individual MERCOSUR countries;
      - development of Customs Cooperation and Mutual Assistance Arrangements;
      - development of cooperative arrangements in the areas of labour and environment, taking into account related discussions at the World Trade Organization and International Labour Organization, with a view to fostering the participation of civil society of both Parties in bilateral trade and investment relations;
      - dialogue on regulatory reform and development of mutual recognition of conformity assessment procedures in specific sectors to be identified;
      - consultations and, as appropriate, coordination in the negotiation and implementation of the Free Trade Area of the Americas;
      - consultations on areas of mutual interest in the Cairns Group; and
      - cooperation in the World Trade Organization and other appropriate fora regarding any issue of common interest.

   b. Promotion of trade and investment

      - exchange of information on international trade and on business opportunities in all economic sectors;
      - encouragement of small and medium-sized enterprises to participate in bilateral trade and economic cooperation
      - promotion of business missions, trade fairs, strategic venturing initiatives, symposia, conferences and technical presentations;
      - promotion of efforts of the private sector of both Parties in third country markets;

- fostering of joint partnerships in the area of environmental technologies; and,
- cooperation between official institutions responsible for trade and investment promotion.

3. The present Action Plan will be reviewed periodically and revised as appropriate by the Consultative Group.

CUSTOMS CODE OF MERCOSUR

IN VIEW: The art. 13 of the Treaty of Asunci6n, art. 10 of Decision 4/91 of the Common Market Council and;

WHEREAS:

By Resolution GMC 13/94, was commissioned to prepare the Draft SGT 2 of the MERCOSUR Customs Code;

Are required to draw up a basic law that comprise the discipline of defining and institutes that regulate customs matters within MERCOSUR, in view of the Customs Union as of 01/01/95;

That all States Parties should apply a basic common customs legislation within MERCOSUR;

THE COMMON MARKET COUNCIL DECIDES:

Article 1 - To approve the MERCOSUR Customs Code, attached as Annex to this Decision.

PROTOCOL ON THE CUSTOMS CODE OF MERCOSUR

The Argentine Republic, the Federative Republic of Brazil, the Republic of Paraguay and the Eastern Republic of Uruguay, hereinafter "States Parties";

Whereas the Treaty of Asuncion signed by States Parties on March 26, 1991;

Conscious of the need to adopt a common customs legislation allowing uniform application of Community rules within MERCOSUR;

Recognizing that for the entry into force of the Customs Union on 01.01.95, it is essential to adopt a Community Customs Code;

Agree:

TITLE I PRELIMINARY PROVISIONS

CHAPTER 1 SCOPE AND BASIC DEFINITIONS

Article 1

This Code and its Implementing Rules are applicable customs legislation:

a) the entire customs territory of the Southern Common Market-MERCOSUR, established by the Treaty of Asuncion, March 26, 1991, unless the special Community or resulting from international agreements;

b) the trade of MERCOSUR Member States with third countries.

Article 2

One. The territory comprises the MERCOSUR customs:

a) the territory of the Republic of Argentina;

b) the territory of the Federative Republic of Brazil;

c) the territory of the Republic of Paraguay;

d) the territory of the Republic of Uruguay, and

e) the territory of any State which becomes an integral part thereof.

2nd. Included in the MERCOSUR customs territory territorial waters, exclusive economic zones and airspace of States Parties.

3rd. The permanence of goods in the Free Zone and Special Customs Area is not subject to the usual customs controls.

Article 3

For the purposes of this Code, the following definitions apply:

1 "Customs Territory" means the entire territory of States Parties to the MERCOSUR, which applies to Community customs legislation.

2nd. Enclave: It is understood by the Community customs enclave, part of the territory of another country, in whose geographic scope is allowed the application of Community customs legislation;

3rd. Exclave: It is understood by customs exclave, part of the territory of MERCOSUR, in whose geographic scope, does not apply to Community customs legislation.

4th. "Person":

a) an individual;

b) the legal person.

5th. "Person established in the customs territory":

a) in the case of individuals, the same one that has his habitual residence or domicile and permanent legal;

b) in the case of a corporation, the same one that has its headquarters, its management or permanent establishment.

6th. "Customs authority" means the authority competent for the application of customs legislation.

7th. "Decision": administrative act that decide a case concerning the application of customs legislation.

Eight. "Merchandise" means any goods liable to a customs operation.

9th. "Community goods":

a) obtained in the customs territory in accordance with the provisions of origin set out in this Code;

b) those imported from third countries or territories and shipped for consumption in free circulation in the customs territory;

10. "Non-Community goods":

a); those not covered by item 7;

b) those who lose their Community status by being permanently exported from the customs territory.

11. "Customs Tax Obligation": the obligation of a person to pay the amount of tax credit under the customs legislation.

12 "Destination Customs of the goods"

a) the application of a procedure

b) the introduction in the Free Zone or Special Customs Area;

c) re-export;

d) destruction;

e) abandonment in favor of the Treasury.

13. "Customs procedure":

a) the order for consumption;

b) the reimportation;

c) temporary admission;

d) temporary admission for inward processing;

e) export;

f) the temporary export;

g) the temporary export for outward processing;

h) customs transit;

i) the customs warehouse

j) processing under customs control;

14. "Declaration of arrival" communication to the customs authority, as provided, the goods arrive to an area under the jurisdiction of customs.

15. "Presentation of the goods": the act of putting the goods available to the Customs for customs formalities.

16. "Declarant": sender, consignee or person entitled to dispose of the goods, acting on their behalf or through duly authorized representative, to submit a declaration for a customs procedure.

17. "Declaration for a customs procedure" act by which, as prescribed by Customs, the declarant describes the goods, indicating the customs procedure applicable to it and provides the information necessary for their implementation.

18. "Early Delivery": College of the customs authority to make the goods available to the interested before the full completion of the formalities of customs clearance.

19. "Simplified Procedure" is the set of actions that customs clearance, the characteristics of the goods or the circumstances of the transaction actually helps cut, dispensing with the prior formalities, customs control through minimum necessary to ensure compliance with customs Community.

20. "Community provisions" normative acts and regulations laid down jointly by the States Parties within MERCOSUR, and application in the customs territory;

21. "Provisions in force": the Community provisions and complementary national, provided that the national standards are not contrary to this Code.

22. "Customs Operation" means any operation of loading, unloading, input, output, handling, storage or transit of goods subject to foreign trade and subject to Customs control;

23. "Customs Control": a set of measures adopted by the customs authority to enforce the provisions of this Code and its Implementing Rules;

24. "Clearance" means all procedures and formalities that must be met to obtain the release of the goods, whatever the customs procedure applied;

25. "Customs Verification": the procedure whose purpose document analysis and verification of merchandise as well understood as a sequence of actions taken by the customs authority in order to prove the correctness of the declaration submitted and compliance with legal and regulatory requirements, corresponding to the respective customs regime.

26. "Primary Zone" means the area of land or water, continuous or discontinuous, occupied ports, airports and the area adjacent to the border points, bonded by the customs authority, to freight, vehicles and / or people.

27. "Crew member" means any person who is in the service of the vehicle during the course of the trip commercial or military.

28. "Vehicle" means any means of transport used to carry people or goods from one place to another.

29 "traveler" means any person who enters or moves into the customs territory or leaving the same, and that is not crewmember.

CHAPTER 2

GENERAL PROVISIONS RELATING TO THE RIGHTS AND OBLIGATIONS

PEOPLE FACE TO CUSTOMS RULES

Section 1

Right of Representation

Article 4

One. The shipper, the consignee, or person entitled to dispose of the cargo, it may act directly, through employee with permanent employment or through a representative, in the processing of customs operations, the conditions laid down in the Rules of Application.

2nd. The representative must be customs broker, authorized and registered in the State party of the transaction.

3rd. The customs agent must be a person of good moral character and proven economic entitling him to exercise the technical skills required to function under conditions laid down in the Rules of Application.

4th. Each State Party shall provide for the compulsory intervention of customs broker in foreign trade operations.

Section 2

Inquiries Concerning Customs Enforcement

Article 5

One. When applying the customs authority a decision on the application of customs legislation, the person will provide all the elements necessary for that purpose.

2nd. Applications should be submitted in writing, on such terms and conditions set forth in the Rules of Application.

3rd. Decisions, substantiated by the customs authority, shall be communicated in writing to the applicant within the time limits set out in the Application of Standards, and will be implemented immediately, except as provided in Title on Resources.

Section 3

Information

Article 6

One. Any interested person may apply to the customs authority information on the application of customs legislation in relation to specific cases.

2nd. Information will be provided free of charge to the applicant. However, when the same special cause costs to Customs, they may be borne by the applicant in accordance with the Rules of Application.

Section 4

Other Provisions

Article 7

The customs authority shall adopt, in accordance the provisions in force, the control measures necessary for the correct application of customs legislation.

Article 8

People interested in exchanging operations provide goods, the customs authority, the documents and information necessary for the application of customs legislation, in the manner and within the period specified in the Application of Standards.

Article 9

Information provided to the Customs Administration or obtained by it because of its legal duties, the character will be booked in accordance with the provisions laid down by the national legislation of each State Party, while not edited their community norm.

Article 10

For purposes of customs control, the parties shall retain documents relating to customs operations for a period of five (5) years, commencing on the first day of the calendar year following that of the taxable event, observing the specific provisions of this Code .

Article 11

For purposes of conversion into national currency values in foreign currency related to foreign trade transactions, the exchange rate to be used will be a force in the State Party on the date of registration of the declaration for a customs procedure as set Standards Implementation .

CHAPTER 3

EXERCISE OF CUSTOMS AUTHORITY

Article 12

One. The customs authority shall be held permanently in the customs territory of MERCOSUR, and all that is within its area of authority and jurisdiction, the customs administration and tax their servers take precedence over other bodies exercising its powers in him.

2nd. The precedence that the previous item implies the obligation of the other authorities, to provide immediate assistance, whenever required, to fulfill the activities of customs control and put at the disposal of the customs administration, people, facilities or equipment necessary for the performance of their duties.

3rd. The server Customs may request the assistance of the federal, state or municipal, when necessary to perform its functions.

Article 13

One. The discipline of entry, stay, exit and movement of people, vehicles, cargo units and cargo in the primary zone is the competence of the customs authority, the form and conditions will be set out in the Application of Standards, without prejudice to the powers of other bodies .

2nd. The issue of standards whose purpose is to regulate the activities of other bodies involved in foreign trade transactions, involving or affecting implementing controls customs, should be preceded by the manifestation of the customs authority.

Article 14

The customs authority shall, when it deems necessary, and may undertake investigations or procedures that aim to investigate violations typified this Code and its implementing rules and even request information from other agencies with responsibilities to control the entry, residence and exit of goods from the customs territory.

TITLE II ELEMENTS OF THE BASIS FOR APPLICATION OF CUSTOMS CHARGES

CHAPTER 1 COMMON EXTERNAL TARIFF AND CLASSIFICATION OF GOODS TARIFF

Article 15

One. The charges levied on the taxable event of a customs tax liability will be based on the Common External Tariff (CET).

2nd. Other measures prescribed by Community provisions on the exchange of goods are applied according to the tariff classification of the goods.

3rd. The Common External Tariff includes:

a) Common Nomenclature;

b) any other nomenclature established by specific Community provisions, which is wholly or partially Common Nomenclature or adds any subdivisions;

c) the rates and other systems charge normally applicable to goods understood by common classification;

d) preferential tariff rates contained in agreements which MERCOSUR has negotiated with a given country or group of countries;

e) measures which provide for reduction of the duties applicable to certain goods;

f) other tariff measures and / or trade protection provided by EU legislation.

4th. The measures contemplated in paragraphs "d" and "e" of the previous item shall be applied instead of those provided in paragraph "c", only in cases where the customs authority finds that the goods that it meets the conditions of those points .

5th. The measures that treat the letters "d" and "e" in item 3 of this Article, which is set maximum volumes shall be limited to their volume.

6th. It is understood by the tariff classification act by which a commodity is coded according to common classification.

7th. The tariff classification of goods in the nomenclatures referred to in paragraphs "a" and "b" of paragraph 3 of this Article shall be determined by applying the rules of these additional classifications.

Article 16

One. The favorable tariff treatment to certain goods that are entitled will be subject to the conditions set forth in the Application of Standards.

2nd. It is understood by "favorable tariff treatment," regardless of whether there contigenciamento, any reduction of tariffs for certain goods subject to trade.

3rd. The reduction of charges referred to in paragraph "and" Item 3 of Article 15 shall be established by the competent authority of MERCOSUR.

Article 17

The foreign trade statistics MERCOSUR will be prepared based on the common classification referred to in paragraph "a" of section 3 of Article 15.

Article 18

Products from the Free Zone Area and Special Customs, apply the provisions of the Standards Implementation or specific Community legislation.

CHAPTER 2

ORIGIN OF GOODS

Section 1

Rules of Origin Not Preferred.

Article 19

One. Goods originating in a country the goods wholly obtained in its territory, in the manner and conditions in the Application of Standards.

2nd. It is understood by goods wholly obtained in a country:

> a) the products of the mineral kingdom, plant and animal, including hunting and fishing, extracted, harvested or caught, born and raised in its territory or in its territorial waters and exclusive economic zones;
>
> b) seafood products, extracted outside their territorial waters and exclusive economic zones by vessels flying its flag, duly registered or recorded in that country or leased by companies established in its territory and processed in its economic zone, even when they have been subjected the primary processes of packaging and preservation, needed for marketing and exchanges not involving the classification nomenclature;
>
> c) the products obtained on board factory ships from those referred to in the previous paragraph, originating in that country, when such factory ships are registered or recorded in the same and fly its flag;
>
> d) products extracted from marine soil or subsoil outside the territorial sea upon which this country has exclusive exploitation rights;

e) the tailings and waste resulting from operations or development, collected in its territory, and that may serve only for the recovery of raw materials;

f) goods produced in that country solely from those mentioned in the preceding paragraphs or their derivatives, at any stage of manufacture.

Article 20

One. Unless otherwise set forth in the Application of Standards, are considered to originate from a state party goods produced in the territory of that State Party, using the same non-originating materials, as the result of a process of substantial transformation conferring a new individuality, characterized even because they are identified by a code in the nomenclature other than those mentioned materials.

2nd. A substantial transformation process excludes transactions consisting only fitting, dovetails, division into lots or volumes, selection or classification, marking, the gaming goods or other similar operations or processes.

3rd. Goods whose production involved more than one country, it is from the country where substantial transformation occurred, as provided in Rules Application, duly proved before the customs authorities.

Article 21

For the purposes of Article 20, it is understood that the term "materials" includes raw materials, inputs, intermediate products and parts used to manufacture the products.

Section 2

Rules of Determination of Origin Preferred

Article 22

Products from the Free Trade Zone or Special Customs Area apply the requirements of the Standard Application specific on the matter.

Article 23

One. The rules of origin for goods with tariff preferences that treats the "d" Item 3 of Article 15 shall be established in accordance with their agreements or by the competent authority, when arising from the MERCOSUR ruling.

Section 3

General Provisions

Article 24

One. The origin of the goods must be shown by presenting documentation.

2nd. The customs authority may request information regarding imported products whenever there is doubt as to meet the requirements of origin or the veracity or authenticity of the source documentation presented.

3rd. The information provided will be strictly confidential.

Article 25

I. The import procedures can not be interrupted by questions of origin, unless there is sufficient evidence of fact as to the falsity or adulteration of documentation.

2nd. For questions about the origin of goods or lack of documentation, the customs authority may require the importer or his legal representative sufficient guarantee, established under the provisions in force, or take other necessary measures to protect the fiscal interests.

CHAPTER 3

CUSTOMS VALUE OF GOODS

Article 26

One. 0 for determination of the customs value of import levies on imported goods, introduced in any capacity in the customs territory shall be determined according to the rules of the Agreement on Implementation of Article VII of the General Agreement on Tariffs and Trade - GATT.

2nd. No customs value shall include the following elements:

a) the cost of transport of the imported goods to the port or place of importation;

b) the expenses relating to the loading, unloading and handling associated with transportation of imported goods to the port or place of importation, and

c) the cost of insurance.

3rd. The port or place of import mentioned in item 2 will be the point of entry of the goods into the customs territory.

Article 27

The customs value of imported goods shall be the basis for application of the Common External Tariff or any other charges no tariffs established by Community provisions relating to special import.

Article 28

One. The control of the customs value shall be made selectively, as set out in the Standards Implementation.

2nd. When, for whatever reason, the survey of documentary evidence and information necessary for a correct determination of the customs value retrospectively, can cause delay in delivery of goods, it may be released, by lodging a security, as the set Application of Standards.

Article 29

The determination of the customs value shall be conducted in accordance with Community rules on special in the following cases:

a) goods brought by travelers, within the concept of luggage;

b) goods intended for:

1) diplomatic or consular permanent and its members;

2) representations of international organizations permanent, that a State Party is a member, and its employees, experts, technicians and consultants;

c) funeral urns containing human remains, and

d) goods conceptualized as postal orders and international flights, not subject to the general import, as required under the domestic law of each State Party.

Article 30

The mechanisms and procedures for determining the value referred to in this Chapter shall be established in the Standards Implementation.

Article 31

The customs administration has exclusive competence attesting the veracity and accuracy of all information, document or declaration presented by the parties for the purpose of valuation of goods at all customs operations.

TITLE III PROVISIONS APPLICABLE TO GOODS BROUGHT INTO THE CUSTOMS TERRITORY UNTIL THEY ARE ASSIGNED A DESTINATION CUSTOMS

CHAPTER 1 INTRODUCTION OF customs territory

Article 32

Goods brought into the customs territory shall be subject to controls and subject to inspection by the customs authority, since its introduction to its destination Customs, under the provisions in force.

Article 33

One. Goods brought into the customs territory shall be conducted immediately by those who have made or by whom this introduction, in case of overflow, has assumed its transport after introduction into that territory, fulfilling the formalities laid down by the customs authority, a local bonded or authorized by it.

2nd. The provisions of paragraph 1 above shall not apply to goods which are on board ships or aircraft, calling the customs territory, crossing the territorial sea or airspace of States Parties, where your destination is a third country.

Article 34

When, by fortuitous event or force majeure, it can not fulfill its obligation under Article 40, the person responsible for transporting immediately inform the customs authority that situation. If there has been a total or partial loss of the goods, the customs authority shall be informed of the location where the event occurred and, if so, where they meet.

CHAPTER 2

DECLARATION OF ARRIVAL AND DISCHARGE OF GOODS

Article 35

Goods which, by application of Article 33 to reach Aduana or anywhere else bonded or authorized by the customs authority, shall be declared by the person who has entered into the customs territory or, if applicable, the person responsible for your transportation, soon after its introduction.

Article 36

One. The declaration of arrival may be done before or in conjunction with the introduction of the goods and must contain information necessary for their identification, as prescribed in the Rules of Application.

2nd. The declaration of arrival will be made by those who have entered the customs territory or by its representative.

Article 37

The customs authority may authorize the correction of the declaration of arrival, as stated in the Standards Implementation.

Article 38

The total goods intended place of arrival should be discharged on the same, except that the board whose stay is permitted by the customs authority.

Article 39

One. Goods may only be unloaded or transhipped from the means of transport that are subject to authorization by the customs authority and local bonded or authorized to do so.

2nd. You can do without the authorization in case of imminent danger requiring immediate unloading of goods, in whole or in part. In this case, the customs authority shall be informed immediately.

CHAPTER 3

OBLIGATION TO GIVE AN ALLOCATION TO CUSTOMS GOODS

Article 40

The goods subject to a declaration of arrival shall receive the allocations provided for the same customs, under the terms and conditions set forth in the Application of Standards.

CHAPTER 4

TEMPORARY STORAGE OF GOODS

Article 41

One. From the moment of discharge and until they receive a destination

Customs, the goods will be subject to condition of Temporary Storage.

2nd. The goods in Temporary Storage can only remain in bonded warehouses or in places authorized by the customs authority, as laid down by it.

3rd. Will be jointly responsible for any customs tax obligation that may be caused by goods in Temporary Storage, the depositary and the person entitled to dispose of them

Article 42

One. The goods in Temporary Storage can not be subject to further manipulations to ensure that their conservation in the state where they are, without modifying their appearance or technical characteristics.

2nd. Notwithstanding the preceding item, interested parties may examine or take samples of the goods, as prescribed in the Rules of Application.

Article 43

The customs authority shall take the necessary measures to preserve the tax credit, as set Standards Enforcement, for goods that have not been subject to a destination under customs laid down in Article 40.

CHAPTER 5

CLASSES AND CONDITIONS OF DEPOSITS CUSTOMS

Article 44

It is understood by all the local customs bonded warehouse in which goods can enter, with the permission and under the control of the customs authority.

The customs authority may enable or authorize customs warehouse, on a temporary basis, to receive goods for exhibitions, fairs and other events of the same gender.

Article 45

One. The deposit is classified in customs:

a) public, where it can be used by any person to deposit goods;

b) private, when for the deposit of goods by the depositary.

2nd. The deposit customs administration may be state or private, regardless of class.

3rd. It is understood by:

a) custodian, the person authorized to administer the customs warehouse;

b) the depositor, the person bound by the record of admission of goods in customs warehouse, or one who has been transferred rights and obligations of such first person, as set out in the Standards Implementation.

Article 46

One. The alfandegamento a customs deposit will only be granted to person established in the customs territory, as provided in the Application of Standards.

2nd. The customs authority may enable or authorize customs warehouse, on a temporary basis, to receive goods for exhibitions, fairs and other events of the same gender.

Article 47

The depositary shall be liable:

a) to ensure that the goods during their stay in the customs warehouse, are not removed from customs supervision;

b) to carry out the obligations arising from the storage of goods which are on deposit and customs to observe the particular conditions specified in the authorization;

c) to pay the corresponding levies in cases of faults or failures when it is alleged that responsibility.

Article 48

One. Except as provided in paragraph "c" of the preceding article, may be held to the order of consumption goods damaged or damaged by fortuitous event or force majeure, before his departure from the customs warehouse, upon payment of the duties due on the corresponding import to the state meet.

2nd. The goods stored in a customs warehouse they are destroyed or irretrievably lost, by fortuitous event or force majeure shall not be subject to the payment of tariffs on imports, provided that such destruction is duly established to the customs authority.

Article 49

The customs authority shall require that the depositary submit warranty in relation to the fulfillment of its obligations in accordance with the Standards Implementation. When the depositary for the state will be given the presentation warranty.

Article 50

The custodian shall maintain, as required by the customs authority, records the existence of all goods admitted in the customs warehouse.

TITLE IV ALLOCATION OF GOODS CUSTOMS

CHAPTER 1 GENERAL PROVISIONS

Article 51

One. The goods subject to a declaration of arrival may receive any destination customs regardless of their nature or quantity, source, origin or place of destination, the conditions set forth in this Code and the Standards Implementation.

2nd. The provisions in the preceding paragraph shall not prevent the application of prohibitions and restrictions dictated by reasons of morality and public safety, protection of health and life of humans, animals and plants and the environment, protection of artistic, historic or archaeological national or those for protection of industrial and commercial property, among others, of an economic nature.

CHAPTER 2

CUSTOMS PROCEDURES

Section 1

Inclusion of goods in a

Customs Regime

Article 52

One. All merchandise to be included in a customs procedure shall be subject to a declaration to this end.

2nd. Customs procedures for import and export may be on a permanent or temporary, with the latter requiring the customs tax obligation will be suspended as set forth in the Application of Standards.

Article 53

The declaration for a customs procedure will be performed as follows:

a) in writing, or

b) using a computerized procedure, authorized by the customs authority, or

c) in any other manner set forth in the Application of Standards.

Article 54

One. The declaration must be made in the form established by the Standards Implementation, be signed by authorized person or electronically identified and include all information necessary to implement the relevant provisions under the customs procedure indicated.

2nd. The documentation required for the application of customs procedure specified in the declaration must be submitted on time and in the manner established in the Standards Implementation.

Article 55

A statement meeting the requirements of the preceding Article shall be registered by the customs authority in accordance with the Standards Implementation.

Article 56

One. The statement, once registered, will be unchanged.

2nd. Nevertheless, the customs authority shall authorize the rectification, modification or supplement thereto, when the inaccuracy arises from the statement itself or the documents referred to in paragraph 2 of Article 54, and is not intended to cover up whenever a customs offense and is requested in advance to top any monitoring procedure.

Article 57

One. The customs authority, founded upon request of the declarant may revoke a declaration already registered.

2nd. Nevertheless, when the customs authority has decided to examine the goods, the cancellation of the declaration shall be subject to the result of that.

3rd. There shall be no cancellation of the declaration after customs clearance.

4th. There shall be no cancellation of declaration when detected evidence of alleged customs violations.

5th. The annulment of the declaration does not exempt the declarant from liability for any violations or offenses linked to it.

Article 58

The rules governing the procedure for which the goods are declared shall be those prevailing at the date of registration of the declaration, unless otherwise noted.

Article 59

To prove the veracity of the declaration to the customs authority may proceed to document analysis, and verification of goods, if any, to the removal of samples, request technical reports and any other action it deems necessary in the course of customs clearance.

Article 60

One. The declarant shall be entitled to attend the acts of examination of goods and removal of samples. The customs authority shall, where appropriate, require the presence of the declarant or his representative.

2nd. Incumbent upon the declarant the transport of goods to places they should examine the goods and, if necessary, removal of samples for tests and preparation of technical reports, as well as all the manipulations necessary to do so.

3rd. The costs of removal of samples and their analysis as well as the preparation of technical reports, may be borne by the declarant in accordance with the Rules of Application.

4th. The customs authority may require the assistance of specialized personnel in the examination of goods or withdrawal of samples of special goods, fragile or dangerous, being the declarant bear the costs.

Article 61

One. When the scan takes place only part of the goods subject to the same statement, the results of this will be extended to all other

2nd. However, the declarant may request a further check the goods where it considers that the results of the partial examination are not valid for the remainder of the goods declared.

3rd. For the purposes of paragraph 1 of this Article, when the declaration includes several tariff codes, each shall be considered a separate statement.

Article 62

One. The customs authority shall take measures to identify the goods where it is necessary to guarantee the fulfillment of the conditions of the customs procedure for which they have been declared.

2nd. The identification placed the goods or means of transport can only be removed or destroyed by the customs authority, or with his authorization, except in situations of unforeseeable circumstances or force majeure.

Article 63

Once made the controls and verifications that apply, and where the goods are not subject to any prohibition or restriction, the customs authority shall clearing the same, without prejudice to Article 64.

Article 64

Only be cleared in advance or delivered the goods object declaration, the record implies the recognition of a deferred tax, if any paid or guaranteed amount.

Article 65

One. The customs authority may provide for disposition or sale, destruction or procurement of commodities under statement, in the following cases:

a) when it has not performed to check the goods on time, for reasons attributable to the declarant;

b) when it has not been delivered documentation;

c) when it has not been paid or guaranteed tax obligation within established customs;

d) if the goods are subject to a prohibition or restriction;

e) when it has granted customs clearance and are not withdrawn within its.

2nd. The Standards Implementation regulate the exercise of those faculties.

Article 66

The customs authority may permit the use of simplified customs procedures, including early delivery of goods under conditions laid down in the Rules of Application.

Article 67

One. After clearing customs, the customs authority may also carry out control of commercial documents and data relating to the importation or exportation, as well as the inspection of the goods and their valuation, to prove the accuracy of the data declaration.

2nd. When in that control or verification it is found that the rules governing the customs procedure covered have been applied on the basis of inaccurate or incomplete, the customs authority in accordance with applicable law, adopt the necessary measures and, if appropriate, apply the sanctions.

Section 2

Dispatch for Consumption

Article 68

The order is for the consumption of final import customs regime which gives the character of Community goods to a non-Community goods, and involves the completion of customs formalities and other natures, as well as the payment of the corresponding levies.

Article 69

The goods cleared for home use, with a reduction or waiver of charges because of their use for specific purposes, remain under control after customs clearance, as provided in the Rules of Application.

Section 3

Reimportation

Article 70

This scheme will allow clearance for use of Community goods exported, on a permanent or not, upon request of the interested party, where:

a) is made by the exporter who was there for them;

b) are the same goods;

c) complying with the terms and conditions set forth in the Application of Standards.

Section 4

Suspensive procedures Import

A - General Provisions

Article 71

The suspensive import include the following modalities:

a) customs transit;

b) customs warehouse;

c) temporary admission;

d) temporary admission for inward processing;

e) processing under customs control.

Article 72

The use of any suspensive procedure requires prior authorization for import customs.

Article 73

The suspensive import will be considered completed when the goods or, if applicable, the resulting products included in the scheme receive a new destination customs planned.

Article 74

The rights and obligations of the holder of a suspensive procedure of import may be transferred, with the prior permission of the customs authority to other persons who meet the requirements for admission of merchandise to the corresponding regime.

B. CUSTOMS TRANSIT

Article 75

One. The customs transit system will transport from one point in the customs territory to another point of destination within the same or its output of goods:

a) non-Community, with suspension of payment of import charges and applying restrictions of economic character;

b) Community, released for export, for his exit from the customs territory;

c) the object of trade between the States Parties, as the case

2nd. Non-Community goods in transit customs will be transported in accordance with the Rules of Implementation and the determination in International Agreements signed by MERCOSUR Member States.

3rd. The customs transit procedure shall apply without prejudice to specific provisions under another customs procedure suspension of the goods that are submitted.

Article 76

The customs transit procedure shall be deemed complete when the goods are delivered and the corresponding documentation in a timely manner, the Aduana target, as set forth in the Standards Implementation.

Article 77

The customs authority may require the provision of security, as set forth in the Application of Standards, in order to ensure payment of any tax credit, subject to the provisions of International Agreements signed by MERCOSUR Member States.

Article 78

The carrier shall be jointly and severally liable to the beneficiary for compliance relating to customs transit procedure, without prejudice to International Agreements signed by MERCOSUR Member States.

C. CUSTOMS DEPOT

Article 79

One. This scheme allows the entry of non-Community goods to a customs warehouse, with suspension of payment of liens; import and application of restrictions of economic character, in the following ways:

a) storage tank: - the goods in this condition can only be the object of operations to ensure its recognition, preservation, division into lots or volumes, and any that do not change its value or modify its nature or condition;

b) commercial deposit: - In this condition the goods may be subject to operations to facilitate its commercialization, such as improving your presentation, prepare for distribution or resale, and any other similar transaction which has the aim to increase its value, without modifying its nature or status;

c) industrial warehouse: - in this condition the goods may be subject to operations to modify its nature or state, including the industrialization of raw materials, semi-finished products, assembly, installation and operation of any other similar transformation.

2nd. The manipulations included in the previous section will be performed under the conditions established in the Standards Implementation.

Article 80

One. The Standards Implementation may set deadlines during which the goods in the customs warehouse regime.

2nd. When goods in the scheme exceed the time limit, the customs authority shall take the necessary measures to preserve the interests of the Treasury, in accordance with the Rules of Application.

3rd. The ownership of the goods in the customs warehouse regime may be transferred as set out in the Standards Implementation.

Rule 81

When circumstances warrant, the customs authority may authorize, under the responsibility of the beneficiary of the scheme, the temporary withdrawal of goods from warehouses to submit them to the operations set out in Article 79.

Rule 82

The customs authority may allow goods included under the customs warehouse are transferred from one tank to another, under customs control under conditions laid down in the Rules of Application.

Article 83

Notwithstanding the assurances relevant to the depositary of the goods, the customs authority may require the beneficiary of the scheme, when the operations required under Articles 79, 81 and 82, providing security, in order to ensure payment of any customs tax obligation .

D. TEMPORARY ADMISSION

Article 84

One. This scheme allows the use in the customs territory, with total or partial suspension of the payment of the duties and import restrictions applying economic, non-Community goods, for a specified period and may not be modified, except normal depreciation for its use .

2nd. The means of transport that community, with the purpose of carrying passengers or goods reach the customs territory and reside temporarily therein, without changing their status, are subject to temporary admission, regardless of any paperwork.

3rd. The containers, wrappers and packaging needed to freight not staying temporarily in the Community customs territory, without changing their status, are subject to temporary admission, regardless of any paperwork.

Rule 85

The temporary admission will be granted, upon prior request of and with the securities that result due in accordance with the Rules of Application.

Rule 86

The customs authority shall fix the time and conditions of use of the system, in accordance with the Standards Implementation.

E. Temporary Admission for ASSET ENHANCEMENT

Rule 87

This scheme allows entry into the customs territory, with suspension of payment of import charges and applying restrictions of an economic, non-Community goods for improvement and subsequently re-exported in the form of the resulting products.

Rule 88

One. Means for processing operations:

a) the processing of goods;

b) the production of goods, including its assembly, assembly and fitting them to other goods;

c) the repair of goods, including restoring them and putting into working order.

2nd. It is understood by the resulting products: the products obtained as a result of processing operations.

3rd. It is understood by coefficient of performance: the amount or percentage of resultant products obtained from the processing of a given quantity of goods permitted in this regime.

4th. This scheme allows the use of some goods, determined according to the procedure set forth in the rules of application, which does not incorporate the resulting products, but which allow or facilitate the production of these products, yet they are entirely or partially during use, as well as those that because of commercial usage are exported with the resulting products.

Rule 89

The customs authority may allow the resulting products are obtained from goods previously imported into the customs territory for consumption and can make up these replacement for equivalent goods, as set Standards Enforcement.

Rule 90

The temporary admission for inward processing shall be granted. by the customs authority, where requested by the person established in the customs territory, and fit the requirements of the Standards Implementation.

Article 91

One. The customs authority shall state the period within which the resulting products will be exported or expected to receive another destination customs. This term will be determined taking into account the time needed to carry out the processing operations and marketing of the resulting products.

2nd. The customs authority may require guaranteed by liens suspended in accordance with the Standards Implementation.

Article 92

The customs authority shall determine the coefficient of performance of the operation, the manner and conditions in which they determine the same, and methods of control, as defined in the Standards Implementation.

Article 93

Application of Standards establish the circumstances and conditions under which goods without improving or the resulting products can be shipped for consumption.

Rule 94

All or part of the resulting products, or goods without improving, may be temporarily exported for further processing that should be done outside the customs territory, with the permission of the customs authority, under the conditions laid out for the regime of temporary export for outward processing .

Article 95

Waste products resulting from the improvement will be subject, in the case of clearance for consumption, the corresponding levies its import.

F. PROCESSING UNDER CONTROL

CUSTOMS

Article 96

This scheme allows you to enter in the customs territory, non-Community goods to subject them to operations that modify its kind or condition, with suspension of payment of the duties and import restrictions applying economic, and subsequent clearance for consumption of products derived obtained from these operations, with the import levies which are theirs. These styling products will be processed products.

Article 97

The terms and conditions of use of the system will be established in the Standards Implementation.

Rule 98

This scheme will only be granted by the customs authority:

a) the person established in the customs territory;

b) where it is possible to identify the products processed non-Community goods;

c) when the species or the status of non-Community goods at the time of registration of the declaration of goods can not be economically restored after processing.

d) when the use of the system can not cause deviation from the rules of origin, quantitative restrictions and other conditions of the policy.

Rule 99

Apply to this regime, as applicable, Articles 91, 92 and 95.

Section 5 Export

Article 100

This scheme allows the final output, the customs territory of the Community or a commodity that has acquired this condition, subject to the formalities provided for in the Rules and Application, if applicable, the payment of export encumbrances, to receive incentives or benefits, as well as compliance requirements to it themselves.

Article 101

The goods which enjoy tax incentives or benefits during his final export, shall be subject to controls and conditions that determine the Rules of Application.

Article 102

Community goods destined for export are under customs control, since the registration of the declaration until the moment they leave the customs territory, or is revoked the declaration.

Section 6 Suspensive arrangements Export

A. GENERAL PROVISIONS

Article 103

The suspensive export include the following modalities:

a) Customs Transit;

b) Deposit Customs;

c) Temporary Export;

d) Temporary Export for Outward Processing.

Article 104

The use of suspensive export requires prior permission of the customs authority.

Article 105

The suspensive export will be considered completed when the goods or, if applicable, the resulting products included in these schemes are definitely re-imported or exported.

B. CUSTOMS TRANSIT

Article 106

The customs transit procedure laid down in Articles 75 to 78 shall apply, mutatis mutandis Community goods released for export, in order to control its exit from the customs territory.

C. CUSTOMS DEPOT

Article 107

This scheme allows the entry of Community goods to a customs warehouse, in order to be exported under the conditions and deadlines established in the Standards Implementation.

D. EXPORT TEMPORARY

Article 108

The regime of temporary export permits to leave the customs territory, with suspension of payment of levies and export restrictions applying economic, community of goods, conditional on reimportation without having undergone modifications, except those relating to depreciation caused by normal their use.

Article 109

One. The regime of temporary export shall be granted by the customs authority, upon prior request of and with the provision of guarantees that are required, in accordance with the Rules of Application.

2nd. The transportation of goods or passengers, registered or recorded in any of the States Parties, when they leave the customs territory temporarily in transport activity, are subject to the system of temporary export, regardless of any administrative formalities and should return in the same state.

Article 110

The customs authority shall fix the time and conditions of use of the system, in accordance with the Standards Implementation.

E. TEMPORARY EXPORT TO OUTWARD.

Article 111

The regime of temporary export for outward processing allows to leave the customs territory, for a fixed period, with suspension of payment of levies and export restrictions applying economic, Community goods intended to be perfected and the subsequent re-importation in the form of products resulting, subject to the application of customs charges that are theirs, on the value added.

Article 112

Apply to this scheme, the settings of items 1 to 3 of Article 88.

Article 113

One. The regime of temporary export for outward processing shall not be granted to goods which have been cleared for home use with full exemption from import charges, linked to their use for specific purposes, as long as they apply the conditions for granting this exemption.

2nd. Standards Enforcement may determine other exceptions to the grant of the regime.

Article 114

The regime of temporary export for outward processing shall be granted by the customs authority, where requested by the person established in the customs territory and fit the requirements of the Standards Implementation.

Article 115

1 The customs authority shall determine the period within which the resulting products will be shipped for consumption or receive other destination customs. This period is determined taking into account the time needed for performing the processing operations.

2nd. The customs authority may require guaranteed by liens suspended. in accordance with the Standards Implementation.

Article 116

The customs authority shall determine coefficient of income from operations, manner and conditions in which it will be determined and the methods of control, according to the Rules of Application.

Article 117

One. When the processing operation whose purpose is the repair of goods temporarily exported under this regime, reimportation will be performed with total exemption from import levies on goods employed by case, if proven, the customs authority, that the repair has been carried out so Free, for reasons of contractual or statutory obligation guarantee.

2nd. Item 1 of this Article shall not apply where the defective condition has already been taken into consideration at the time of clearance for consumption goods.

TITLE V SPECIAL PROVISIONS

CHAPTER 1 MERCADORIAS WITH BANS AND RESTRICTIONS

Article 118

When non-Community goods into the customs territory, because of prohibitions or restrictions of any kind, can not be included in a customs procedure shall be reembarcadas destined for third countries, considered destroyed or abandoned in favor of the Treasury, under the terms and conditions set out in the Standards Implementation.

CHAPTER 2 RE

Rule 119

Non-Community goods ingressadas temporarily, may leave the customs territory by re the request of the Company, provided that:

a) requested by the beneficiary of the suspension system;

b) are the same goods;

. C) complying with the terms and conditions set forth in the Application of Standards.

CHAPTER 3

DESTRUCTION

Article 120

One. Goods brought into the customs territory of endangering public safety, the health and life of humans, animals or plants or the environment, may, based on technical information and the judgment of the competent authority of the customs administration, be returned to its origin receive another destination customs or destroyed in accordance with the Rules of Application, subject to applicable penalties to the offender.

2nd. In the case of the previous item, the applicant shall be notified, running for his account of the costs.

CHAPTER 4

ABANDONMENT

Article 121

Non-Community goods into the customs territory which, in time and form, have not been included in a customs procedure, re-exported, ingressadas in a Free Trade Zone or Special Customs Area or reembarcadas will be considered abandoned to the Exchequer, which can have the same standards as set forth in the Application, subject to the penalties to which they are subject.

CHAPTER 5

SUBSTITUTE GOODS

Article 122

One. The customs authority will allow goods imported or exported goods are replaced by the same tariff classification, commercial quality, value and technical characteristics, when the merchandise is sent free replacement as a result of a contractual or statutory warranty.

2nd. In the case of imports, the merchandise may be returned replaced its origin, destroyed under customs control, customs or receive other destination.

3rd. In case of export, the goods replaced may enter the customs territory free of encumbrances.

4th. The manner and conditions for applying this Article shall be established by the Standards Implementation.

TITLE VI TREATMENTS SPECIAL CUSTOMS

CHAPTER 1 EXPRESS SHIPMENTS

Article 123

Called Express Shipping or "Courier", the activity of legal entities legally established in any of the States Parties, namely the shipment to third parties through international transportation, correspondence, documents, and certain goods that require urgent transport, in the form and conditions in the Application of Standards.

CHAPTER 2

SAMPLES

Article 124

One. It is considered a sample of no commercial value amount, fragments or part of any commodity, strictly necessary to make known its nature, type and quality.

2nd. The form and conditions of entry or exit from the customs territory of samples will be established in the Standards Implementation.

CHAPTER 3

POSTAL SHIPMENTS

Article 125

One. The Customs administration will perform flow control of postal consignments entering, leaving or transiting through the customs territory, respecting the jurisdiction and powers of the postal administration.

2nd. Customs control shall be exercised directly on the international postal, whatever the recipient or the sender and whether or not for commercial purposes.

3rd. The form, limits and conditions established in this Article shall be those provided for in the Rules of Application.

4th. The postal administration will hear the customs administration of any action that may be taken with respect to the flow of international postal items affecting customs controls.

CHAPTER 4

BAGGAGE

Article 126

One. It is considered the new objects or luggage a traveler used, consistent with the circumstances of your trip, you can allocate for your personal use or consumption, as well as for gifting, where, in terms of quantity, quality or variety, not allowing assume import or export for commercial or industrial.

2nd. The tax exemption, as well as common or special taxation on the goods members of travelers' luggage and conditions of any category, including the crew, will have its terms, limits and conditions set out in the Standards Implementation.

CHAPTER 5

UNITS OF CHARGE

Article 127

One. It is considered charging unit for the purposes of this Code and its Implementing Rules, the containers, standardized according to international standards and specifications and community, indelibly marked, and trailers, semi-trailers and the like, for the carriage of cargo unitized.

2nd. The entry and exit into the customs territory of the same, the cargo units shall be conducted in accordance with the standards set forth in the Application.

CHAPTER 6

SUPPLY BOARD

Article 128

One. It is considered as delivery on board the supply of products or consumer goods or use their own vessel or aircraft, its crew and its passengers.

2nd. Will be considered as exports, as established in the Standards Implementation, providing board the ships and aircraft of foreign flag, as well as those long-haul or international trip, enrolled or registered in States Parties.

3rd. The manner and conditions in which the supply of board will be held will be established in the Standards Implementation.

CHAPTER 7

BORDER TRADE

Article 129

Customs control and the tax treatment applicable to goods brought them to third countries or brought by residents in cities located on land borders, the movement characteristic of border trade will be established in the Standards Implementation.

CHAPTER 8

MEANS OF TRANSPORT MILITARY AND POLICE

Article 130

The means of transport military and police will have their entry and circulation in the customs territory, or their departure from it, performed in accordance with standards set out in the Application, subject to the agreements signed by the States Parties.

CHAPTER 9

Free shops (FREE SHOP)

Article 131

One. Duty-free shops are establishments in the primary zone of bonded port or airport by the customs authority for the commercialization of goods from the customs territory or not, free of taxes.

2nd. The terms and conditions for installation and operation of duty free shops, arrival or departure, will be established in the Standards Implementation.

TITLE VII FREE ZONES AND SCAS

Article 132

The Free Zones are part of the territory of States Parties, especially marked in the entry and exit of non-Community goods are free from encumbrances and the application of economic constraints, while not used or consumed under conditions other than those set out in the Standards Implementation .

Article 133

The entry, stay and exit of goods in a free zone will be subject to Customs control, and should be made in the manner and subject to the conditions set forth in the Application of Standards.

Article 134

In the Free Zone can be performed any industrial activity, commercial or service in ways and conditions in the Application of Standards.

Article 135

The goods leaving a free zone should be included in the customs procedures provided in the manner and conditions in the Application of Standards.

Rule 136

The Special Customs Areas are parts of the territory of States Parties particularly bounded, in which the goods will be subject to special treatment in the form and conditions in the Application of Standards.

Article 137

States Parties may establish Free Zones Areas and Special Customs in their territories, in the manner and conditions in the Application of Standards.

TITLE VIII CUSTOMS DUTY TAX

CHAPTER 1 FACT GENERATOR

Article 138

One. It is a fact giving rise to customs tax, the introduction or exit of goods from the customs territory.

2nd. Also considered will be introduced into the customs territory of the goods contained in the manifest or equivalent documentation, the lack of which is determined by the customs authority.

Article 139

It is also a triggering event of customs tax liability:

a) the disappearance of merchandise entered into Free Trade Zone or Special Customs Area;

b) the consumption or use of goods in the Free Zone or Special Customs Area, in breach of the conditions set forth in the Application of Standards.

Article 140

Not be considered existing customs tax liability, relating to specific goods, if the person proves that the breach or failure to comply with obligations under the arrangements corresponding results from the total destruction or permanent loss of the goods, because of their nature, unforeseeable circumstances or force majeure or by a decision of the customs authority to determine its destruction.

CHAPTER 2

DETERMINATION OF TAX CREDIT REQUIREMENT AND CUSTOMS

Article 141

The amount of customs tax credit will be determined taking into account the customs value of the goods, its origin, tariff classification and by applying the corresponding tax rate.

Article 142

One. For the purposes of calculating the charges, it is the triggering event occurred on the date of registration of the declaration for a customs procedure;

2nd. When the registration is not made the declaration for a customs procedure, the charges will be calculated based on the date of the fact that originated the tax liability or, when this is not known, the date of its finding, subject to available regarding infractions.

Article 143

The payment of custom charges will be made on the date of registration of the declaration for a customs procedure, without prejudice to the requirement of any differences later cleared.

Article 144

The payment of customs tax credit must be made in cash or by any other means with tender, as establishing the Standards Implementation.

_Artigo 145

One. Application of Standards establish the manner and conditions for collection of fines and liens owed.

2nd. The customs authority, in the situation described in the previous section, require the payment of default interest, subject to the restatement, as established by law in the States Parties.

CHAPTER 3

LIABILITIES SUBJECT

Article 146

One. The taxpayer will be the sender or the consignee who is entitled to dispose of the goods.

2nd. For these act through a representative, this will be jointly responsible for the customs tax obligation, along with the person on whose behalf the statement is made, except where proof has fulfilled obligations is your responsibility.

CHAPTER 4

WARRANTY

Article 147

When, in accordance with the provisions of this Code, is required to lodge a guarantee, shape, condition of enforceability, performance and release shall be governed in accordance with the Standards Implementation.

Article 148

The customs authority may refuse the security proposed, when it considers that it does not ensure payment of the tax credit.

CHAPTER 5

EXTINCTION OF CUSTOMS TAX CREDIT

Article 149

The tax credit will be abolished customs:

a) the payment due;

b) for compensation;

c) by prescription;

d) by reference;

e) the court passed final.

Article 150

One. Compensation as a form of extinction of customs tax credit, will be effected in accordance with the standards set forth in the Application.

2nd. The remission of customs tax credit may be granted only by special arrangement Community.

Article 151

One. The action to demand payment of the tax credit customs prescribe within five (5) years from the first day of the calendar year following the date on which it originated.

2nd. The prescription will be suspended or terminated in the manner and conditions in the Application of Standards.

CHAPTER 6

REFUND AND CANCELLATION OF liens CUSTOMS TAX CREDIT

Article 152

One. It will be preceded repayment of liens import or export whenever it is proved that they were wrongly paid.

2nd. Will proceeded to cancel the customs tax credit, where it is shown that its amount was not legally owed.

3rd. The provisions of paragraphs 1 and 2 above shall be made at the request of the interested party, in the manner and conditions in the Application of Standards.

Article 153

It will be carried out, also, upon request of the interested party, the refund of the duties paid on the importation or exportation, when a declaration for a customs procedure is aborted.

Rule 154

The action of interested to apply for the refund of the amount of the charges referred to in Articles 143 and 144 shall prescribe in five (5) years from the first day of the calendar year following the date of payment.

Rule 155

Where it is established that the refund of the duties or the cancellation of customs tax credit was improper, this will again be payable within the period of 5 (five) years, contacted from the first day of the calendar year following the refund or cancellation.

TITLE IX CUSTOMS OFFENCES

CHAPTER 1 GENERAL PRINCIPLES

Article 156

Infraction is any action or omission voluntary or involuntary, resulting in failure on the part of individuals or legal entities, the established norm or disciplined by this Code and its Implementing Rules.

Article 157

In the area of customs offense will apply the following principles:

a) in case of doubt applies whichever is more favorable to the accused;

b) no person may be punished only once for the same act;

c) will apply the standard punitive force at the time of occurrence of the violation, except that subsequent law comine penalty less severe than provided for in current legislation at the time of their practice, since this does not change the tax or customs treatment of goods;

d) will be applied to a more specific rule in preference to general legislation on the same matter.

CHAPTER 2

SPECIES OF INFRINGEMENT

Rule 158

Are species of offense:

a) smuggling;

b) defrauding;

c) the inaccurate statement.

CHAPTER 3

PENALTIES

Article 159

One. Penalties can be up to a fine, confiscation of goods, or both together, and where applicable, also the forfeiture of the vehicle carrier in accordance with this Code and its Implementing Rules.

2nd. Fines will be determined according to the value of the infringing goods and graded according to the circumstances, the nature and gravity of the offenses and the antecedents of the offender, as set Standards Enforcement, unless specific provision of this Code.

3rd. The customs authority may also impose administrative penalties on violators, such as warnings, suspensions and overcoats temporary or permanent, in the manner and conditions in the Application of Standards.

Article 160

In the event that the appropriate penalty is confiscation of the goods object of the offense and that, for whatever reason, can not be effected, it will be replaced by a fine that will be based on the value of the merchandise.

Article 161

The action to impose penalties for infractions customs extinguished:

a) for amnesty;

b) by prescription;

c) to pay the corresponding fine when it is the only applicable penalty in the manner and conditions in the Application of Standards.

Article 162

The action to impose penalties for customs offenses prescribe in five (5) years from the first day of the calendar year following that in which the offense has been committed, or that in which it was recorded, when it is not possible to determine the date of occurrence.

Article 163

The interruption of prescription for the imposition of penalties occurs by:

a) initiation of administrative or judicial action;

b) commission of another offense customs.

CHAPTER 4

NOTICE OF VIOLATIONS

Article 164

One. Corresponding penalties are cumulative when it actually constitutes more than one offense.

2nd. If the events are independent, the penalties will be imposed corresponding to each of the offenses.

CHAPTER 5

RESPONSIBILITY

Article 165

One. The shipper, the consignee or who is entitled to dispose of the goods are liable for offenses committed by the provisions of this Code.

2nd. A person or entity is jointly liable with their agents, the customs offenses committed by them in the exercise of their functions.

3rd. The directors and officers of a corporation are jointly liable for the payment of fines imposed by the same customs offenses.

4th. The representative is jointly and severally liable to the shipper, the consignee or who is entitled to dispose of the goods, for offenses they may commit in the exercise of their duties, unless there is prove complied with its obligations in charge.

5th. The carrier is responsible for customs offenses committed in connection with the exercise of transportation activity or action or omission of its agents.

6th. Ignorance of the existing provisions or mistake of fact or law does not relieve the offender penalty, except as expressly provided in this Code and the Standards Implementation.

7th. Unless otherwise noted, the responsibility for customs offense irrespective of the intention of the offender or the person responsible and effectiveness, nature and extent of the effects of the act or omission.

Eight. It is responsible for customs offense arising out of acts committed by incompetent, who has the custody or under his care.

CHAPTER 6

CONTRABAND

Article 166

It is considered contraband for the purposes of this Code, any action or omission that has for its object the introduction or exit from Customs Territory of particular goods, with evasion of customs control, which could result in damage to the Treasury or in violation of the conditions set in laws or specific regulations, but not customs, the provisions of this code and the Application of Standards.

Rule 167

One. Apply, the customs offense of smuggling, the following penalties:

a) forfeiture of the goods object of the infraction;

b) Forfeiture of means of transport that leads to finding merchandise at the time of the violation, whether belonging responsible for this;

c) a penalty of 100% of the value of the vehicle, the person responsible for the violation, when it does not belong to the offender and his owner proves no competitive, actively or passively, for the offense;

d) when the value of the goods on offense is notoriously disproportionate to the value of the vehicle subject to the penalty of forfeiture and its owner is not relapsing particular, this applies to a fine of 3 (three) times the value of the goods in violation;

e) in all cases provided for in this Article, will, cumulatively, to a fine of 30% of the value of the goods;

2nd. Applies to trying to smuggle the same penalties for the infraction consummated.

3rd. Penalties will be applied without prejudice to establish that the criminal law of each State Party.

CHAPTER 7

DEFRAUDATION

Article 168

It is considered defrauding any action or omission that violates legal provision or regulation, customs or not, or implies injury to the Treasury, where the fact not configure smuggling or inaccurate statement.

Article 169

Apply the following fines proportionate to the value of the goods, to defraud offenses characterized as:

One. 80% when relating to:

a) price and customs value of the goods;

b) tampering or falsification of any document.

2nd. 40% when relating to:

a) use of imported goods with exemption, reduction or suspension of payment of charges in different activities or purposes than that for which it was authorized;

b) breach of the terms of the scheme in which they are imported.

3rd. 15% when relating to:

a) Breach of deadlines;

b) Loss or lack of merchandise expressed or discharged into Customs Territory.

c) Waive requirements or other formalities prescribed in this Code or its implementing rules.

CHAPTER 8

Misstatements

Article 170

It is considered that the declaration for a customs procedure is inaccurate when the customs authority at the customs check to see that information, data or statements provided by the declarant imply underpayment of the duties owed to the Treasury, the incentives or benefits in excess of what the declarant would be entitled if the statement was made correctly, or in breach of customs legislation, or of any other nature, and any other formality.

Rule 171

Apply the following penalties proportionate to the value of the goods to offenses characterized as inaccurate statement.

1 From 10% when related to:

a) species, origin or provenance diverse class or superior or inferior or of different sizes, or recorded with higher taxes;

b) the weight or quantity greater or less;

c) unmanifested goods where no configure smuggling.

2nd. When the difference between the declared value and determined by the customs authority exceeds 100%, the inaccurate statement shall be deemed to defraud and punishable by fine provided for in paragraph 1 of Article 169.

CHAPTER 9

OTHER PROVISIONS

Article 172

Where in any case the goods are infringing object restriction will apply even the penalty of forfeiture thereof.

Article 173

When the goods in violation is subject to penalty of loss and this can not be effected, it will apply a fine of 100% (one hundred percent) of the value of the merchandise.

Rule 174

The variation is not an infraction, more or less, not exceeding ten percent (10%) about the price and five percent (5%) as the quantity.

TITLE X RESOURCES

Article 175

A person who considers their rights undermined by application of customs legislation, may use when they are affected in a direct, personal and legitimate.

Article 176

One. The right of appeal may be exercised:

> a) in the first instance, before the customs authorities designated for this purpose by the States Parties;
>
> b) on appeal before a higher authority, under the provisions in force in the States Parties.

2nd. The appeal procedure will be established in the Standards Implementation.

Rule 177

One. An appeal shall not suspend the implementation of the contested decision.

2nd. Nevertheless, the customs authority may, at request of a party and a reasoned decision to suspend execution for reasons of public interest of States Parties, or to prevent serious harm to the person concerned, or when it is alleged, justifiably, absolute nullity.

3rd. When the contested decision has the effect of requiring liens import or export, the suspension will depend on the constitution of warranty.

TITLE XI GENERAL PROVISIONS

CHAPTER 1 Legal effects DICTATED ACTS BY STATES PARTIES

Rule 178

Decisions regarding specific cases, checks and controls, the measures taken or documents issued by the customs authority of a State Party, the application of this Code and its implementing rules, legal effect on the entire customs territory.

CHAPTER 2

CUSTOMS CODE COMMITTEE

Article 179

It creates the Customs Code Committee, comprising representatives of States Parties chaired by one of them, the rotation system.

Rule 180

One. The Committee is responsible for resolving doubts concerning the application of this Code and its Implementing Rules and ensure its proper implementation, as well as examine issues related to customs rules presented on the initiative of its Chairman or at the request of one of its members.

2nd. The Committee may establish Technical Committees with the objective of providing you with advice on matters within its competence.

3rd. The decisions of the Committee will be established in the Standards Implementation.

Article 181

The Committee shall establish its rules of procedure, as well as the Technical Committees are formed and organization of their competence.

TITLE XII TRANSITIONAL PROVISIONS

CHAPTER 1 OF EXCHANGES BETWEEN THE PARTIES

Article 182

Customs control of exchanges between States Parties, its form and arrangements will be set out in the Standards of application, until it in its fullness as MERCOSUR.

CHAPTER 2 OF EXCHANGES BETWEEN THE PARTIES AND THIRD COUNTRIES

Article 183

Until that conforms to its fullest MERCOSUR:

a) goods from third countries which are assigned to persons established in a State Party other than that in which they were introduced, subject to payment of customs charges on import of the State Party to which it is intended;

b) The goods leaving the customs territory, bound for third countries, by a State Party other than that in which the statement was made to a customs procedure of export, subject to payment of the duties on exports or receive corresponding benefits in customs the exporting State Party.

TITLE XIII FINAL PROVISIONS

Article 184

This Code is mandatory for all terms in all States Parties.

Article 185

This Protocol is an integral part of the Treaty of Asunción.

The accession by any State to the Treaty of Asunción entail ipso jure accession to the present Protocol.

This Protocol shall enter into force thirty (30) days after the deposit of the second instrument of ratification.

Rule 186

The Government of the Republic of Paraguay shall be the depositary of this Agreement and the instruments of ratification and shall send duly certified copy thereof to the Governments of other States Parties.

ALBA-TCP AGREEMENT

The Presidents Hugo Chávez Frías, on behalf of the Bolivarian Republic of Venezuela, Evo Morales Ayma, on behalf of Bolivia and Fidel Castro Ruz, on behalf of the Republic of Cuba, gathered in the City of Havana on the 28th and 29th of April, 2006, decide to sign the present Agreement for the construction of the Bolivarian Alternative for the Peoples of Our America (ALBA) and the Trade Agreements between the Peoples of our three countries.

General Provisions:

Article 1: The Governments of the Bolivarian Republic of Venezuela, of Bolivia and of Cuba, have decided to take concrete steps towards the process of integration, based on the principles inscribed in the Joint Declaration, signed on December 14th, 2004, between the Bolivarian Republic of Venezuela, Republic of Cuba and to which the Government of Bolivia adheres and welcomes.

Article 2: The countries will implement a strategic plan to guarantee the most beneficial and productive complementarities on the basis of rationality, use of existing advantages in the countries, resources saving , extension of employment, access to markets or another consideration underpinned by a real solidarity, which promotes our peoples.

Article 3: The countries will exchange integral technological packages, developed in these countries by the parties, in common areas of interest which will be facilitated for its use and exploitation based on the principles of mutual benefit.

Article 4: The countries will work together, in coordination with other Latin-American countries, to eliminate illiteracy in these countries, using massively evidence-based and efficient methods, which have been put successfully into practice in the Bolivarian Republic of Venezuela.

Article 5: The countries agree to execute investments of mutual interest, which can adopt the form of public, binational, mixed, cooperative companies, joint management projects and other forms of association which they decide to establish. Priority shall be accorded to the initiatives that strengthen the capacities of social inclusion, the industrialization of the resources, food safety, within the framework for respect and environmental conservation.

Article 6: In cases of binational or three-nation companies with strategic connotation, the parties will do their best, as long as the nature and cost of the investment allow it, for the host country to hold at least 51% shares.

Article 7: The countries will be able to agree upon the opening of state-owned bank subsidiary of a country on the national territory of the other country.

Article 8: to facilitate the payments and collections relative to commercial and financial transactions between the countries, the conclusion of swap arrangements between the banking institutions designated for the purpose by the Governments.

Article 9: The Governments will be able to practice mechanisms of commercial compensation of goods and services to the extent that this proves to be mutually suitable in order to extend and deepen the commercial exchange.

Article 10: The Governments will promote the development of joint cultural plans which keep into account the particular characteristics of the different regions and the cultural identity of the peoples.

Article 11: The Governments Party will deepen the cooperation regarding communication, taking the necessary actions to strengthen its capacities at levels of infrastructure, in terms of transmission, distribution, telecommunication, among others; as well as at level of capacities of production of information, cultural and educational contents. Accordingly, the Governments will continue supporting the communicational space of integration secured through Telesur, strengthening its distribution in our countries, as well as its capacities of content production.

Article 12: The Governments of Venezuela and Cuba recognize the special needs of Bolivia as a result of the exploitation and plunder of its natural resources during centuries of colonial and neocolonial rule.

Article 13: The Parties will exchange knowledge in the scientific-technical field in order to contribute to the economic and social development of three countries.

Article 14: In the light of all of the above, the Government of the Republic of Cuba, the Government of the Bolivarian Republic of Venezuela and the Government of the Republic of Bolivia, decide to execute the following actions:

Actions to develop by Cuba in its relations with Bolivia in the framework of ALBA and the TCP (People's Trade Agreement))

FIRST: To create a Cuban - Bolivian non-profit entity which guarantees free quality ophthalmological operation to all those citizens of Bolivia who lack the necessary economic means to cover the highest prices of these services, with a view to preventing tens of thousands of poor Bolivians from losing the sight every year or suffering serious limitations, which are often disabling as to the visual function.

SECOND: Cuba will provide the highest technology equipment and the ophthalmological specialists needed in the initial stage, and those, with the support of young Bolivian doctors trained in the Latin-American School of Medical Sciences (ELAM) as residents, or other doctors and bolivian residents or coming from other countries, will offer diligent care to the bolivian patients.

THIRD: Cuba will cover Cuban medical staff salaries in the framework of the present actions.

FOURTH: Bolivia will guarantee the necessary facilities to offer the service, and the latter could be buildings intended for medical purposes or adapted for these aims. From the three donated ophthalmology centers offered within the Bilateral Agreement signed on 30 December last year, Cuba will raise that previous number to six.

FIFTH: Six centers would be located in La Paz, Cochabamba, Santa Cruz, Sucre, Potosi and Copacabana town of La Paz Department. Those six ophthalmology centers will be able to operate on no less than 100 thousand persons every year. Such capacities will be able to expand if required.

SIXTH: Cuba ratifies Bolivia's offer of 5 thousand scholarships for the training of doctors and specialists in Integral Family Medicine or other areas of the Medical Sciences: 2.000 in the first quarter of 2006, are already undergoing basic training in Cuba; 2.000 in the second semester of the present year, and 1.000 in the first semester of 2007. In the subsequent years, the established quota will be renewed with new entrants. They are included among these new scholarship holders; some 500 young Bolivians who have already been studying medicine at Faculties of Cuban Medical Sciences.

SEVENTH: Cuba will maintain in Bolivia for as long as that brotherly country considers it necessary, 600 medical specialists who travelled to Bolivia on the occasion of the serious natural disaster which occurred in January of this year and affected all the Bolivian departments. Likewise, it will donate 20 field hospitals with surgery, intensive therapy, and emergency care to the victims of cardiovascular accidents, laboratories and other medical resources sent on the occasion of the mentioned disaster for the most affected areas.

EIGHTH: Cuba will continue contributing to Bolivia through its experience, didactic material and the necessary technical means for the literacy program in four languages: Spanish, Aymara, Quechua and Guarani, which could be offered to the entire needy population.

NINTH: In the education sector, the exchange and collaboration will extend to the assistance of methods, programs and techniques of the teachers' and educational process that are of interest for the Bolivian party.

TENTH: Cuba will convey its experiences to Bolivia regarding energy saving and will cooperate with this country in an energy saving program, which will be able to bring about important resources in convertible currencies.

UNDÉCIMO: Every state investment and Bolivian mixed companies, including the private Bolivian capital in Cuba are exempted from taxes on profit, during the period of recovery of the investment.

TWELFTH: Cuba grants the Bolivian airlines the same facilities which the Cuban airlines have as to the passenger transport and cargo to and from Cuba and the use of airport services, or any other kind of facilitation, as well as the domestic passenger transport and cargo on the cuban territory.

THIRTEENTH: The exports of goods and services coming from Cuba will be able to be paid for by means of bolivian products, in the national currency of Bolivia or in other mutually accepted coins

Actions to be developed by Venezuela in its relations with Bolivia in the framework of the ALBA and the TCP

FIRST: Venezuela will promote a wide collaboration in the mining and energy sector, which will include: institutional strengthening of the Ministry of Hydrocarbons and Energy and of the Ministry of Mines and Metallurgy of Bolivia, through legal-technical assistance; extension of the supply of the crude oil, refined products, LPG and asphalt, covered by the Energy Cooperation Agreement of Caracas, up to the volumes needed to satisfy the domestic demand of Bolivia, establishing compensation mechanisms with Bolivian products for the total invoice cancellation for these items ; technical assistance to Bolivian Fiscal Oilfields "(YPFB)" and "COMIBOL"; development project of adequacy and extension of infrastructures and petrochemicals, steel products, industrial chemicals, as well as other forms of cooperation that the parties agree upon.

SECOND: All state investment and Bolivian mixed companies in Venezuela are exempted from paying taxes on profits during the period of recovery of the investment.

THIRD: Venezuela ratifies the offer of 5000 scholarships for studies in different areas of interest for the productive and social development of the Republic of Bolivia.

FOURTH: Venezuela will create a special fund of up to 100 million dollars for the financing and productive infrastructure projects.

FIFTH: Venezuela will donate thirty million dollars to attend to needs of social and productive character of the Bolivian people as determined by its Government.

SIXTH: Venezuela will donate asphalt and an asphalt mixing plant that contributes to the maintenance and construction of pathways.

SEVENTH: Venezuela will increase significantly the imports of bolivian products; especially those which help raise its strategic food reserves.

EIGHTH: Venezuela will grant fiscal incentives to projects of strategic interest for Bolivia on its territory.

NINTH: Venezuela will grant preferential facilities to aircraft flying a Bolivian flag on the Venezuelan territory within the limits allowed by its legislation.

TENTH: Venezuela puts its infrastructure and airlift and maritime transport assets in a preferential manner at the disposal of Bolivia in order to support the economic and social development plans of the Republic of Bolivia.

ELEVENTH: Venezuela will grant facilities so that Bolivian public or mixed companies can be set up for the downstream transformation of raw materials.

TWELFTH: Venezuela will collaborate with Bolivia in research studies on biodiversity.

THIRTHEENTH: Venezuela will support the participation of Bolivia in the promotion of endogenous development hubs by sharing the experience of the Mission Vuelvan Caras (Change Faces).

FOURTEENTH: Venezuela will develop agreements with Bolivia in the sphere of telecommunications, which might include the use of satellites.

Actions to be developed by Bolivia in its relations with Cuba and Venezuela in the framework of ALBA and TCP

FIRST: Bolivia will contribute with the export of its mining, agricultural, agroindustrial, livestock and industrial products which are needed by Cuba or Venezuela.

SECOND: Bolivia will contribute to the energy security of our countries with its surplus hydrocarbon production at hand.

THIRD: Bolivia will exempt all state investment of mixed companies that are set up between Bolivia and the States of Venezuela and Cuba, from taxes on profits.

FOURTH: Bolivia will provide all its experience in the study of the indigenous peoples both in theory and in the investigative methodology.

FIFTH: Bolivia will take part with the Governments of Venezuela and Cuba in the exchange of experiences for the study and recovery of ancestral knowledge in natural medicine.

SIXTH: The Government of Bolivia will take part actively in the exchange of experiences for scientific research on natural resources, agricultural genetic patterns, and farmers

Joint actions to be developed by Cuba and Venezuela in their relations with Bolivia in the framework of ALBA and TCP

FIRST: The Governments of the Bolivarian Republic of Venezuela and the Republic of Cuba eliminate in an immediate manner the duties or any type of non-tariff barrier applicable to all the imports from all customs areas, made by Cuba and Venezuela, and which come from the Republic of Bolivia.

SECOND: The Governments of the Bolivarian Republic of Venezuela and the Republic of Cuba guarantee Bolivia that they will purchase the quantities of products of the oilseed chain and of other agricultural and industrial products exported by Bolivia, which may be left with no market, as a result of the application of a Treaty or Free-Trade Treaties, promoted by the government of The United States or of the European Governments.

THIRD: The Governments of Venezuela and Cuba offer Bolivia their financial, technical collaboration and human resources for the establishment of a bolivian state airline, which is genuinely national.

FOURTH: The Governments of Venezuela and Cuba offer Bolivia their collaboration in the development of sport, including the facilities for the organization and participation in sports competitions and training bases in both countries. Cuba offers the use of its facilities and equipments for anti-doping controls on the same conditions than those granted to the Cuban athletes.

FIFTH: The Governments of Cuba and Venezuela will promote, in coordination with Bolivia, the actions that prove to be necessary to support the Bolivian just demand for the cancelation, without conditionalities, of its foreign debt, which constitutes a serious obstacle to the fight of Bolivia against poverty and inequality.

New measures of economic and social character will be added to the present Agreement between the three signatory Parties.

Bolivia, Venezuela and Cuba will fight for the union and integration of the peoples of Latin America and the Caribbean.

Bolivia, Venezuela and Cuba will fight for peace and international cooperation

FUNDAMENTAL PRINCIPLES OF THE PEOPLES' TRADE TREATY (TCP)

1. Trade with complementariness, solidarity and cooperation, so that together we reach a worthy life and living well, promoting trade rules and of cooperation for the well-being of people and in individuals of the underprivileged sectors.

2. Sovereign trade, without conditioning nor interference in internal affairs, respecting the political constitutions and the laws of the States, without forcing them to accept conditions, norms or commitments.

3. Complementary and solidary trade among the peoples, the nations and their companies. The development of the socio-productive complementation on cooperation bases, advantage of existing capacities and potentialities in the countries, the saving of resources and the creation of uses. The search of complementarity, cooperation and solidarity between the different countries. The constant technical – scientific exchange, cooperation and collaboration as a for of development, having in consideration the strengths of the members in specific areas, with a view to constituting a critical mass in the field of the innovation, science and the technology.

4. Protection of national production interest, for the integral development of all the peoples and nations. All the countries can become industrialized and diversify their production for an integral growth of all the sectors of their economy. The rejection to the premise "export or die" and the questioning of the model of development based on exporting enclaves. The privilege of the production and the national market that the satisfaction of the necessities of the population through the internal factors of production impels, mattering what is necessary and exporting the excesses of complementary form.

5. The solidary treatment for the weakest economies. Cooperation and unconditional support, with the end for them to reach a level of sustainable development, that allows to reach the supreme social happiness.

While FTAs impose equal and reciprocal rules for the big and small, the TCP proposes a trade that recognizes the differences between the different countries through rules that favors to the smallest economies.

6. Recognition of the sovereign States role in the socioeconomic development, the regulation of the economy. The fortification of the State like central actor of the economy from a country at all the levels, facing the opposite private practices the public interest, such as the monopoly, oligopoly, the cartelization, hoarding, speculation and usury. The TCP supports the nationalization and the recuperation of companies and natural resources to which the peoples have the right to, establishing legal defense mechanisms of aforementioned.

7. Promotion of the harmony between the man and the nature, respecting the Rights of the Mother Earth and promoting an economic growth in harmony with the nature. The Rights of Mother Earth are recognized and the sustainability in harmony with nature is promoted.

8. The contribution of trade and investments to strengthening of the cultural and historical identity of our peoples. While the FTAs aims to convert the whole humanity in simple consumers standardizing the patterns of consumption to extend therefore the markets of the transnational companies, the TCP impels the diversity of cultural expressions in the trade.

9. The favoring to the communities, communes, cooperatives, companies of social production, small and medium companies. The Joint promotion towards exports markets of our countries and of productions that result actions of productive complementation.

10. The development of the sovereignty and food security of the member countries based on a social and integral quantity and quality food for our peoples. Support to food policies and national production to guarantee the access to the population of an adequate quantity and quality feeding.

11. Trade with tariff policies fit to the requirements of the developing countries. The elimination between our countries of all barriers that constitute an obstacle to the complementation, allowing to the countries to raise its tariffs to protect its infant industries or when they consider it necessary for its internal development and the well-being of its population with the purpose of promoting a greater integration between our peoples. Asymmetric and nonreciprocal tariff reduction that allow the less developed countries to raise their tariffs to protect their infant industries or when they consider it necessary internal development and the well-being of its population.

12. Trade protecting the basic services as human rights. The recognition of the sovereign right from the countries to control it services according to its priorities of national development and to directly provide with basic and strategic services through the State or in mixed investments with partner countries.

In opposition to the FTA that promotes the privatization of the basic services of water, education, health, transport, communications and energy, the TCP promotes and strengthens the role of the State in these essential services that allow for the full compliance to human rights.

13. Cooperation for the development of different servicessectors. Priority to cooperation directed to the development of structural capacities of countries, searching for social solutions in sectors such as health and education, among others. Recognition of the sovereign right of countries to control and regulate all services sectors seeking for promotion of its national services companies. Promotion of the cooperation among countries for the development of the different services

sectors prior to the impulse of the free unfair competition between services companies of different scale.

14. Respect and cooperation through Public Purchases. Public purchases are a planning tool for the development and promotion of national production that must be strengthen through participation, cooperation and the joint execution of purchases when convinient.

15. Execution of joint investments in trade issues that can adopt the form of Grand National companies. The association of state companies of different countries to impel a sovereign development and of mutual benefit.

16. Partners and no bosses. The exigency that foreign investment respects national laws. Unlike FTAs which impose a series of advantages and guarantees in favour of transnational companies, the TCP looks for a foreign investment that it respects the laws, re invest the utilities and solves any controversy with the State like any national investor.

The foreign investors will not be able to demand to the National States nor the Governments for develop policies of public interest.

17. Trade that respects the life. While FTAs promote the patents of the biodiversity and the human genome, the TCP protects them as a common patrimony of humanity and the mother earth.

18. The overlapping of the right to development and health to intellectual and industrial property. Unlike FTAs which look for patenting and extending the duration of the patent of inventions that are fundamental for the human health, the preservation of the mother earth and the growth of the developing countries, -many of which have been made with funds or public subventions- the TCP overlaps the right to the development and the health to intellectual property of transnational companies.

19. Adoption of mechanisms that entail monetary and financial independence. Promotion of mechanisms that help to strengthen the financial, monetary sovereignty, and the complementariness in this matter between the countries.

20. Protection of the labor rights and the rights of the indigenous peoples. Promotion of the total use of such and the sanction to the company and not to the country that fails to fulfill them.

21. Publication of trade negotiations in order that the peoples can exert its protagonist and participative role in trade. Nothing of secret negotiations and behind the back of the population.

22. The quality as the social accumulation of knowledge, and its application in the production based on the satisfaction of social needs of the peoples, according to a new concept of quality within the framework of the ALBA-TCP so that the standards do not become obstacles to the production and the trade exchange between the peoples.

23. The free mobility of the people as a human right. The TCP reaffirms the right to free human mobility, with the intention to strength the bndss of brotherhood between all the countries of the world.

AGREEMENT FOR THE ALBA APPLICATION

One the one hand, the President Hugo Chávez Frías, on behalf of the Bolivarian Republic of Venezuela, and on the other hand, the President of the Council of State, Fidel Castro Ruz, on behalf of the Republic of Cuba, gathered in the city of Havana on December, 14th , 2004, on the occasion of the celebration of the 180th anniversary of the glorious victory of Ayacucho and of the Convocation to the Anfictiónico Congress in Panama, have considered extending and modifying the full Cooperation Agreement betweenCuba y Venezuela, subscribed on October 30th, 2000. To this end, it was decided to sign the present agreement on the tenth anniversary of the first encounter of the President, Hugo Chávez with the Cuban people.

Article 1: The governments of Venezuela and Cuba have decided to take concrete steps towards the process of integration based upon the principles, which are laid down in the Joint Declaration signed as of this date between the Bolivarian Republic of Venezuela and the Republic of Cuba.

Article 2: Since the bolivarian process has been consolidated following the decisive victory in the revocatory referendum of 15 August, 2004 and in the regional elections of 31 October, 2004, and Cuba being in position to ensure its sustainable development,the cooperation between the Republic of Cuba and the Bolivarian Republic of Venezuela will as of this date, not only be based upon the principles of solidarity , which will always be present, but also upon a maximum possible extent of the exchange of goods and services which prove beneficial to the social and economic needs of both peoples.

Article 3: Both countries will implement a strategic plan to ensure the most beneficial and productive complementarity on the basis of rationality, of the exploitation of the existing benefits in a manner or another, of saving in resource, of extension of helpful employment, of access to markets or any other consideration underpinned by a real solidarity that enhances the strengths of both parties.

Article 4: Both countries will exchange comprehensive technological packages developed by the parties, in areas of common interest, which will be facilitated for its utilization and use, based upon the principles of mutual benefit.

Article 5: Both parties will work together in coordination with other Latin-American countries, to eliminate the illiteracy in third countries, using evidence-based and efficient methods of massive application, which have successfully been put into practice in the Bolivarian Republic of Venezuela. Also, they will collaborate in health programs for third countries.

Article 6: Both parties agree to execute investments of mutual interest on equal conditions than those realized by national entities. These investments can adopt the form of mixed companies, cooperative productions, projects of joint administration and other partnership modalities that they may decide to establish.

Article 7: Both parties will be able to agree on the opening of state-owned bank subsidiaries of a country on the national territory of the other country.

Article 8: In order to facilitate the payments and collections corresponding to commercial and financial transactions between both countries, the conclusion of a Reciprocal Credit Agreement between the banking institutions designated for the purpose by the Governments was agreed on.

Article 9: Both governments accept the possibility of practicing countertrade to the extent that this turns out to be mutually suitable to extend and to deepen the commercial exchange.

Article 10: Both governments will stimulate the development of cultural joint plans that take into account the particular characteristics of the different regions and the cultural identity of both peoples.

Article 11: In reaching the present Agreement, the political, social, economic and juridical asymmetries between both countries have been taken into account. Cuba, throughout more than four decades, has created mechanisms to resist the blockade and the constant economic aggression, which allow for a great flexibility in its economic and commercial relations with the rest of the world. Venezuela, for its part, is a member of international institutions to which Cuba does not belong. All of these aspects must be considered when applying the principle of reciprocity within the commercial and financial agreements which are agreed upon by both governments.

Article 12: Accordingly, Cuba proposed the adoption of a series of measures directed to deepening the integration between both countries and as expression of the spirit of the joint declaration signed on this date about the Bolivarian Alternative for the Americas. Considering the solid arguments exposed by the Cuban party and its high convenience as an example of the integration and the economic unity to which we aspire, this proposal was understood and accepted by the Venezuelan party in a brotherly and friendly fashion, as a constructive gesture that expresses the great reciprocal confidence that exists between both countries.

The actions proposed by Cuba are as follows:

1st: The Republic of Cuba eliminates in an immediate way the duties or any type of non-tariff barrier applicable to all the imports made by Cuba and whose origin is the Bolivarian Republic of Venezuela.

2nd: Each and every state investment, together with Venezuelan mixed companies, including the private Venezuelan capital in Cuba, is exempted from taxes on profits during the period of recovery of the investment.

3rd: Cuba grants the Venezuelan-registered ships the same treatment than the ships flying a cuban flag in all the operations that they execute in Cuban ports, as part of the relations of exchange and collaboration between both countries, or between Cuba and other countries, as well as the possibility of taking part in cabotage services between Cuban ports, on equal conditions than the ships flying a cuban flag.

4th: Cuba grants the Venezuelan airlines the same facilities which the Cuban airlines have regarding the transportation of passengers, cargo to and from Cuba and the use of airport services, facilities or any other type of facility, as well as the domestic transportation

5th: The price of the oil exported by Venezuela to Cuba will be fixed on the basis of the international market price, as stipulated in the current Agreement of Caracas in force between both countries. Nevertheless, taking into accounts the traditional volatility of the oil prices, which have occasionally made the Venezuelan oil price fall below 12 dollars a barrel, Cuba offers to Venezuela a guaranteed price not lower than 27 dollars per barrel, always as per the commitments assumed by Venezuela inside the Organization of Petroleum-Exporting Countries

6th: Concerning the investments of state Venezuelan entities in Cuba, the Cuban party eliminates any restriction to the possibility that such investments could be 100 % the property of the Venezuelan investor, who is the State.

7th: Cuba offers 2.000 annual grants to young Venezuelans so that they can attend higher education in any area that could be of interest for the Bolivarian Republic of Venezuela, including the areas of scientific research.

8th: The imports of goods and services coming from Cuba will be able to be paid by means of Venezuelan products in the national currency of Venezuela or in other mutually acceptable currencies.

9th: Concerning the sport activities which have gained territory in Venezuela within the Bolivarian process, Cuba offers the use of its facilities and equipments for anti-doping controls, on the same conditions than those granted to the Cuban athletes.

10th: In the sector of education, the exchange and collaboration will extend to the assistance in methods, programs and techniques of the process of instruction and education which are of interest for the Venezuelan party.

11th: Cuba puts at the disposal of the Bolivarian University the support of more than 15.000 medical professionals that take part in the Barrio Adentro (Into the Neighborhood) Mission , for the training of all the integral doctors and health specialists , including candidates who wish to be considered for scientific qualifications, accordingly to the needs of Venezuela, and of all the pupils of the Mission Sucre who want to study Medicine and subsequently graduate as integral General Practitioners, which, being put together, could amount to tens of thousands over a period no longer than 10 years

12th: The integral health services offered by Cuba to the population who is cared for by the Mission Barrio Adentro (Into the Neighborhood) and whose number is over 15 million persons, will be provided on conditions and economic terms that are highly preferential and will have to be mutually agreed upon.

13th: Cuba will facilitate the consolidation of multi-focused tourism products coming from Venezuela without fiscal surcharges or restrictions of another type.

Article 13: The Bolivarian Republic of Venezuela, for its part, proposed the following actions orientated towards the same aims set forth in the Article 12 of the present agreement.

1st: Transfer of own technology in the energy sector.

2nd: The Bolivarian Republic of Venezuela eliminates in an immediate way any type of non-tariff barrier to all the imports made by Venezuela and whose origin is the Republic of Cuba.

3rd: Any state investment and Cuban mixed companies in Venezuela are exempted from taxes on profits over the period of recovery of the investment

4th: Venezuela offers the scholarships which Cuba needs for studies in the energy sector or in any other one that is of interest for the Republic of Cuba, including the scientific and research areas.

5th: Financing of productive and infrastructure projects, among others, energy sector, electrical industry, road paving and other roadways projects, port development, aqueducts and sewage, agro-industrial and services sector.

6th: Tax incentives to projects of strategic interest for the economy.

7th: preferential Facilities to ships and aircraft flying a Cuban flag on Venezuelan territory within the limits which its legislation allows it.

8th: Consolidation of multi-focused tourist products coming from Cuba without fiscal surcharges or any other type of restrictions.

9th: Venezuela puts at the disposal of Cuba its infrastructure and equipments of air and maritime transport on preferential bases to support the plans of economic and social development of the Republic of Cuba.

10th: Facilities for mixed companies with Cuban capital for the processing of raw materials downstream to be established.

11th: Collaboration with Cuba in research studies on biodiversity.

12th: Participation of Cuba in the consolidation of endogenous community centers on a binational level.

13th: Venezuela will develop agreements with Cuba in the field of telecommunications, including the use of satellites.

Signed, in the city of Havana, on the 14th day of December, 2004.

ANDEAN TRADE PROMOTION AND DRUG ERADICATION ACT ATPDEA

Participating Countries : Bolivia
Colombia
Ecuador
Peru
United States

Statutory Provisions: Law HR 3009 "TRADE ACT OF 2002"
Term: From December 4, 2001 to December 31, 2006
Effective Date: Retroactive to December 4, 2001

1. INTRODUCTION

Back in 1991, the United States enacted the "ANDEAN TRADE PREFERENCE ACT - "ATPA", for the purpose of promoting economic development among four Andean countries fighting against drugs (Bolivia, Ecuador, Colombia and Peru).

Being this program the commercial component of the North American administration in the "War against Drugs", one of the goals is to promote alternatives to coca leaf growth and production, providing easier access to thousands of products from the Andean region to the North American market. Another goal is to stimulate investments in nontraditional sectors diversifying the exportation bases in the Andean countries.

This commercial cooperation mechanism that expired on December 4, 2001 was postponed and expanded, after the US Senate gave its final approval (on August 1st, 2002) for the trade bills that included the postponement and expansion for this trade cooperation mechanism. The new law was designated "ANDEAN TRADE PROMOTION AND DRUG ERADICATION ACT, ATPDEA"

The passing of ATPDEA provided the possibility to export with "zero duties" goods that were originally exempted from such preferential treatment (shoes, leather goods, petroleum byproducts, clocks-watches and components, and textiles, these last ones however, subject to requirements of eligibility).

2. BENEFICIARY PRODUCTS

The previous ATPA provided for total duty exemption for almost all products subject to duties, except for products such as textiles and manufactured goods; canned tuna fish, petroleum and byproducts, shoes, leather gloves, rubber and plastic; luggage, purses and other hide products; leather apparel; clocks-watches and components; rum and tafia.

The ATPDEA currently in effect, shows clear evidence of the expansion from the previous APTA providing duty exemptions for the following products:

- Shoes: When not benefiting from the preferential treatment under the General Preference System.
- Petroleum and its byproducts, contemplated under item 27.09 (crude oils from petroleum or bituminous minerals; and preparations where such oils are the base element.
- Clocks-watches and components: Containing materials produced by Afghanistan, Cuba,

Laos, and North Korea.

- Purses, suitcases, plain articles, work gloves and leather apparel.

Receiving these benefits are likewise, **Andean articles and creations,** produced or assembled with parts originating from the United States or beneficiary countries (Bolivia, Colombia, Ecuador, Peru), **or** with parts produced locally but insufficient to cover the demand; will be subject to duty free importation, without quantitative restrictions or consultation levels through ATPDEA.

- The possibility described in the above paragraph will be viable for creations or articles sawn or assembled in: a) one or more beneficiary countries; b) the United States of North America; or, c) both; starting with the combination of eligibility criteria for preferential treatment without quotas of any kind.

- Additionally, preferential treatment is foreseen for creations and assembled in one or more beneficiary countries, with material or components manufactured in one or more beneficiary countries, starting with threads or yarns totally made in the United States of North America or in beneficiary countries. This possibility is subject to the application of the 2% entitlement to importations into the United States of America. Such percentage will be proportionally increased every year by 0.75%, starting on October 1, 2003, not to increase 5% for the period starting October 1, 2006.

- Preferential treatment will also benefit, materials or fabrics for which the President of the United States establishes, at the request of the interested party, that the domestic demand cannot be covered on time and commercial quantities required by the local industry.

- The ATPDEA establishes preferential treatment for creations made or weaved by hand, as well as for folkloric handicrafts certified as such, by the competent national authority in the beneficiary country of origin.

- It should be noted as well, that Andean creations containing trimmings and preparations or some interlinings, originating from third countries, will be eligible for preferential treatment when and as long as the cost of the same does not exceed 25% of the total cost of components in the assembled product.

- To conclude, the eligibility is foreseen for those creations containing fiber or thread not entirely made in the United States or in one or more beneficiary countries, as long as the total weight for such fiber or thread, does not surpass 7% of the total weight of such creations (De Minimis).

3. QUALIFICATION CRITERIA

If the following conditions are met, the products are considered as adequate to enter duty free:

3.1. The merchandise is directly exported from a beneficiary country to customs territory of the United States of America;

3.2. The merchandise is produced in the beneficiary country. This requirement is met when:

a) the same has been produced or manufactured in a beneficiary country, or;
b) it has been substantially changed into a new and different commercial article in the

beneficiary country, as established by the US Customs Service.

3.3. No less than 35% of the taxable value of the article imported into the United States of America shall consist, in reference to cost or value, of materials produced in one or more ATPDEA beneficiary countries, and/or the processing operations shall take place in one or more of such countries.

The cost or value of materials produced in the territory of the United States of America may be considered, but only to a 15% maximum, of the taxable value for the imported product. The cost or value of materials imported by the beneficiary country from a non beneficiary country, shall be included when estimating the 35% required for the taxable value if the materials are substantially changed into a new or different commercial article and are used, additionally, as materials incorporated to manufacture the product.

In order for Andean products to enter the North American market duty free, compliance with the mentioned rules of origins shall be confirmed, submitting Certificate of Origin type "A".

NEW ANDEAN TRADE BENEFTS

The Bush Administration today announced that Colombia, Bolivia, and Peru will be granted new trade benefits available under the recently renewed and expanded Andean trade preference program, the Andean Trade Promotion and Drug Eradication Act (ATPDEA).

The United States is continuing to work closely with the Government of Ecuador in order to be able to recommend that Ecuador receive benefits in the near future.

U.S. trade preference programs like the ATPDEA, which was expanded as part of the Trade Act of 2002, demonstrate American leadership and are important tools for building prosperity and openness, and furthering economic integration.

*The Andean Trade Promotion and Drug Eradication Act (ATPDEA)*The Andean trade preference program provides the four Andean countries with duty-free access to U.S. markets for approximately 5,600 products. The program expired in December of 2001 and was renewed as part of the Trade Act of 2002.

All existing provisions were renewed, each country enjoys the same benefits as under the original program, and the program was extended by 700 additional products. The law requires a country certification process for the new, expanded portion of the program, which included receiving public input on each country's eligibility.

In addition, for some of the new products, the Administration must review the impact of providing duty-free access on U.S. producers. These reviews must be completed before realization of the new benefits.

Today's announcement means that Colombia, Bolivia and Peru will receive the new benefits of the program, pending the review for certain sensitive products and a Presidential proclamation to implement the program.

THE PROCESS AND THE COUNTRIES

Before extending the new benefits, the President must determine whether the countries meet the eligibility criteria established in the law. On the basis of an interagency review that included public comments, and certain actions and assurances by the governments of Colombia, Bolivia, and Peru, the President will grant these countries the full benefits available under the program.

The Administration is analyzing several Federal Register submissions as part of the public comment process related to Ecuador, which arrived at the end of the public comment period.

ATPDEA IN ACTION

The Trade Act of 2002 expanded trade benefits for developing countries by more than $1.2 billion. U.S. trade preference programs like the ATPDEA, which expanded the Andean Trade Preferences Act (ATPA) as part of the Trade Act, demonstrate U.S. leadership and are important tools for building prosperity and openness, and furthering economic integration.

As an example of the success of the Andean Trade Preference Program in promoting economic development and providing incentives for these four Andean countries to diversify their economies away from narcotics production, Colombian exports to the U.S. market under ATPA have increased in value and as a percentage of total Colombian exports every year since 1993.

According to the Colombian Ministry of Foreign Trade, between 1992 and 1999, ATPA generated a total of $1.2 billion worth of output and more than 140,000 direct jobs in Colombia.

According to the government of Peru, in 1994, only 16 percent of Peruvian exports went to the United States. In the last year, with ATPA preferential tariff benefits, nearly 30 percent of Peru's exports went to the United States. ATPA has helped to bolster the Government of Peru's alternative development programs aimed at promoting the cultivation of crops such as coffee and cacao in areas of illicit coca cultivation. According to the Bolivian government, the ATPDEA will boost exports of jewelry, leather, and lumber products - all important economic sectors for Bolivia.

Under the expanded ATPDEA, apparel assembled in the Andean region from U.S. fabric or fabric components or components knit-to-shape in the United States may enter the United States duty free in unlimited quantities. Apparel assembled from Andean regional fabric or components knit-to-shape in the region may enter duty-free subject to a cap. The cap is set at 2 percent of total U.S. apparel imports, increasing annually in equal increments to 5 percent. These countries currently account for only about one percent of U.S. apparel imports.

Other new benefits of the program include: tuna in pouches, leather products, footwear, petroleum and petroleum products, watches and watch parts. For all of the new products except for apparel and tuna, the President must determine that the imports are not sensitive before those products can be granted duty-free treatment.

ANDEAN TRADE PROMOTION AND DRUG ERADICATION ACT

By the President of the United States of America

A Proclamation

1. Section 3103 of the Andean Trade Promotion and Drug Eradication Act (title XXXI of the Trade Act of 2002, Public Law 107-210) (ATPDEA) amended section 204(b) of the Andean Trade Preference Act (19 U.S.C. 3203(b)) (ATPA) to provide that certain preferential tariff treatment may be provided to eligible articles that are the product of any country that the President designates as an "ATPDEA beneficiary country" pursuant to section 204(b)(6)(B) of the ATPA, as amended, provided that the President determines that the country has satisfied the requirements of section 204(b)(5)(A)(ii)(I) of the ATPA, as amended, relating to the implementation of procedures and requirements similar to those in chapter 5 of the North American Free Trade Agreement (NAFTA).

2. Section 3103(a)(2) of the ATPDEA amended section 204(b) of the ATPA to authorize the President to proclaim duty-free treatment for any article described in section 204(b)(1)(A) through (D) of the ATPA, as amended, that is the growth, product, or manufacture of an ATPDEA beneficiary country, that is imported directly into the customs territory of the United States from an ATPDEA beneficiary country, and that meets the requirements of section 204 of the ATPA, as amended, if the President determines that such article is not import-sensitive in the context of imports from ATPDEA beneficiary countries, provided that the President determines that the country has satisfied the requirements of section 204(b)(5)(A)(ii)(I) of the ATPA, as amended, relating to the implementation of procedures and requirements similar to those in chapter 5 of the NAFTA.

3. Section 3103(a)(2) of the ATPDEA amended section 204(b) of the ATPA to provide that eligible textile and apparel articles of a designated ATPDEA beneficiary country shall enter the United States free of duty and free of quantitative limitations, provided that the President determines that the country has satisfied the requirements of section 204(b)(5)(A)(ii)(I) of the ATPA, as amended, relating to the implementation of procedures and requirements similar to those in chapter 5 of the NAFTA.

4. Section 3103(a)(2) of the ATPDEA amended section 204(b) of the ATPA to provide that eligible tuna products of a desig-nated ATPDEA beneficiary country shall enter the United States free of duty and free of quantitative limitations, provided that the President determines that the country has satisfied the requirements of section 204(b)(5)(A)(ii)(I) of the ATPA, as amended, relating to the implementation of procedures and requirements similar to those in chapter 5 of the NAFTA.

5. Section 203(e)(2)(A) of the ATPA (19 U.S.C. 3202(e)(2)(A)) requires the President to publish in the **Federal Register** notice of proposed action under section 203(e)(1) of the ATPA (19 U.S.C. 3202(e)(1)) at least 30 days prior to taking such action. Section 212(e)(2)(A) of the Caribbean Basin Economic Recovery

Act (CBERA) (19 U.S.C. 2702(e)(2)(A)) requires the President to publish in the **Federal**

Register notice of proposed action under section 212(e)(1) of the CBERA (19 U.S.C. 2702(e)(1)) at least 30 days prior to taking such action.

6. In order to implement the tariff treatment provided under the ATPDEA, it is necessary to modify the Harmonized Tariff Schedule of the United States (HTS).

7. Section 604 of the Trade Act of 1974 (19 U.S.C. 2483) (1974 Trade Act) authorizes the President to embody in the HTS the substance of the relevant provisions of that Act, and of other acts affecting import treatment, and actions thereunder, including the removal, modification, continuance, or imposition of any rate of duty or other import restriction.

NOW, THEREFORE, I, GEORGE W. BUSH, President of the United States of America, acting under the authority vested in me by the Constitution and the laws of the United States of America, including section 604 of the 1974 Trade Act, do proclaim as follows:

(1) I have designated the following countries as ATPDEA beneficiary countries pursuant to section 204(b)(6)(B) of the ATPA, as amended, and have determined that these countries have satisfied the requirements of section 204(b)(5)(A)(ii)(I) of the ATPA, as amended, relating to the implementation of procedures and requirements similar to those in chapter 5 of the NAFTA:

Bolivia
Colombia
Ecuador
Peru.

(2) In order to provide for the preferential treatment provided for in section 204(b) of the ATPA, as amended, the HTS is modified as provided in the annex to this proclamation.

(3) The functions of the President under section 203(e)(2)(A) of the ATPA and section 212(e)(2)(A) of the CBERA with respect to publishing notice of this proclamation are delegated to the United States Trade Representative.

(4) Any provisions of previous proclamations and Executive Orders that are inconsistent with this proclamation are superseded to the extent of such inconsistency.

(5) This proclamation is effective on the date of signature.

IN WITNESS WHEREOF, I have hereunto set my hand this thirty-first day of October, in the year of our Lord two thousand two, and of the Independence of the United States of America the two hundred and twenty-seventh.

ANDEAN TRADE PROGRAM

PERU

The Andean Trade Program (ATP, part of the Andean Trade Program and Drug Eradication Act or ATPDEA) retroactively renews and builds upon the recently-expired Andean Trade Preferences Act (ATPA) to further open U.S. markets to Peruvian products.

ATP is a critical element of a strategy to promote broad-based economic development, diversify exports, defeat the scourge of drug trafficking, and consolidate Democracy in Peru. The growing importance of the U.S. market for Peruvian exporters is reflected by the fact that the U.S. share of Peru's total exports grew from 16.6 percent in 1994 to over 30 percent in 2000.

As the leading ATPA exporter, in 2000 Peru accounted for 42.7 percent of U.S. imports under ATPA. Over 43 percent of Peru's $1.99 billion in exports to the U.S. entered under the ATPA. U.S. imports from Peru under ATPA increased in 2000 to $846 million, compared to $631 million in 1999.

ATPA generated significant job opportunities in a variety of sectors in Peru through increased duty-free export of metal products (copper cathodes and zinc plates), jewelry, non-traditional fruits (mangos) and vegetables (fresh asparagus), and cacao and coffee production. The area under coffee cultivation doubled since 1997, growing to 19,422 hectares in 2000, while the area under cacao cultivation nearly tripled to 4,882 in the same period. Meanwhile, Peru's area under coca cultivation dropped by 66 percent in 2000.

ATP will allow quota-limited duty-free imports of clothing made in Peru from regional fabric or other fabric dyed and finished in the U.S. Textile preferences could generate up to 120,000 new textile jobs and 300,000 to 400,000 cotton cultivation jobs in Peru by 2006. Under ATP, the President may proclaim duty-free treatment for Peruvian footwear not determined to be import sensitive. Tuna packed in pouches in Peru will enjoy duty-free, quota-free access to the U.S. market under ATP.

SOCIAL SAFETY NETS IN LATIN AMERICA

1. PRIVATIZATION AND SOCIAL SAFETY NETS

After more than a decade of development as a generalized regional phenomenon, privatization in Latin America can be finally evaluated from a "social" angle. The "social evaluation of privatization" risks being limited to its direct effects on employment, prices, the quality of goods supplied by the new enterprises, etc. While these markers are important, a wider vision places them in a more complex context closer to reality. Hopefully this will lead to the successful implementation of a strategy to correct negative effects such as unemployment and greater poverty.

The establishment of "social safety nets" in the era of "post-privatization", as suggested in the title of this conference, forces a new examination of the phenomena of poverty and marginality. This is no longer the old debate on the "dual society" of Latin America, although some authors still try to maintain this argument as the principal support of such examination (Jaguaribe E. 1993, pg. 91). In fact it is necessary to understand the globalization movement and all of its implications (acceleration of technological change, rapid emergence and decline of productive systems, the retreat of governmental power, the sequence and overlap of financial, social, political, military and other turbulence, etc.).

During the last two decades, in countries in different stages of development, distinct experiences of privatization have been followed by the spectre of unemployment and political and unionized resistance. In numerous cases, privatizations have continued existing processes of restructuring.

In the United Kingdom, for example, since the late 1970s, restructuring and privatization had a negative impact on employment. Between 1978-1979 and 1982-1983 the number of individuals employed in the steel industry declined from 186,000 to 81,000. In British Leyland, employment fell from 177,000 to 107,000, and in British Airways from 56,000 to 35,000 (Domingues R.M., 1988, pg. 52). The movement towards privatization was extended during the 1980's to other Western European countries such as France and Italy.

Later, in Argentina, the restructuring process started in 1990 when the 13 largest public enterprises underwent a reduction in employment from 222,000 to 42,000 by the end of 1993. Under such reduction, 66,000 employees were expected to transfer to the new privatized companies, 10,000 were forced to retire and 95,000 took early voluntary retirement (through indemnities and compensations). When considering all public firms during the same period, the number of individuals employed fell from 250,000 to approximately 60,000.

The privatization of the "Sociedad Mixta Siderurgica Argentina (SOMISA)" is a case in point. In 1991 the firm, located in San Nicholas and being the chief employer in the city, employed 12,000. In slightly over 4 months, 6,200 employees, in addition to 1,700 from its subsidiaries, accepted voluntary early retirement packages.

During the six months that followed, SOMISA disbursed approximately US$ 100 million in compensation as part of those packages. During that period, the ex-employees used the compensation packages to maintain and frequently increase their level of expenditures (purchases of appliances, automobiles, home repairs, etc.) and to start small enterprises with little previous research, such as market research. Thus, San Nicolas experienced an explosive surge of "micro-businesses" (kiosks, paddle ball courts, etc.) which in less than a year went from 9 to 120, but finally ended massively bankrupt.

The level of disappointment was such that the municipal authorities started a project financed by UNDP under the advice of ILO (PREALC). The project consisted in the establishment of a technical unit within the local municipality aimed at training workers for the creation of new enterprises, using existing infrastructure and technical and financial support from the programme (di Rocco E.L., 1993, pg. 203). The naive expectation of a spontaneous and improvised conversion of employees into entrepreneurs, without prior market evaluations or specific technical training, was considered the most critical error of that experience, which might have been avoided if a programme of social conversion had been in place beforehand.

2. THE CRISIS WITHIN THE STATE

The SOMISA case questions the level of efficiency available within the State to resolve the problems of social reintegration caused by its own conversion. This leads us to the subject of the crisis within the State in Latin America and its relationship with the privatizations of the 1980's and 1990's. In this sense, the Latin American case must be considered within the widespread decline of statist economies in their different versions, viz. Keynesian in developed countries, socialist in the ex-Soviet States, protectionist in developing countries).

This decline is partially due to globalization. The development of extensive global economic networks implies the emergence of systems highly autonomous from national powers, not only at the financial or commercial level but also at the technological, cultural and political levels.

Nevertheless, the Latin American experience of crisis within the State and of privatization is clearly different, particularly in its social implications, from the experiences of Western Europe in the 1980's (which were relatively "orderly and soft", and stimulated a certain renewal of the capitalist culture) and Eastern Europe (particularly in the ex-USSR, which were generally chaotic, catastrophic and plagued with the emergence of organized crime). In Latin America, the developing mixed economies followed a different road.

The statism which originated in the 1930's and was aggravated in the 1940's through large-scale nationalizations and the creation of parastatal enterprises caused the degeneration of the State apparatus into hypertrophied structures overwhelmed by inefficient bureaucracies. In many cases, the State became a hospital or junkyard of enterprises. For example, by the mid-1980's, Argentina had 527 State-owned enterprises and Mexico had 1155, in an environment in which irrelevant companies such as manufacturers of tortillas, gym shoes, hotels and hostels, coexisted with important firms in the mining, steel and energy sectors (Minsburg N., 1993, pg. 1061).

A perverse and mutually parasitic relationship developed between State bureaucracies and private firms which engaged in a predatorial attack on the public sector through arbitrarily priced contracts to supply goods and services, disputable financial operations, etc. Thus, the analysis of the decadence of the State should be included in the context of the culture of underdevelopment, which includes both corrupt bureaucrats and entrepreneurs, both parties showing a poor level of professional responsibility.

The debt crisis was not the only stimulus of change. The financial impasse triggered a situation of evident decadence highlighted by technological retardation, organizational irrationality, overexpenditure, etc. In all their different national manifestations, privatizations took place within a situation of State crisis.

3. PRIVATIZATION, UNEMPLOYMENT, POVERTY

Latin American privatization should be placed within the context of a social landscape seriously worsened by the economic recession of the 1980's and its impact on a structurally weak productive apparatus. This explains the multiplied negative effect on employment caused by the conversion of State enterprises into private firms. Between 1981 and 1990, regional per capita GDP declined at an average annual rate of 1.2 per cent (from US$2,188 to US$1,946). On the other hand, according to ECLAC, poverty and destitution affected approximately 110 million Latin Americans in 1970, 135 million in 1980 and 195 million in 1990 (Minsburg N., op.cit., pg. 1064).

In other words, privatization took place in impoverished societies, with increasing social marginalization. The dis-industrialization of the 1980's seriously affected the productive culture and, in addition to the deterioration of the State, operated as a brake on the process of labour reconversion.

	Evolution of Minimum Urban Wages, 1984-1990 Average annual indices (1980 = 100)			
	1984	1986	1988	1990
Argentina	167.5	110.0	93.5	40.2
Brazil	87.4	89.0	68.7	53.4
Colombia	113.5	114.2	109.9	107.9
Costa Rica	104.4	118.7	114.6	120.5
Chile	80.7	73.6	73.9	87.5
Ecuador	62.8	65.0	53.4	36.2
Mexico	72.3	64.9	54.2	45.5
Peru	62.3	56.4	52.0	23.4
Uruguay	88.0	88.5	84.5	69.1
Venezuela	66.5	90.4	89.5	59.3

Source: ECLAC, 1992

The exclusive nature of the global technological environment contributed to the negative legacy of the 1980's. Computerization, biotechnology, new materials, reduction in energy consumption and other components of the technological revolution tend to reduce employment, chiefly through the introduction of systems which increase quality while reducing the imperfections of direct human participation (computerization, etc.) or by simply displacing traditional productive structures (e.g. introduction of isoglucose, which marginalized the production of sugar cane).

Globalization and the development of labour-saving (mostly unskilled) technologies are virtually inseparable. Furthermore, the problem goes beyond skilled and unskilled labour, involving an acceleration of the rate of emergence and obsolescence of skills. The flexibility and adaptability of systems of professional training becomes a decisive factor.

Thus, in the era of globalization, development is differentiated from underdevelopment not only by a superior accumulation of wealth but also to a large degree by the ability to adapt to technological change. The chronic technological unemployment prevailing in industrialized countries is worse in developing nations. The entrepreneurial, labour and State structures of Latin America, with a weak potential for productive adaptation, bear the consequences of globalization through unemployment and marginalization.

This does not imply that the creation of highly technological employment is the only valid response to compete in a global economy. Labour alternatives should be available for varied market places, whether local or international, whether demanding high- or low-technology goods. It is essential to find alternative survival and development mechanisms, associating specific niches with feasible products and technologies appropriate to precise commercial objectives.

The establishment of projects of social development at the labour or entrepreneurial level must be based on rigorous interrelationships between markets, products and technologies. In this sense, the organization of social promotion projects based on local economic realities could constitute an appropriate response in developing countries.

4. INFORMAL ECONOMY

The crisis within the State can be explained by globalization, the decadence of State bureaucracies and the acceleration of the technological revolution. The examination of the expansion of the informal sector is also very useful in the development of social safety nets. The informal sector appears as an expression of autonomy and social discontent in the face of the State, and has been in continuous expansion for the last twenty years to the point of becoming a significant global phenomenon.

Informal economic activities are defined as those not registered in official statistics and thus marginalized from the State. They cover legal and illegal activities, range from the technically rudimentary and of very limited geographical reach (food production in areas of extreme poverty) to highly technological sophistication (software production) and with international projection (financial flows). Informal activities run parallel to globalization and are an irresistible socio-economic tide in both developed and developing countries, enjoying in the latter higher relative weight in the overall economy. These activities are independent of deteriorated statal machinery and employ a significant proportion of low-income urban populations.

In Latin America by the mid-1980's, the informal sector was responsible for a significant portion of the national economy. In Mexico, Argentina and Colombia the informal sector represents approximately 25 per cent of all economic activity, reaching 30 per cent in Peru and 50 per cent in Bolivia. In Mexico alone, informal GDP increased from 10 per cent of total GDP in 1970 to 32 per cent in 1985. Projections in Peru point to an increase of up to 60 per cent by the year 2000

The recent history of Latin America shows the joint emergence of globalization (and the rapid dissemination of technological innovations that it generates), together with the deterioration of the State, widespread privatizations and the extension of the informal economy. The establishment of social development networks in poor areas must take into consideration not only the generally low level of efficiency of the State apparatus but also the existence of widely extended mechanisms of survival and entrepreneurial development, beyond State control and at the level of the lower-income sectors of medium and large urban centres. These sectors grow following economic parameters which are different from those found in more advanced systems (in terms of rate of return, commercial activity, innovation, etc.) and which should be rigorously examined as a base for future strategies of support to that segment of the economy.

How to get full use of the creative forces in the informal sector is a mystery, since neither conventional macroeconomic approaches nor the managerial models based on the "excellence" of global high-technology firms have managed to fully explain this amazing micro-economy. Its current importance, which will be even greater in the coming years, demands the development of a specialized kind of management which will be essential to the success of social development projects.

Curiously, the Latin American privatizations, especially those of very large enterprises (steel, telecommunications, airlines, railroads, etc.) appear as the consummate expression of globalization, combining technological and managerial modernization with their integration into transnational enterprises, and definitely in sharp contrast with the gray universe of the urban informal sector. However, both processes share the same origin: the decline of the modern underdeveloped State. Many ex-employees of the privatized public enterprises survive and in some cases prosper as small entrepreneurs when they are left to their own initiative, without official programmes of labour conversion. In general, they have managed to find and exploit concrete commercial opportunities re-utilizing and/or re-tooling their own technical expertise. These experiences constitute an invaluable source to be taken into consideration in the formulation and implementation of micro-strategies of social development.

5. MANAGEMENT OF MICROSYSTEMS OF SOCIAL DEVELOPMENT

It is normally held that there is a need to relate economic growth to social investment as a means of overcoming poverty. This equation is usually completed with proposals for programmes of social development focused on well-delimited population groups, in order to avoid the dispersion common in over-generalized initiatives. The need to focus social policy appears as a major obligation of the State after the crisis of the 1980's and the subsequent wave of privatizations (Infante T., 1992 and Aedo C., 1993). This type of approach merits three observations.

In the first place, economic growth within the context of globalization appears as a necessary but not sufficient condition of social development. Furthermore, recent experiences show us that entrepreneurial modernization is indivisible from advanced technologies which generally reduce the need of unskilled or obsolete labour. On the other hand, those social groups (particularly urban) which are left outside the modern (globalized) entrepreneurial systems do not remain outside the culture of globalization: they participate in it mostly as spectators, unemployed and/or underemployed producers in informal survival structures. The media and other urban networks inform everybody of the changes and novelties and nobody can escape from the spectacle of cultural globalization, or take refuge in a separate autonomous space.

The general lack of economic growth produces a drastic increase of unemployment (as in the 1980's), but growth is also often followed by a significant increase in unemployment, especially in the case of rapid global integration. Privatizations fall within this logic.

Secondly, social investments, even those focused on the neediest, are a necessary complement to growth but also insufficient for poverty eradication.

Finally, the State can be reformed, adapting it to the new era. However, even such a necessary achievement is insufficient from the point of social development. Growth is a potential basis of resources for governmental and non-governmental organizations, and focused social investments carried out by an efficient State can create a good support base, but both become pointless without opportunities available to the majority.

These three observations compel us to pay attention to the concept of social development powered by small innovative projects based on a combination of surveyed niche markets, goods specifically designed for those niches, and labour and entrepreneurial training aimed towards those commercial opportunities.

The management of micro-systems is closely related to the development of social, labour and commercial projections. Training of managers of micro-enterprises of a diverse technological range (from artisans to internationally competitive initiatives) appears to be an essential component of social development. From a macro-economic perspective, productive systems are needed in which interacting sub-systems coexist. At one extreme are those globalized firms which need to constantly renew their technological base, while at the other end of the spectrum are firms generating a sufficient return for their survival. There is ample scope between these extremes for the development of interrelated initiatives through markets, cultural exchanges, etc.

PRIVATIZATION AND THE FUTURE OF LATIN AMERICA

Economic reform in Latin America is a work in progress—and a work under assault. From President Caldera's departure from orthodoxy to the collapse of the Mexican peso to the dramatic reversal of capital flows that is affecting the whole region, there is a sense that the reforms of the recent past are at risk. The hemispheric outlook has gone almost overnight from white to black or, at least, to grey. Investors, national and international, who only months ago were prepared to commit an ever larger share of their porfolios to the region are cancelling new investments and re-evaluating those which had already been made; the general perception in the investment community is that risk has risen dramatically while returns have fallen equally fast. The resulting shift in capital flows has caused a dramatic retrenchment of economic policies, whether in reaction to crisis (Mexico) or in order to forestall one (Argentina). Growth is slowing in all countries and actual declines in output are likely in some.

The obvious question is whether the region's apparent recovery from the growth-numbing debt crisis of the 1980's was ephemeral; whether the economic growth model was somehow fatally flawed. Central to that model, of course, has been privatization—defined not just as the sole of State-owned assets, but as a profound shift of the boundary between the public and private sectors in favour of the latter. This shift, financed by private capital flows and assuming the continuous availability of new flows, was designed to move the fulcrum of economic activity to the private sector. The result was intended not only to get governments out of the business of making steel or generating electricity or flying airplanes, but to change how growth was generated and financed. Private savings and investment, supplemented by private foreign capital flows, would replace the old process of governmental borrowing to finance public-sector economic, industrial and perhaps even social investments.

It is the thesis of this paper, first, that the privatization-based model of economic reform remains viable and, second, that in the absence of a continuing move toward greater private ownership and policies to support the private sector, the countries of Latin America will once again be caught up in a vicious circle of inflation, recession, and financial market crises. The challenge to policy makers is to persevere in strategies which rely on private sector investment and entrepreneurship, resisting the knee jerk reaction to frustrate market forces or to return to the bankrupt model of State intervention and ownership. The further challenge is to continue to create conditions which maximize the possibility of private sector success—including continued privatization—even when it would easier (at least in the short run) and more natural for the State to resume a leading role in the economy.

Arguably, the governments and countries which survive the current crisis most successfully will be those which most aggressively reinforce the strategies of the recent past; more privatization, more tax reform, more incentives to invest and save, more transparent capital market conditions, more efforts to liberalize labour markets, more predictable policy environments, and more competition. The countries which continue to move in such a direction, rather than ones which either retreat toward the statist past or even ones which pursue orthodox stabilization programmes to an extreme which debilitate the private sector, are likely to prosper.

PRIVATIZATION

The world-wide rush to privatization over the past decade has changed the economic landscape not just of Latin America, but of many countries around the world. Airlines, hotels, banks, telephone and electrical utilities, newspapers, and innumerable other companies have been sold by governments eager to redefine how they intervene in the day-to-day functioning of their economies. When the dust from all this activity finally settles, the result will be a dramatic transformation in how these economies work, in the fabric of international commercial and financial relations, and in the very distribution of economic and, consequently, political power within and between countries.

Whether motivated by pragmatism or ideology—or simply because the owners were broke and needed money—there has been, and continues to be, a global fire sale of assets. Some of these sales were unqualified successes with immediate financial, commercial and economic benefits. And some of these sales did not attract qualified buyers or sufficient finance or were badly structured or lacked the proper macroeconomic or regulatory framework. But both failure and success have had important economic and political consequences.

Indeed, in most so-called emerging markets, particularly in this hemisphere privatization has been not only an essential part of practically every government's economic strategy, but a key measure of their leaders' commitment to political and economic reform. Just as the debt crisis and the initial wave of democratization defined Latin America in the 1980's, the sale of State-owned enterprises has been the most consequential characteristic of Latin governments (and countries) in the 1990's.

Privatization, at least as it has been conducted in Latin America, needs to be understood first in a political context and—more particularly—in the political context which existed at the start of the post-debt crisis reform process. At that point, most reform proposals enjoyed little inherent political support and excited fierce opposition. Neither Presidents Menem nor Salinas were elected with much of a mandate to undertake the sort of profound structural changes which became their governments' trademarks. Entrenched interests, including unions, consumers, suppliers, bureaucrats and politicians had long benefited from government control of important parts of the countries' industrial and service infrastructures, even if, in broad terms, the whole country had suffered from public stewardship. Sustained economic reform requires new political constituencies with stakes in the reformed economic system; privatization was one of the few ways in which such political constituencies could be quickly created.

But Latin American economic history meant that privatization played a second important political role. Governments and their leaders had often proclaimed commitments to reform. However, traditionally, Latin presidents proved their patriotism, if not their economic good sense, by nationalizing investments in oil, banking and other sectors; politicians sustained their political machines by creating jobs in State-owned enterprises and built their fortunes through the contracts those companies controlled. Throughout the hemisphere, monuments abounded to these heroes of statism in the form of overmanned, inefficient, often corrupt State companies; as in the Soviet Union and Eastern Europe, not until those statues were torn down would long-suffering people and hesitant investors believe that a new era had really dawned.

In addition, there were also important economic considerations which made privatization a central part of post-debt era economic strategies. The most obvious is that State ownership was not working anywhere in Latin America. This is an empirical, not an ideological observation, which is as true in this hemisphere as elsewhere in the world. For example, an analysis of the 500 largest non-U.S. mining and manufacturing companies in 1983 concluded that private corporations are substantially more profitable and more efficient than State-owned companies (see Anthony

Boardman and Adrian Vining, 1989, "Ownership and performance in competitive environments", Journal of Law and Economics 32, 1-33). In Latin America most State-owned enterprises were inefficient, overmanned, undercapitalized, without adequate access to modern technology, unable to compete without government subsidy, and generally without defenders among the public once the possibility of divestiture began to be discussed. If nothing else, the popularity of privatization, demonstrated in poll after poll in country after country, suggested that consumers of the output of these government-owned companies recognized that private owners could do better.

Moreover, most of these companies were significant drains on already overburdened government budgets. Regardless of how proceeds were used, the need for deficit reduction demanded privatization, if only to remove operating losses from the governments' books.

Most importantly, privatization offered the opportunity to attract new investors, new capital, new technology, and new management skills, as well as the chance to become integrated into the world economy. At a time when governments were largely unable to raise money in international markets, asset sales became the vehicle which not only provoked the return of massive amounts of flight capital, but stimulated new investors to invest in local stock and bond markets. Without these inflows, the region would have become an economic backwater, moving toward African rather than Asian economic conditions. Indeed, the core challenge facing policy makers in the mid-1980's was to design a new engine of growth, replacing Prebisch's statism with Adam Smith's reliance on markets. Privatization was a necessary element of that effort.

However, privatization alone could not accomplish the profound transformation of Latin America's economies which was needed after the debt crisis—although that transformation could not have been achieved without privatization. And, more obviously after the onset of the recent Mexican financial crisis, a fully articulated economic modernization strategy built around privatization could not eliminate the possibility either of policy failures or of swings between periods of growth and periods of recession. But the shift in the boundary between the public and private sectors opened up new possibilities of growth which neither existed nor seemed to be in prospect ten years ago, when commentators routinely worried about the Africanization of Latin America.

It is not necessary to recap the spectacular recovery of the Latin economy after 1988 or to make a resume of the liberal economic and financial strategy which to a greater or lesser degree was adopted throughout the hemisphere. Trade liberalization, fiscal reform, implementation of conservative monetary policy, debt renegotiation, regulatory reform, labour law reform, de-indexation, improvements in capital market and banking oversight as well as privatization were common elements of that strategy. Naturally, there were important differences—Argentina's convertibility law versus Mexico's crawling peg, Uruguay's rejection of privatization versus Chile's aggressive embrace—but the similarities defined a clearly recognizable "Latin American model" whose core was constructed upon the development of the private sector as the leading edge of economic growth and development.

How necessary was—and is—privatization to the success and prospects of this model? There is a growing body of empirical evidence that privatization played a central role. A recent study of 61 companies from 18 countries (including several Latin countries) in 32 industries shows that privatization significantly increased profitability, productivity, efficiency and, most surprisingly, total employment. (See William Megginson, Robert Nash and Matthias von Randenborg, 1994, "The Financial and Operating Performance of Newly Privatized Firms", Journal of Finance). Another study, by a team of World bank economists (Ahmed Galal, Leroy Jones, Pankaj Tandon and Ingo Vogelsang, 1992, Welfare Consequences of Selling Public Enterprises. The World Bank, Washington, D.C.) looked at twelve privatizations in four countries (including Mexico) and concluded that in eleven of the twelve case studies there were positive welfare gains for society as a whole. Again, the biggest surprise in the study was that workers as a whole were not disadvantaged by privatization and in some cases that they gained, largely because of higher wages and appreciation of shares granted to or purchased in the privatization process as well as because of substantial severance payments for those whose jobs disappeared. The table below summarizes the study's conclusions. Evidence from particular privatizations in Brazil, Mexico, Argentina and Chile closely track the conclusions of these international studies.

Winners and Losers: New Welfare Changes

Workers:	Not worse off; sometimes clear winners.	
Consumers:	Lose in a number of cases as prices rise to an economically efficient level with larger societal benefits.	
Governments:	Immediate fiscal effect usually positive.	
Competitors:	When relevant (i.e. non-monopoly situations)	clear gains.
Foreigners	When foreigners are involved, they generally do quite well	
vs. Nationals:	but nationals do even better.	

Source: Galal, Jones, Tandon and Vogelsang, Welfare Consequences of Selling Public Enterprises.

These improvements in efficiency and productivity have been important contributors to the economic successes of the past few years. And there was, at least until recently, every reason to believe that the positive effects on privatization would continue. Indeed, the World Bank study cited above concluded that for a typical developing economy, privatization, if embedded in a broader market-oriented economic reform strategy, would have continuing benefits:

"(a) ... capable of producing annual welfare gains of around 5 to 10 per cent of predivestiture annual sales;

(b)if half the public enterprise sector were to be divested, the annual gains would be about 1 per cent of GDP, and

(c)additional benefits might follow from such indirect effects as unleashed private entrepreneurial activity and accelerated capital market development."

Nevertheless, the Mexican financial crisis and consequent flight of capital from Latin America have raised new questions about the viability of the hemisphere's reliance on portfolio capital flows to finance growth. Commentators from President Zedillo to The New York Times have opined that reliance on speculative capital—so-called "hot money"—puts the fate of great nations in the hands of 28-year-old traders with no commitment beyond the next trade and no horizon beyond the news flash on a computer screen. It is a short leap from this criticism to an argument that the hemisphere has been too dependent on foreign capital (i.e. current account deficits have been too high and savings rates too low), to an argument that the private capital flows are unstable and private investment unreliable as a linchpin of economic growth, to questions about whether the private sector is the right platform on which to base a sustainable economic strategy. This somewhat tortuous chain of logic could become more persuasive, or at least more popular, if private capital flows (which have overwhelmingly gone to private sector addresses over the past five years) dry up, if recently privatized companies fail in Mexico or elsewhere and are rescued (that is, re-nationalized) by governments, or if the economic growth does not quickly revive.

The immediate issue, then, is not whether to continue to privatize or whether privatization has worked. Privatization has produced sufficient tangible economic and financial benefits to make the case that private ownership is usually preferable to public ownership. The question, rather, is how to sustain the momentum toward a private-sector driven economy —including continuing privatization where the process is as yet immature—in the face of adverse changes in international and regional conditions. The answer lies partly in an examination of some of the lessons of the Latin privatization experience and partly in a discussion of future policies which governments should consider.

It is possible to cull a number of lessons from the Latin experience with privatization, some of which address future privatizations, some of which concern the viability of past privatizations.

First, governments typically face a buyers', not a sellers', market, although they just as typically fail to recognize this. The consequence may be lower prices and less restrictive conditions than expected when domestic political circumstance and national pride may demand higher prices and more restrictions. There is always severe competition for scarce capital and scarcer technical expertise. As a result, some privatizations will fail and, as a result, some loss-making enterprises will (or should) simply disappear. For example, there may not be a market for all of the airlines now owned by Latin governments, when there is an obvious excess supply of airline services internationally. This does not mean that the State-run airlines should be kept flying; the public welfare may be best served by permanently grounding some of them.

Second, privatization is an intensely political process. This does not mean it is corrupt, but rather that the government has to cope with important domestic forces whose aim is to frustrate or pervert the process. The government can be caught between the demands of entrenched interests and those of the potential investors; too often the result of trying to please both simply produces bad policy. The rule should be: when in doubt, favour the investors.

Third, privatization should be defined primarily in industrial rather than financial terms. Asset sales can raise money and extinguish debts. But the long-run success of these sales depends on the injection of new management, capital and technology. Thus, the organizing principles should be to improve economic efficiency, promote technological development, and provide enhanced services rather than to maximize receipts. To the extent that privatization is seen primarily as a way to raise revenues for the government or an alternative to debt strategy, it will ultimately fail, even if, along the way, individual deals are completed. The sale of banks in Mexico to the highest bidders rather than to the most qualified may have helped produce the solvency problems which are increasingly evident.

Fourth, the sale of a public-sector monopoly to the private sector requires the careful elaboration of a new regulatory framework. Private-sector owners and investors are inherently more likely to manage more efficiently to introduce new technologies, and to allocate capital on economic rather than political criteria, if only to maximize profit. Monopoly powers can be abused, however, and the dilemma is how to give the new owner enough protection to earn a fair return, especially in the early post-privatization period, while protecting the public interest.

However, private monopolies pose their own problems. Different governments have approached the problem differently. In Argentina, the telephone monopoly was divided into two regional, but not competing companies; in Mexico, the company was sold intact with a national concession. In both cases, however, competition has subsequently been introduced by allowing new entrants to offer services based on new (wireless) technologies. Moreover, Mexico, like Chile before it, will soon open even basic local and long distance services to direct competition.

The growing reality is that the evolution of technology is transforming the nature of what traditionally were considered to be natural monopolies. In almost all industrial and service activites competition can and should be introduced to maximize the public welfare.

Fifth, it is a general rule of thumb that the success of privatization depends on the ultimate distance from the political process of the privatized entity. The more the post-privatization decision-making process in an entity is depoliticized, the more likely the company is to make economically based decisions. This is true, for example, in the case of electricity or telephone companies; if privatized utilities have to bargain with politicians over each price increase, their independence (and their profitability) will inevitably suffer.

Sixth, governments often have a hard time understanding the difference between their roles as owners or as regulators. It is essential that the post-privatization regulatory environment be specified prior to sale, not only to maximize revenues from the privatization but to maximize the likelihood that the privatized company will be able to operate successfully. But it is also important that governments recognize that they need to let private companies operate freely, succeeding or failing on their own. For example, in technology-intensive businesses—like telecommunications—the government should regulate services, not pick technologies. There is a critical difference between defining the framework and managing a business and, in a privatized world, only the former is within the appropriate purview of the government. But many governments, out of habit or conviction, too readily interfere in what should be operational decisions.

PROMOTING PRIVATIZATION

What can governments do to assure the continued success of privatization and of privatized companies even as the Mexican induced financial crisis threatens to curtail capital flows to the whole region? The basic answer is to sustain a stable growth-oriented macroeconomic framework which recognizes the priority of maintaining the viability and competitiveness of the private sector. The crucial modification to the economic strategy of the recent past should be a greater emphasis on measures to promote domestic savings, to improve the transparency and efficiency of capital markets and to raise the quality of local financial institutions; one element of such an approach should be the rapid privatization of social security systems, as pioneered by Chile. This would reduce dependence on external portfolio capital flows. At the same time, countries should look at measures which reduce the velocity of cross-border capital flows, carefully balancing the liquidity needs of investors against the stability needs of the users of capital. The risk, of course, is that the distance between such measures as minimum investment periods and capital controls may be too short in the minds of some investors (and, indeed, some politicians).

One of the present dilemmas facing several countries in the region, particularly Mexico, is that the sort of orthodox adjustment programmes mandated by official lenders as well as by conventional wisdom require dramatic fiscal and monetary tightening. Positive real interest rates and budget surpluses are appropriate to certain situations, but could transform a recession into a depression if too much damage is done to private financial and non-financial companies. There is a real, urgent need for new thinking about how to stabilize financial markets when government finances are basically sound and when the growth strategy is predicated on continuing private sector credit flows to private sector addresses.

Even in the midst of financial crisis, governments should seek to reinforce the privatization processes which they have launched. Indeed, it is possible that just as the early Chilean, Argentinean and Mexican privatizations captured the imaginations of investors, a new wave of privatizations now could entice owners of capital to resume much needed flows. This suggests several observations:

First, it is essential that contractual commitments made to privatized firms are rigorously observed. Venezuela's harassment of CANTV has done almost as much damage to the market's perception of the country's investment climate as any of its other policies.

Second, the economic rationale underlying the decision to privatize should not be lost when fiscal pressures suddenly balloon. Just as privatization should not be a substitute for debt policy, it should not be a substitute for fiscal policy or the long-run commercial consequences may not be viable. Rushed, badly designed, unprofessional privatizations will not work.

Third, governments should be prepared to let privatized companies fail. The absence of market discipline was a principal source of the inefficiency of State-owned companies and would have a similar corrosive effect on private ones. Saving privatized companies will do little to impress potential investors and will do nothing to improve the viability of the economy.

Fourth, perhaps the single greatest mistake in the early wave of Latin privatizations was the failure by some governments to create full blown post-privatization regulatory environments before divestiture. Success in the future requires the establishment of a known, predictable policy framework. This is even truer in the midst of crisis conditions when investors are being asked to undertake long-term commitments, than it was when conditions were more positive.

Fifth, as little distinction as possible should be made between foreign and domestic capital. There is no economic case for such distinctions—indeed, there is a strong case in favour of allowing unfettered foreign investments—and the political case is usually exaggerated. Where outright asset sales to foreigners are thought to be too sensitive, more subtle methods of incorporating foreign capital and technology—joint ventures between private and public firms, concessions to operate, etc.—can come close to approximating privatization.

Sixth, for privatization to flourish, indeed, for private sector to fulfil its leading economic role, there must be profound judicial and legal reform throughout the hemisphere.

From today's vantage point it seems likely that privatization will remain an essential element of the Latin American economic strategy. In a world where wealth is primarily created in the private sector, government's role will increasingly be limited to one of setting and maintaining the rules within which private forces interact. This requires a profound change in how politicians and bureaucrats think about economics. For example, there is little in the administrative tradition of most Latin countries which is consistent with the exercise of open, impartial regulatory processes; Latin bureaucrats are typically more comfortable mandating activities rather than in simply establishing and administering parameters within which companies are allowed wide latitude to operate.

The companion to this observation is that most Latin American governments and bureaucracies do not seem to have yet embraced the full implications of market-driven economics. For example, in discussions about the framework for the post-Telmex telephone liberalization, Mexican government officials have worried aloud that too many market entrants will lead to over-investment and that the country can ill afford such waste. Similar examples of a reluctance to give up the vestiges of dirigiste thinking abound and

will only disappear if leaders insist that market forces predominate.

Finally, the governments of Latin America have little choice but to reinforce the strategies which produced success during recent years. There are no substantial pools of capital outside the private sector and there is no willingness on the part of the leading industrial countries to finance alternative models of development. Indeed, there is no credible alternative model.

The opportunity—and the challenge—is to consolidate the gains of past privatizations and to promote new ones. After all, what would be a more spectacular affirmation of continuing commitment to radical economic change than the privatization of PEMEX or Petrobras?

VI. COUNTRY PAPERS

1. PRIVATIZATION IN ARGENTINA

Before privatization, public enterprises (PEs) in Argentina had a significant and growing economic and political role. Their share in the economy did not differ significantly from the average country, in which PEs contribute 16.5 per cent of capital formation and 9.5 per cent of gross domestic product (GDP).

Argentina had approximately 300 public financial and nonfinancial enterprises in 1982. These usually took the form of public corporations. They supposedly combined managerial autonomy of operations with political control and oversight. The overall share of the Argentine PE sector before the long privatization process, which started in 1989, was approximately 7 per cent of GDP, 30 per cent of gross fixed investment, 56 per cent of the public sector deficit, 26 per cent of external debt ($58.5 billion) and 2.8 per cent of the total labour force (290,000 employees).

These enterprises were principally public utilities—energy, transport, telecommunications and water resources (90 per cent of the overall sector), and industries—mainly Ministry of Defence productive enterprises, which were about 10 per cent of the total sector, mainly in steel, metalworking, chemicals and petrochemicals. There were also some productive and service enterprises which were rescued by the State and later liquidated or returned to the private sector. Employment was concentrated heavily in the railways (FA), telecommunications (ENTEL) and postal services (ENCOTEL), which provided about 60 per cent of total sectoral employment.

Although their evolution and origins were diverse, one can usually trace some of the following motives: ideological, market, national security, industrial development strategy, nationalization, employment and distributive factors. Each one had a different weight and depended on the particular political, social and economic setting. However, the recent period witnessed a major shift in many of the driving forces backing the public enterprise sector.

Since the debt crisis started in the early 1980's, Argentina's investment capacity was reduced to a level that did not allow even the maintenance of its capital stock, both public and private. Investment dropped from 20 per cent of GDP during the 1970's to 10 per cent in the 1980's. This led to a short-sighted lack of investment in maintenance and improving the productivity of existent operations, because of overall cuts in current expenditures. Although this was the turning-point which made privatization the only possible outcome, it also worsened institutional investment programming, policy-making and planning process at the sectoral level.

Ideological changes stressed the need for liberalization, "market-friendly" policies and the "subsidiary State", and the perceived limitations of bureaucratic management. New contestable markets and technological changes also affected market structures and shifted borders while management capacity matured and indigenous entrepreneurs got better access to capital markets. Thus, when the debt crisis erupted in the early 1980's, the overall financial performance of PEs imposed a burden on the fiscal accounts. The consequent adjustment process seriously eroded the quality of services, productive performance and the capital base in many sectors, contributing to the popular endorsement of privatization policies.

The above-mentioned changes and limitations created the conditions to start profound stabilization and reform processes of which privatization was a part.

Therefore, Argentina began an overriding, rapid and widespread "sell first" policy without extended restructuring, which took into account its fiscal restraints and temporary political capital, sectoral support and weak opposition, which would have vanished if a more gradual step-by-step approach had been adopted.

To understand this overall and speedy privatization process, the policy has to be analyzed in its particular setting. Argentina confronted at least two hyperinflationary episodes in mid-1989, with a second one early in March 1990. This situation caused serious fiscal problems, due to adjustment fatigue and the lag in counterinflationary interventions. This exhausted public policy tools and access to public sector borrowing. The main source of funds was privatization through outright sale of public assets or of long-term concessions.

2. Former institutional structures

Argentine PEs operated amidst a complex institutional and regulatory network with multiple and inconsistent objectives and policies. The Ministry of Public Works and Services (MOSP) was responsible for the main service PEs through its four sectoral Secretariats that were held directly accountable for each area. The productive enterprises were under the aegis of the Ministry of Defence. The rescued PEs were under the charge of the National Development Bank (BANADE). In 1985, a Secretariat of Growth Promotion was established to increase divestiture options, but was eliminated in 1986 due to its negligible effect. During the same year, the Secretariat of Control of Public Enterprises (SECONEP) was created to advise the Government on PE policies and control: this was also soon dissolved.

The Directorate of Public Enterprises (DEP) was instituted in 1986. At first, it tried to promote the institutional reform of PEs by means of decentralization management contracts, restructuring and privatization. Later, it centralized power and decision-making in the DEP and MOSP and appointed directors and management staff in PEs. It tried to implement deregulation and demonopolization policies, but with limited success, and was abolished in 1989.

The Sindicatura General de Empresas Publicas (SIGEP) became the oversight body for PEs. It audited legal compliance, accounting and management (operational) procedures by participating in PE board meetings. However, most audits were ex post and formal, given the lack of clear ex ante management objectives and policies for most PEs.

The first phase of privatization started in 1985 and was able to privatize only a few public enterprises that had been rescued from bankruptcy and some others in which the State had a minority stake.

The new administration, which took office in July 1989, emphasized the need to advance towards State reform and presented an ambitious legislative package to Congress for its enactment and implementation. As mentioned above, the initial political thrust, the overall social and political impact that the recent hyperinflationary process had, and the diverse political base and constituency, gave the Government the support it needed to start this policy.

The second privatization phase had two parts. The first, between July 1989 and February 1991, was conducted by the Ministry of Public Works and Services (MOSP), during which controlling shareholdings of Argentine Airlines and ENTEL (telecommunications) were sold. Minor stakes in petrochemical firms, television stations and highway concessions were awarded. The second part began in 1991 amidst a successful stabilization package (the Convertibility Plan) and was managed by the Ministry of Economy and Public Works and Services (MEOySP), which shared the responsibility for enterprises belonging to the Ministry of Defence.

This was part of a learning process for both the public and private sectors. It used the existing monitoring capacity as a stepstone for its success.

Between 1990 and 1994, after legal changes and break up into independent business units, approximately 115 enterprises were privatized through outright sale of assets, concessions and franchises. Also public offerings of YPF shares and concessions for primary and secondary oil production areas were made. Total sale proceeds were $16.3 billion. During this period there was an overall personnel reduction in most sectors leaving about 100,000 employees in the privatized firms after retrenchments.

The dimension, diversity, complexity and time constraints of the privatization process required appropriate coordination, coherence and sequencing to allow the attainment of its different objectives and goals.

3. Privatization process

(a) Objectives

The policy statement on privatization declared that "anything that the private sector can undertake itself will not be done by the national State; that everything that the provinces can do autonomously will not be done by the national State; and that all that can be done by the municipalities will not be done by the national State" (Presidential Message to Congress, July 1989).

The objective of this policy was to increase fiscal revenues to service foreign debt, to contribute to stabilization and to improve the quality and coverage of public services. This process had support and assistance from the World Bank and UNDP through the sectoral Public Enterprise Reform Adjustment Loan and a Technical Assistance PE Reform Loan as well as other sector loans and projects. These provided the necessary funding for both sectoral adjustments and tailor-made privatization plans.

Because of the pace and size of the privatization process, the important fiscal needs, the sale of control stake—all aspects of the privatization policy and strategy, there was a lag in the development of relative regulatory capacity, or the burden was too heavy, which created serious challenges to the regulatory agencies.

(b) Modalities

The choice of modality of privatization was based on market structure, required period for investment recovery, competitive conditions and the amount of the State's stake. Modalities were: (a) outright sale of asset for firms that operated in competitive markets, such as in electricity generation, YPF peripheral activities and most productive PEs; (b) share offerings, as with YPF and most residual stakes; (c) concessions, franchises and licences, for periods that varied between 10 and 95 years for roads, railways, subways, telecommunication networks, water and sewerage infrastructure, and facilities for transportation and distribution of electricity and gas and oil production.

(c) Macroeconomic conditions

The so-called Technical Operative Group, which was set up within the Secretariat of Finance, conducted the financial, fiscal, price and tariff monitoring of all PEs during the whole process. This task was useful to determine the overall cash and debt requirements and sector goals and to build different scenarios for privatization. It also analyzed the possible inflationary and fiscal impacts of changes in tariff levels and structures and tax cuts in the stabilization and deregulation process, and the external balance and debt impact of different privatization strategies. During this phase, due to the improvement in fiscal conditions, Argentina got an IMF Extended Fund Facility and later started negotiations to be eligible for the Brady Plan, which allowed rescheduling of foreign debt that was carefully monitored by the IMF, World Bank and commercial banks. Therefore, waivers and other conditions had to be met before privatization of PEs. These accounted for about 26 per cent of the external debt.

The strict and widespread current and capital financial constraints, set by the Secretariat of Finance, caused deviations which led to an increase of liabilities during the privatization and transfer process. This could have been avoided with a more flexible and piecemeal approach towards control of revenues and expenditures.

The aforementioned information was used mainly by the Secretariat of Finance, but could have had a more extended use in the Undersecretariat of Privatization, the ad hoc Privatization Commissions and other sectors.

(d) Techniques and procedures

Other preparations included transfers of rights, statutory reforms based on privileges, attention to competitive and market conditions, and necessary regulations, with preference given to partial owners, employees (Programme for Participated Property (PPPs or ESOPs), users and consumers or producers of inputs (cooperatives).

In many cases there was business unbundling through horizontal restructuring, such as in freight and passenger railways and highway toll networks, or vertical restructuring, such as with gas and electricity transport and distribution. This was intended to reduce the firm's market power, introduce competition or facilitate privatization, through break up of networks. The task entailed identifying business units, separating infrastructure and assets, administrative and accounting information, allocating personnel and other operational aspects as well as establishing boundaries and contractual forms of access and integration.

Preparation also involved statutory, legal and institutional reforms of PEs which were restructured to facilitate divestiture. After these transformations, public corporations became stock corporations. This facilitated later sales of equity.

The sales were made through assignment of control stakes to groups which were formed by a sectoral operator with confirmed experience of running utilities of significant size. Formal guarantees were obtained for investment commitments, quality of service and maintenance, and safeguards for public service assets, according to the conditions of each particular business.

Golden shares were not retained by the public sector. The only contractual condition related to share ownership and foreign investors (who have the same rights as domestic investors) was the obligation to inform the Government of any change in the control group. The firms were subject to concession contracts and regulatory framework conditions set for public services in terms of service standards, investment commitments, consumer rights, monitoring and information disclosure, access conditions, review periods and other key issues. The selection procedures included public bidding, public contests and auctions—with or without baseline prices, share offerings in different markets and direct contracts.

(e) Valuations

Appraisals by national, provincial or municipal public agencies were required. International and national professional appraisers were hired when valuation by the public sector was not feasible.

In most cases, there were asset valuations at the net present values of businesses, based on their discounted projected cash flows. From this information, baseline prices were set for each bidding process. Depending on the outcome, this threshold could be lowered or removed. Since values changed with macroeconomic conditions, this also affected the acceptable mix between cash, debt and transfer of liabilities. Public offerings were based on reasonable price-earnings ratios for similar firms, adjusted by the rated country risk.

(f) Administrative arrangements

The "sell first" and comprehensive privatization strategy required strong political commitment, centralization, coordination, monitoring and control to proceed without affecting transparency, accountability, competition and other aspects.

Debt-equity swaps could be used for partial payment to reduce the debt load and also provide external backing. There were also provisions for protecting employment conditions and social security to mitigate negative social impacts. The policies towards labour were broad and established general intentions which served to reduce employee opposition, but lacked patterns to be dealt with in the process. The Government assumed most PEs' total liabilities in order to facilitate the privatization process, although some were transferred to licensees.

During the second phase, Decree 2408/91 set the time-frame, sequence and conditions for the privatization process, which was to be terminated by the end of 1992. It set the deadlines for drafting legislation, transfer of services, bidding, tender, concession conditions and restructuring plans and programmes. It established the basis for coordination and agreement with provinces in areas of shared competence related to privatizations and concessions. Responsibility was assigned for submitting projects to the National Executive Power (PEN) with the regulatory framework and service standards, inspection and control, consumer protection and safeguards for State assets included in concessions, privatizations and decentralization, prior to issue of corresponding bidding terms and conditions. External debt conversion and capitalization could be requested by the enforcing authority and approved by PEN, after approval of the MEOySP. The discount rate of debt was set by the MEOySP and their review was shared by the Secretariat of Finance with the Central Bank (BCRA).

The MEOySP had a policy-making role. It also coordinated progress and received monthly reports from the implementation units on the fulfilment of the proposed schedules, highlighting particular issues. The Undersecretariat of Privatization became, from then on, the so-called Enforcing Entity, administering and monitoring the procedures, while the Minister of Economy (MEOySP) became the Enforcing Authority with power to contract legal, accounting and economic consultants, both domestic and international, to issue the calls to tender, approve all regulations and general and specific bidding terms and conditions, issue all administrative acts and carry out all necessary steps for the fulfilment of the Decree.

Resolution MEOySP 4178/91 placed the rules and procedures for presentation of progress reports, monitoring and control of the privatization process with the Congressional Committee. Enforcement was by the Ministry and coordinated by the PEN. The annex specified 37 administrative acts, starting with the declaration of what was "subject to privatization". It also instituted a Privatization Commission, and dealt with selection and contracting of technical, financial and legal consulting firms (with or without external control), approval of the regulatory framework, restructuring, appraisal procedure, sale conditions, pre-qualification and award commissions, bidding process and consultations, pre-qualification and award, appointment and establishment of the directorates of regulatory bodies, performance guarantees, the signing of contracts and transfers. For each step there were specific mechanisms which were pre-determined. Centralized decision-making and decentralized implementation allowed a strong rhythm to comply with the set schedule.

The Privatization Commissions contracted extensive legal, technical, financial and economic consulting capacity. This was used to prepare specific privatization strategies and policies, draft the institutional, legal and statutory changes, set the employment and investment conditions, make appraisals of enterprises and business units, set bidding, award, contract and transfer conditions, design regulatory frameworks and other necessary aspects. There were many problems concerning personnel, inventories, assets, billing and infrastructure information update which had consequences on the bidding and transfer procedures, when defining business units, conditions and residual revenues. The Employee Property Shared Programmes have not been totally implemented to date, mostly because they were used to avoid trade union opposition, but did not fully solve the equity and other implementation problems. In many cases trade unions seriously affected operations and controlled information flow.

Present monitoring of privatization is related to control of the State's residual stake since, after the sale of control packages, the State still has significant participation in many enterprises, amounting to between 10 per cent and 49 per cent including shares held by the Employee Share Ownership Plans. There is also a need for control of the transfer process until all assets and liabilities are totally settled. Here again, there is plenty of room for improvement during the preparatory phase in order to simplify this activity. The experience with transfer of liabilities, retroactive billing, etc., has been quite complicated. It seems that improving reviews and drafting specific contract conditions can avoid future adjustments.

(g) Monitoring

The State Reform Law 23.696, enacted in August 1989, set the rules and procedures for privatization and declared the Administrative Emergency of Public Services and the State. This authorized the appointment by Ministers and sectoral Secretaries of Intervenors in PEs for limited periods (180 days, renewable), and determined their functions and responsibilities. The execution of the programme was supported by sectoral ministries and audited by the regular oversight agencies in their areas of competence, that is, Tribunal de Cuentas for the nonproductive public sector APN, and SIGEP for PEs, to provide external supervision of the process. A Congressional Committee formed by 6 Senators and 6 Representatives was coordinated internally with sectoral Commissions and with the PEN, and was charged with supervision and follow up of procedures. In cases where provincial jurisdictions were affected, the Law required their consent.

For divestiture and participation of private capital, PEs had to be declared "subject to privatization", total or partial, except for minority stakes, which were governed by their own statutory provisions. Inclusion of any enterprise other than those listed in the annex to the Law had to be dictated by the PEN, with approval of Congress.

Immediately thereafter, Decree 1105/89 set the rules derived from the Law. During the same year, various sectoral decrees were enacted to establish the basis for railway concessions, deregulate and demonopolize telecommunication services and deregulate the oil sector. The Directorate for Public Enterprises (DEP) was dissolved and the existing monitoring capacity was transferred to the Ministry of Public Works and Services (MOSP). MOSP created an Executive Reform Committee, responsible for the process at this initial stage. As the reform progressed, Decree 2074/90 added ports, water and sewerage, gas, shipping, electricity, coal production and postal and telegraph services to the original list of sectors and firms.

After years of trying to establish appropriate, reliable, consistent and timely information systems for PEs, a Technical Operative Group (GTO) was set up at the DEP in 1987. This maintained information on all relevant PEs—service and productive—on labour contracts, employment, productivity and personnel management, financial and fiscal data, prices and tariffs, cost structures, some performance indicators and procurement. This unit was able to succeed in its job because it had acquired expertise in the PE budget monitoring process in the Undersecretariat of Budgeting within the Secretariat of Finance and because it started with a tailor-made financial information system implemented at the enterprise level. The system was transferred to the MOSP when the DEP was abolished, and was used to monitor key macroeconomic, labour and microeconomic issues related to the privatization objectives and sectoral process, including direct control of PE cash flows since 1990.

It was subsequently transferred to the Under-Secretariat of Privatizations and finally to the Secretariat of Finance, where it is charged with financial monitoring and tracking the State's residual stake and liabilities in divested enterprises. SIGEP, the audit body for PEs, also maintained and published economic and financial information and performance indicators from the MOSP enterprises, but was interrupted in 1991. The report and audit function are still carried on by its successor SIGEN.

A general overview of each particular divestiture strategy and outcome shows very different patterns which can only be explained by the particular sector circumstances in which each strategy was designed and implemented. Each sector faced different public-and private-sector technical, investment and service expertise, labour conditions and consumer demands. This quite obvious fact is often disregarded when analyzing the privatization process.

Thinned public-sector capacities, bureaucratic resistance and other factors placed a heavy burden on most privatization units, which were intensively supported by external consultants and had appropriate incentive schemes to comply with the privatization strategy. These groups generally participated in all phases of the process, beginning with the intervention of management, setting the particular privatization strategy, following the divestiture procedure and, in many cases, designing and heading the regulatory body. These very compact ad hoc units usually conducted the whole process effectively and in a timely fashion. Careful attention had to be given to transparency, accountability and autonomy when addressing the different issues.

The above-mentioned GTO collected different data which were processed to provide various short-and medium-term indicators. It was able to obtain this information because it provided PEs with systems and models which facilitated their work and it processed the crude data to obtain the key indicators requested by the policy-making authority. The information system that was built had a data base which was continuously updated. This unit could have been vulnerable if not for the fact that it only assumed a monitoring role and had no analytical and assessment capacity. This was known by those subject to monitoring. During the second phase, the World Bank and IMF started using this information for monitoring purposes and soon the authorities realized that they had useful information for macroeconomic and external impact analysis and other aspects related to short and medium-term programming. This gave stronger backing to the task-force which enabled a wider coverage and more timely information.

The other oversight structures were Congress, which had a Bi-Chamber Committee for Supervision of Privatizations, and SIGEP, now Sindicatura General de la Nacion (SIGEN), the central Government's audit agency. They played a limited role, in terms of control and supervision of this process, probably due to their weakened institutional capacities. Recently, the Auditoria General de la Nacion, a congressional oversight body, has been established. It has control responsibilities over the regulatorv agencies.

(h) Constraints

PEs in Argentina were of two very distinct types: (a) public service infrastructure firms, which operate in nontradable and, mostly, noncompetitive markets, appropriate for rent-seekers, and are thus subject to regulation; and (b) industrial enterprises which are exposed to competition. In both cases, indigenous entrepreneurs associated with foreign operators and investors became interested in the prospect of restoring profitability through improved management and investment practices.

The major privatization programme started with the concession of the telecommunication public enterprise (Entel) to two major operators, providing exclusive rights to operate in the basic services during a 7-year period that could be extended, upon compliance of targets, for 3 more years. In that same year Argentine Airline's 85 per cent control stake was sold to private investors, together with the sale of petrochemical firms, award of television station concessions for 15 years, and highway toll concessions for 12 years. During the second phase, generation plants were sold, and electricity transmission and distribution networks were awarded under 95-year concessions; gas transportation and distribution networks were licensed for 35 years; YPF shares were floated in the stock market, providing revenues of $ 3,040 million; freight and passenger railway concessions were awarded for 30 years and metropolitan road accesses were given in concession for 10 years. Furthermore, flotations of residual stakes of privatized firms such as telecommunications, generation plants and one of a gas transportation firm were successfully made in the market.

Since the privatization process started, the major constraints were macroeconomic; related to incipient capital markets; legal and institutional; structural, managerial and labour-related; political (commitment and consistency); and technical competence. These should be appropriately analyzed and addressed when deciding the strategy and policy to follow and probably explain many of the successful outcomes and shortcomings which have occurred.

However, the economic coercion of hyperinflation was a major factor which overcame resistance to privatization within civil society, particularly that of trade unions and PE management. They were overcome by attractive early retirement and employee share ownership plans (PPP) when they realized that this alternative had become inescapable.

Labour contracts, employment, personnel structures, social benefits and labour productivity were analyzed and updated to check compliance with committed goals and specific sector strategies. This information was of paramount importance in supporting negotiations with trade unions and designing the divestiture conditions. However, the quality of the information proved ex post to be partially unreliable since in one privatized enterprise alone there were still close to 900 ghost workers (out of a total estimated work force of 23,000). Corruption and fraud were common in most PEs and reached all employment levels. This was the reason why there was ample room for raising labour productivity under new conditions.

The employee PPPs have not yet been fully implemented. Although these were a useful incentive, they can also serve the objective of worker participation. There were also some microenterprise and labour training and outplacement programmes. Fragile macroececonomic conditions and instability with high inflation created an environment adverse to investment. This raised the internal discount rate, due to the perceived country risk and deteriorating asset values. The overall and protracted fiscal restraint rapidly worsened the technological and operational conditions of most enterprises. This policy, together with cuts in recurrent costs, particularly salaries, left divestiture as the only possible option for PE reform.

Entrepreneurs who had developed their economic base as contractors to PEs, using transfer pricing practices, were aware of the limits to the previous development policy and started to consider the possibility of managing and investing in public service sectors that were subject to severe mismanagement and run-down infrastructure.

Moreover, the distributive dispute which had led to structural constraints and inflation in Argentina, changed because of the effects of adjustment fatigue and the possibility of finding new sources of profit by economic agents. However, not only were domestic conditions modified, but also external economic conditions changed favourably during this period.

Privatization was effected by sale of a controlling stakeholding due to the structural problems that most PEs confronted and the small size of the Argentine stock market when this policy started. Nevertheless, this entails that management is less subject to the discipline of takeover.

During the first privatization phase, the local capital market was small and lacked the density that was needed to absorb new equity issues or large public placements. However, during the second phase the local and international stock markets played a significant role, especially for institutional investors. Because of this, the Government strengthened the Comision Nacional de Valores (Securities and Exchange Commission), which has worked with investment bankers, brokers and other sectors, to establish the conditions for large share offerings and to design other financial instruments to raise capital for private and privatized firms which became public and listed in the stock exchange.

Following the success of the stabilization and reform policies, amidst the depressed international financial markets, the local stock market had a dramatic growth. Its equity traded value grew fivefold and daily operations grew from $ 2-5 million or less to $ 80-100 million at its peak, becoming one of Latin America's emerging stock markets. Capital flight reversed and became capital inflow, surpassing $ 10 billion dollars in recent years. However, it is still an unstable market: recent volatility has had a negative effect on both small shareholders and institutional investors. Government has also tried to institute a loyalty bonus and other means to promote savings and widespread ownership.

Nevertheless, after stabilization and growth policies became effective and credibility recovered, privatized firms were able to place over $ 1.7 billion in financial instruments in markets to finance part of their investments.

Most enterprises, particularly public service ones, faced problems related to size and relative market power which affected the possibility of transfer to the private sector. There were also legal and institutional problems that had to be sorted out to facilitate this shift.

Privatizations during the first phase left market power relatively intact, as with the telecommunications duopoly that was the outcome of splitting Entel into two basic service operators. During the second phase, most enterprises were separated into different business units, such as electricity, gas and railways, while water and sewerage had already been decentralized by creating provincial entities. Trunk highway and metropolitan access networks were given in concession through build-operate-maintenance-transfer (BOMT) or similar contracts with set fees or subsidies.

External financing provided funding for international and indigenous consultant firms and individual consultants for all technical, legal, economic and financial aspects of the process while the State was going through a profound adjustment-cum-reform process.

(i) Impact

Privatizations in Argentina have had positive effects in terms of productive efficiency, quality and coverage of service and fiscal impact, and will continue to do so.

The first privatization phase was fiscally driven and served the purpose of honouring external debt, recovering credibility and reducing country risk. This created a momentum for the overall process, but with insufficient attention given to improvement of allocative efficiency. Nevertheless, this transformation created very strong incentives for productivity and profitability improvements from cost reductions, particularly due to labour retrenchments, and to better management practices. However, incentives for economic efficiency were less than they might have been due to market power. High tariff levels, protected market conditions and a lag in regulation and enforcement capacity contributed to this outcome.

Notwithstanding this, during the second phase, further consideration was given not only to the productive impact of privatization but also, in cases like electricity and gas, the sector separation was aimed at improving allocative efficiency. The contribution of public enterprises to fiscal deficits was dramatically reduced, while tax revenues increased significantly due to high profitability of some firms—mainly in telecommunications, electricity generation and transmission and gas transportation and distribution. For some tradable sectors such as steel and hydocarbons, liberalization was insufficient to curb monopolistic behaviour or collusion and further oversight capacity has to be established to deter non-competitive practices.

Specifically, the fiscal impact was threefold—positive cash revenues, external and domestic debt swaps, and a growing stream of tax revenues, which contrast with the former fiscal deficits and financial requirements for investment.

The outcome in terms of quality of service and investment was also favourable, when compared with past experience in which the efficiency and effectiveness of investment was very low. However, the absolute level of yearly planned investment is not that significant, only 1.5-2 per cent, compared with historical investment and the investment needed for sustained growth. However, most likely, the combination of fiscal deficit reduction and tax revenues derived from these privatized firms may provide resources to finance future infrastructure public service projects with new private participation schemes.

So far, foreign investors have a 60 per cent participation in all privatizations, of which Spain has 15 per cent, the United States 12 per cent, Italy 9 per cent, France 7 per cent, Chile 6 per cent, Canada 3 per cent and the United Kingdom 2 per cent, with minor shares for Switzerland, Belgium and others. This cross-bordering or transnationalization of non-tradable service firms has started recently and is part of the globalization and integration processes, with balance-of-payments, technological and political implications. Also, fifteen large concentrated local economic groups have participated in most privatizations of which four—Perez Companc, Rio, Rocca-Techint, Soldati and Gruneisen-Astra—operate extensively in most sectors .

Given the monopsonist market power, inelastic consumer demand, increased concentration and environment in which these firms operate, there can be a "crowding-out" effect on tradable sectors when they compete in financial markets for scarce funding. There are also problems related to equity changes and distributional effects that have to be accounted for. All these aspects justify the presence of strong sectoral regulation and require anti-trust, trade and consumer regulation to promote competitive practices.

The transfer of enterprises free of liabilities, in generally sound financial condition, with favourable changes in tariff levels and structures and lenient service provision, had a facilitative role, given that some investors considered that their main entry cost was the up-front payment or other initial requirement.

Some economic groups have augmented their annual turnover five-fold during these last few years because of their participation in this process. Given the exposure and leveraged purchases, it will probably be necessary to make a careful scrutiny and review each concessionaire's debt structure, economic and financial performance, investment portfolio and ownership changes. Although the market may provide the solution, in case of mismanagement or default, its public service condition requires careful review by the regulators.

Privatizations also had important consequences on labour productivity in privatized firms since almost 200,000 employees were retrenched. Layoffs and retrenchment were achieved through attractive early retirement and voluntary retirement plans implemented ex ante by the PEs and later by the privatized firms.

There were also distribution effects, as tariff rebalancing in some cases favoured industrial consumers and enhanced sector competitiveness. This has not been appropriately coordinated at the provincial level, so there are some regional inequities which still have to be sorted out. Further attention will have to be given to environmental, technological and regional issues.

Regarding the external impact of privatizations, the outcome is still pending and will depend among other things on future profit remittance policies by foreign investors.

(j) Privatization of public services

ENTEL -National Telephone Company: The privatization of this legal monopolist telecommunications company, which had 3.5 million installed subscribers in a rapidly changing technological sector, led to the sale of 60 per cent of the State's assets to a control group headed by foreign investors—Stet, France Telecom and Telefonica Espanola—which are the service operators.

The company's basic service was split into two main areas: Telecom Argentina in the north and Telefonica Argentina in the south, which provide basic telecommunications services. Teleintar renders international services and Startel contributes with the so-called competitive services (cellular phones, data transmission, telex, etc.) They are owned equally by the two telephone companies. The licensees have monopoly rights for 7 years with an option for extension to 10 providing all basic and long-distance service commitments are met.

Gas del Estado -State Gas Company: The gas sector was broken into two basic parts: transmission (transportation) and distribution. The transportation is being provided by two operators on an open access basis which have transported 20 billion cubic metres of 9,300 kcal gas in 1994, while the distribution is being dispensed to 4.9 million users—households, commercial, industrial, GNC, generation plants and official consumers—by eight operators who have 35 year licences.

Electric Energy Sector -SEGBA, AyEE, HIDRONOR: The electric energy sector has been divided into three segments: power plants which have an installed capacity of 15,000 MW (peak demand slightly exceeds 10,000 MW), consisting of 44.8 per cent hydro, 49.1 per cent thermal and 6.1 per cent nuclear, and operate in a competitive market; the high voltage (500 kV) 7,000 km-long bulk transmission grid is a natural monopoly that connects 80 per cent of the market; and the distribution network which covers approximately more than 5 million industrial, domestic and commercial consumers in the metropolitan area. The transmission system includes an extensive range of lower voltage subnetworks (132 KV) for interconnection between provinces.

OSN -National Water Resources Company: The regulated area has a population of 8.6 million people of which 70 per cent receive drinking water (5.9 million people) and 58 per cent (4.75 million) have sewerage systems. These cover the city of Buenos Aires and 13 districts of the province of Buenos Aires with 2.2 million customers with a 30-year plus 10-year extension concession period. The two treatment plants—Gral. San Martin and Gral. Belgrano—produce 90 per cent of the total water supply, which is estimated at 3.8 million cubic metres/day. Estimated domestic consumption is 280/430 litres per person per day.

Ferrocariles Argentinos and Femesa -National and Metropolitan Railway Companies: The 35,000 km railway system carries 20 billion traffic units, if ton-kilometres and passenger-tons are added together. It was split into three different business units: freight, intercity passenger and suburban passenger for the Buenos Aires Metropolitan Region. The integrated restructuring programme agreed that the freight business (10.2 million tons in 1993) was financially viable. The privatization involved giving concessions for 30 years, with 10 year extensions, and splitting the network into 6 lines to make it technically and financially viable, while developing competition with road haulage. The network may also carry passengers or give access to intercity passenger railways and charge tolls for its use.

The Buenos Aires Metropolitan Region Suburban passenger services, that has a length of 900 km and carries 800,000 passengers per day, was assigned to a firm called FEMESA that was created to cover the 7 lines and the Metro (subway) which is 44 km long and carries 500,000 passengers per day. This part was offered in 5 packages with 10-year concessions and 20 years for the Urquiza and subway-linked network. Intercity linkage for passenger service for the Buenos Aires-Mar del Plata line was transferred to the Province of Buenos Aires. Other provinces are running some passenger services.

D.N.V. (National Road Directorate): The DNV has 12 concession contracts for approximately 9,000 km of roads that span over 20 corridors and carry 2,000-2,500 units per day. They are operated on a toll basis. Awards were made for operation, maintenance and improvement, with an annual subsidy that will later become a fee. The national network has 28,000 km. There is also a toll road access network being built by four metropolitan access companies which will pay a sliding scale annual fee for 22.8 year concessions.

SSP -Undersecretariat of Ports and Navigation (National Port Authority): This sector has been subject to economic and pilotage deregulation and liberalization with the transfer of minor ports to provincial authorities and operative independence given for major ports—Santa Fe, Rosario, Quequen, Buenos Aires, Bahia Blanca, Ushuahia and Rosario). The new Port Law established a regulatory framework that decentralized ports and most port services, with wharf and dock cargo and operation services awarded through concessions of 18-25 years, with baseline prices on a guaranteed freight rate basis. Dredging and buoy maintenance, oversight of concessionaires and port administration are the responsibility of the Port Authority. Its main principles are: decentralization; operative autonomy; competition among and within ports; self-financing; legalized private ports.

ENCOTEL - National Post Office Company: The restructuring that is currently being undertaken has resulted in a new firm, ENCOTE SA, 51 per cent State-owned, 14 per cent by PPP and 35 per cent by members of the Universal Postal Union, which carried 372 million postal parcels in 1993, 70 per cent of the total market share.

(k) Regulation

The main areas of regulation are price-or tariff-setting and the expansion and improvement of quality of service, following the principle of efficiency regulation. The prices have been guided mainly by the price-cap principle—RPI minus X—for electricity, telecommunications and gas, with X being a factor reflecting the Government's or regulator's estimate of the scope for increased efficiency of the utility. However, since this ceiling can have negative effects on the quality of service, it both price and quality have to be supervised. The initial tariff has been set in the concession contracts and will be subject to long-term scheduled review periods. For the rest of the concessions the tariff is set along cost-plus lines.

In most cases, regulation covers not only tariffs and quality of service but also investment commitments and plans.

The activities and geographical areas covered by regulation will probably have to be expanded to encompass different and dynamic technical and economic frontiers. Because of different competencies, provincial frameworks and rules should be compatible with the ones established at the national level.

The privatization strategy that Argentina implemented sets a serious regulatory challenge for these new entities. This is because competition was temporarily curbed to increase revenues, attract local and international investors and advance rapidly. Concentration was allowed as there was insufficient knowledge about the real conditions of infrastructure and capital goods that will require further review.

Regardless of this, experienced investors have probably discounted further regulation when they pursued long-term investment strategies. It may be useful to differentiate investor strategies by sector—industry, service and financial—and by source of capital to understand their different strategies and reactions to diverse conditions.

Approximately 12 regulatory agencies have been established or are being created, including the Direccion Nacional de Control de Servicios Agropecuarios (National Directorate for Control of Agricultural Services). Initial privatizations were effected before regulatory and institutional capacity was in place. The legal instruments used to establish the regulatory agencies have been of different levels—some were laws and others were decrees, which implies different conditions and possibilities for adjustment and repeal.

4. Conclusions

Privatization in Argentina started in 1985 and included a few public enterprises which had been rescued from bankruptcy, some in which the State had a minority stake and others fully State-owned. The second privatization stage, which started in 1989, had two phases. The first, which took place amidst different stabilization packages, policy gyrations and shifts, was done in haste and required further adjustment. The present phase, begun in 1991 amidst a successful stabilization plan conducted by the MEOySP, will be completed shortly with privatization of the post office, nuclear plants, airports and some minor enterprises.

Major constraints were macroeconomic imbalances, unformed capital markets, legal, structural and institutional problems, and managerial and labour resistance.

This massive and impressive privatization process has involved the divestiture of almost all large utilities and service enterprises. The strategy responded to political, economic and social factors which opened a window that the Government, with its important and diverse constituency, exploited favourably.

However, this approach demanded very strong centralized policy-making and coordination together with decentralized operational capacities. Although the State's capacity had severely deteriorated, the external backing provided by the World Bank and UNDP, and particular institutional and technical arrangements, permitted the achievement of set goals with some minor deviations. This was supported by an ad hoc monitoring system which had its shortcomings but was very useful amidst the stabilization and reform programme.

Analyzed with hindsight, as is the usual case, there is always room for improvement and greater efficiency during the privatization and post-privatization processes in terms of further development of overall economic and social regulation for both competitive and monopolistic markets; strengthening of sectoral and intersectoral planning and policy-making capacities, coordination of competencies at the provincial and municipal levels; and oversight, control and enforcement capacities. Also, worker participation schemes have to be fully implemented and the State's control of residual stakes could be strengthened.

Privatization in Argentina has had immediate positive effects in terms of productive efficiency together with medium-and long-term consequences due to improvements in quality, coverage and expansion of services, and a contribution to the reduction of the fiscal deficit and increased tax revenues due to the restored profitability of privatized firms.

This swift move has its costs in terms of a complex and extended regulatory task, with respect to tariff, quality and investment controls. The autonomy and discretional capacities of regulatory bodies deserve further attention because of their effects on credibility, efficiency and sustainability. Careful trade-offs will be required to guarantee due process and diligence together with agility, so as to deter protracted judicial processes.

Although "regulation with a light rein" is difficult during the first stage, due to immature and deteriorated public services, regulation should be considered as a dynamic process which has to be streamlined after pro-competitive and restructuring policies have taken hold, facilitating market entry and increasing productive efficiency and rational resource allocation.

The interest that foreign investors have shown has been beneficial as it reflects credibility and positive capital inflows. Nevertheless, it merits further attention in terms of market, technological and investment strategies, because of their potential impact on local savings, investment capacity and external balance.

SUPPLEMENTS

CUSTOMS UNIONS

Agreement	Date (in force)	Recent reference
Andean Community (CAN)	1988-5-25	L/6737
Customs Union of Belarus, Kazakhstan and Russia	2010-07-1	
East African Community (EAC)	2005-1-1	WT/COMTD/N/14
EU — Andorra	1991-7-1	WT/REG53/M/3
EU — San Marino	2002-4-1	
EU — Turkey	1996-1-1	WT/REG22/M/4
Israel — Palestinian Authority	1994	
Southern African Customs Union (SACU)	1910	WT/REG231/3
Southern Common Market (MERCOSUR)	1991-11-29	WT/COMTD/1/Add.17
Switzerland — Liechtenstein	1924	

MULTILATERAL FREE TRADE AGREEMENTS

WORLD TRADE ORGANIZATION AGREEMENTS

- General Agreement on Tariffs and Trade
  - Agreement on Agriculture
  - Agreement on the Application of Sanitary and Phytosanitary Measures
  - Agreement on Technical Barriers to Trade
  - Agreement on Trade Related Investment Measures
  - Agreement on Anti-Dumping
  - Agreement on Customs Valuation
  - Agreement on Preshipment Inspection
  - Agreement on Rules of Origin
  - Agreement on Import Licensing Procedures
  - Agreement on Subsidies and Countervailing Measures
  - Agreement on Safeguards

- General Agreement on Trade in Services
- Agreement on Trade-Related Aspects of Intellectual Property Rights
- Agreement on Government Procurement
- Information Technology Agreement

OPERATING AGREEMENTS

- ASEAN Free Trade Area (AFTA)
- Asia-Pacific Trade Agreement(APTA)
- Central American Integration System (SICA)
- Central European Free Trade Agreement (CEFTA)
- Common Market for Eastern and Southern Africa (COMESA)
- G-3 Free Trade Agreement (G-3)
- Greater Arab Free Trade Area(GAFTA) - June 1957
- Gulf Cooperation Council (GCC)
- North American Free Trade Agreement (NAFTA)
- Pacific accord
- South Asia Free Trade Agreement (SAFTA)
- Southern African Development Community (SADC)
- Southern Common Market (MERCOSUR)
- Trans-Pacific Strategic Economic Partnership (TPP)

PROPOSED AGREEMENTS

- 2011 Commonwealth of Independent States Free Trade Agreement (CISFTA)
- 2014 Union of South American Nations (CSN)
- 2021 Pacific Island Countries Trade Agreement (PICTA)
- African Free Trade Zone (AFTZ) between SADC, EAC and COMESA
- Arab Maghreb Union (UMA)
- Asia-Pacific Economic Cooperation (APEC)
- Association of Caribbean States (ACS)
- Bolivarian Alternative for the Americas (ALBA)
- Bay of Bengal Initiative for MultiSectoral Technical and Economic Cooperation(BIMSTEC)
- Community of Sahel-Saharan States (CEN-SAD)
- Comprehensive Economic Partnership for East Asia (CEPEA)

- East Asia Free Trade Agreement (EAFTA)
- Economic Community of West African States (ECOWAS)
- Euro-Mediterranean free trade area (EU-MEFTA)
- Economic Community of Central African States (ECCAS)
- Free Trade Area of the Americas (FTAA)
- Free Trade Area of the Asia Pacific (FTAAP)
- GUAM Organization for Democracy and Economic Development (GUAM)
- Intergovernmental Authority on Development (IGAD)
- Pacific Agreement on Closer Economic Relations (PACER and PACER Plus)
- People's Trade Treaty of Bolivarian Alternative for the Americas (ALBA)
- Shanghai Cooperation Organisation (SCO)
- Transatlantic Free Trade Area (TAFTA)
- Tripartite Free Trade Area (T-FTA)
- China–Japan–South Korea Free Trade Agreement

PREFERENTIAL TRADE AREAS

As a free trade areas is basically a preferential trade area with increased depth and scope of tariffs reduction all free trade areas, customs unions,common markets, economic unions,customs and monetary unions andeconomic and monetary unions are considered an advanced forms of a PTA.

MULTILATERAL

- Asia-Pacific Trade Agreement(1976)
- Economic Cooperation Organization (ECO) (1992)
- Generalized System of Preferences
- Global System of Trade Preferences among Developing Countries (GSTP) (1989)
- Latin American Integration Association (LAIA/ALADI) (1981)
- Melanesian Spearhead Group (MSG) (1994)
- Protocol on Trade Negotiations (PTN) (1973)
- South Asian Preferential Trade Arrangement (SAPTA) (1999)
- South Pacific Regional Trade and Economic Cooperation Agreement (SPARTECA) (1981)

BILATERAL

- European Union – ACP countries, formerly via the trade aspects of the Cotonou Agreement, later via Everything But Arms (EBA) agreements
- India – Afghanistan (2003)

- India – Mauritius
- India – Nepal (2009)
- India – Chile (2007)
- India – MERCOSUR (2009)
- ASEAN – PR China (2005)
- Laos – Thailand (1991)

BILATERAL FREE TRADE AGREEMENTS

List of agreements between two states, two blocs or a bloc and a state.

ASEAN has bilateral agreements with the following countries and blocs:

ASEAN Free trade agreements
ASEAN – Australia – New Zealand Free Trade Area (AANZFTA) is a free trade area between ASEAN and ANZCERTA, in effect as of 1 January 2010
ASEAN–China Free Trade Area (ACFTA), in effect as of 1 January 2010
ASEAN–India Free Trade Area (AIFTA), in effect as of 1 January 2010
ASEAN–Japan Comprehensive Economic Partnership (AJCEP), in effect as of 1 December 2008
ASEAN–Korea Free Trade Area (AKFTA), in effect as of 1 January 2010

Caribbean Community (CARICOM) has bilateral agreements with the following countries:

Costa Rica
Cuba
Dominican Republic

People's Republic of China has bilateral agreements with the following blocs, countries, and its two special administrative regions

People's Republic of China
Current FTA's

Proposed Bilateral/Multilateral FTA's
ASEAN, ASEAN–China Free Trade Area
Chile
Hong Kong, Mainland and Hong Kong Closer Economic Partnership Arrangement (CEPA)
Macau, Mainland and Macau Closer Economic Partnership Arrangement (CEPA)
Pakistan, China – Pakistan Free Trade Agreement
Peru, China–Peru Free Trade Agreement
New Zealand, New Zealand – China Free Trade Agreement
Thailand
Singapore
Republic of China (Taiwan), Economic Cooperation Framework Agreement
Costa Rica
Costa Rica has bilateral agreements with the following countries and blocs and took effect on (see date):
Canada (1 November 2002)
Chile (15 February 2002)

China (1 August 2011)
Caribbean Community (CARICOM) (15 November 2005)
Trinidad & Tobago (15 November 2005)
Guyana (30 April 2006)
Barbados (1 August 2006)
Belize (10 March 2011)
Dominican Republic (7 March 2002)
El Salvador Customs union, (1963, re-launched on 29 October 1993)
Guatemala Customs union, (1963, re-launched on 29 October 1993)
Honduras Customs union, (1963, re-launched on 29 October 1993)
Mexico (January 1, 1995)
Nicaragua Customs union, (1963, re-launched on 29 October 1993)
Panama (31 July 1973, renegotiated and expanded for (1 January 2009)
United States (1 January 2009)

EFTA has bilateral agreements with the following countries – including dependent territories – and blocs:

EFTA Free trade agreements
Albania
Canada
Chile
Colombia
Croatia
Gulf Co-operation Council
Faroe Islands (autonomous entity of Denmark)
Egypt
Hong Kong
Israel
Jordan
Lebanon
Macedonia
Mexico
Morocco
Palestinian Authority
Serbia
Singapore
Southern African Customs Union
Tunisia
Singapore
South Korea
Turkey
Ukraine

European Union free trade agreements

EU Free trade agreements
Albania SAA (2009)
Algeria AA (2005)
Andorra CU (1991)
Bosnia and Herzegovina SAA (signed 2008, entry into force pending)
Chile AA (2003)
Croatia SAA (2005)

Egypt AA (2004)
Faroe Islands, autonomous entity of Denmark (1997)
Israel AA (2000)
Jordan AA (2002)
Lebanon AA (2006)
Macedonia SAA (2004)
Mexico AA (2000)
Montenegro SAA (2010)
Morocco AA (2000)
Palestinian Authority interim AA (1997)
San Marino CU (2002)
Serbia SAA (signed 2008, entry into force pending)
South Africa AA (2000)
Switzerland FTA (1973)
Tunisia AA (1998)
Turkey CU (1996)

EU Overseas Countries and Territories
Faroe Islands has bilateral agreements with the following countries and blocs:
Switzerland
Norway
Iceland (The Hoyvík Agreement)

The European Union

Georgia has bilateral agreements with the following countries:
Armenia
Azerbaijan
Kazakhstan (Entry into force: 16 July 1999)
Russian Federation (Entry into force: 10 May 1994)
Turkmenistan (Entry into force: 1 January 2000)
Ukraine
India has bilateral agreements with the following countries and blocs:

India
Current Bilateral/Multilateral FTA's
Proposed/Suspended Bilateral/Multilateral FTA's
SAFTA (Bangladesh, Bhutan, the Maldives, Nepal, Pakistan, Sri Lanka and Afghanistan)
ASEAN (ASEAN–India Free Trade Area)
European Union (final stage)
Sri Lanka
Singapore
Thailand (separate from FTA agreement with ASEAN)
Malaysia (separate from FTA agreement with ASEAN)
Japan
European Free Trade Association (EFTA) (negotiation ongoing)
Canada (negotiation ongoing)
South Korea (India-Korea CEPA)
Japan
Iran has a bilateral agreement with the following country:
Venezuela
Japan has bilateral agreements with the following countries and blocs:

ASEAN (signed in Hanoi as of 1 April 2008)
Chile (signed in 2006)
Brunei (signed in 2007)
Indonesia
Malaysia (Japan-Malaysia Economic Partnership Agreement signed in 2005)
Mexico (took effect in 2005)
Peru
Philippines (signed in 2006)
Thailand (Japan-Thailand Economic Partnership Agreement signed in 2007)
Singapore (signed in 2002)
Vietnam (signed in 2008)
Switzerland (signed in 2009)
Jordan has bilateral agreements with the following countries and blocs:
Algeria
Libya
Syria
Kuwait
Bahrain
Peru
United States (United States-Jordan Free Trade Agreement)
The European Free Trade Association
The European Union
Kyrgyz Republic has bilateral agreements with the following countries:
Kazakhstan (Entry into force: 11 November 1995)
Moldova (Entry into force: 21 November 1996)
Russian Federation (Entry into force: 24 April 1993)
Ukraine (Entry into force: 19 January 1998)
Uzbekistan (Entry into force: 20 March 1998)
Lebanon has bilateral agreements with the following countries and blocs:
Gulf Cooperation Council (GCC)
Iraq
The European Union
Malaysia has bilateral agreements with the following countries:
India
USA
Mexico free trade agreements:

Mexico free trade agreements
Free Trade Agreements
Chile-Mexico Free Trade Agreement
Colombia-Mexico Free Trade Agreement
Costa Rica-Mexico Free Trade Agreement
EFTA-Mexico Free Trade Agreement: Iceland, Liechtenstein, Norway, Switzerland
European Union (EU)-Mexico Economic Partnership:
Austria, Belgium, Bulgaria, Cyprus, Czech Republic, Denmark, Estonia, Finland, France, Germany, Greece, Hungary, Ireland, Italy, Latvia, Lithuania, Luxembourg, Malta, Netherlands, Poland, Portugal, Romania, Slovakia, Slovenia, Spain, Sweden, United Kingdom
Israel-Mexico Free Trade Agreement
Japan-Mexico Economic Association Agreement
(NAFTA) North American Free Trade Agreement: Canada, United States
Nicaragua-Mexico Free Trade Agreement
Northern Triangle)-Mexico: El Salvador, Honduras and Guatemala
Uruguay-Mexico Free Trade Agreement

Framework Agreements

MERCOSUR-Mexico Economic Association: Brazil, Argentina, Uruguay, Paraguay
Partial Preferential Agreements
Argentina
Brazil
Ecuador
MERCOSUR
Paraguay
Panama
Peru
New Zealand free trade agreements:
Australia (as Closer Economic Relations)
Malaysia
Singapore
Thailand
Chile

People's Republic of China (see China-New Zealand Free Trade Agreement)
Brunei (see Trans-Pacific Strategic Economic Partnership)
Hong Kong
Panama has bilateral agreements with the following countries:
Costa Rica
El Salvador
Guatemala
Honduras
Nicaragua
Republic of China (Taiwan)
Republic of China (Taiwan) has bilateral agreements with the following countries:
People's Republic of China Economic Cooperation Framework Agreement
El Salvador
Guatemala
Honduras
Nicaragua
Panama
Peru has bilateral agreements with the following countries:
Canada
EFTA
People's Republic of China
Japan
Mexico
Singapore
Thailand
United States
Serbia has bilateral agreements with the following countries and blocs:
EU (SAA)
EFTA
CEFTA
Russia
Belarus
Turkey
Kazakhstan

United States (GSP)

Singapore has bilateral agreements with the following countries and blocs:
Australia
Chile
India
Japan
Jordan

New Zealand (separate from the Trans-Pacific Strategic Economic Partnership (see above) and is still in force)
Panama
Peru
South Korea
People's Republic of China
the EFTA

South Korea has bilateral agreements with the following countries and blocs:
ASEAN
Chile
EFTA
India (Comprehensive Economic Partnership Agreement)
Peru
Singapore
United States (US) (pending)

Switzerland has bilateral agreements with the following countries and blocs:
Albania (Signed: 17.12.2009: Entry into force: 01.11.2010)
Canada (Entry into force 01.07.2009)
Chile (Entry into force: 01.12.2004)
Colombia (Signed: 25.11.2008. Entry into force: 01.07.2011)
Cooperation Council for the Arab States of the Gulf (GCC) (Signed: 22.06.2009 Entry into force expected 2nd semester 2012)
Croatia (Entry into force: 01.09.2002)
Egypt (Entry into force: 01.09.2008)
European Community (EC) (Entry into force: 01.01.1973; bilateral CH-EC)
EFTA-Convention (Entry into force: 03.05.1960)
Faeroe Islands (Entry into force: 01.03.1995; bilateral CH-Faeroe)
Israel (Entry into force: 01.07.1993)
Japan (Entry into force: 01.09.2009. Bilateral CH-Japan)
Jordan (Entry into force: 01.09.2002)
Republic of Korea (Entry into force: 01.09.2006)
Lebanon (Entry into force: 01.01.2007)
Macedonia (Entry into force: 01.05.2002)
Mexico (Entry into force: 01.07.2001)
Morocco (Entry into force: 01.12.1999)
Palestinian Authority (Entry into force: 01.07.1999)
Peru (Signed: 24.06.2010 (EFTA) and 14.07.2010 (Peru). Entry into force on 01.07.2011)
Serbia (Signed: 17.12.2009: Entry into force: 01.10.2010)
Singapore (Entry into force: 01.01.2003)
SACU (Entry into force: 01.05.2008)
Tunisia (Entry into force: 01.06.2006)
Turkey (Entry into force: 01.04.1992)

Ukraine (Signed 24.06.2010. Entry into force expected 01.06.2012)

Thailand has bilateral agreements with the following countries:
Australia
India
New Zealand
Peru

Tunisia has bilateral agreements with the following countries and blocs:
Morocco

The European Free Trade Association
Jordan
Senegal
Egypt
the Greater Arab Free Trade Area
Algeria
Libya
Mauritania
Turkey
The European Union
United States free trade agreements:

The United States
FTA in force
FTA signed, awaiting ratification
Korea
Colombia
Panama
NAFTA
Canada
Mexico
Australia
Chile
Singapore
Peru
Oman
Morocco
Bahrain
Israel
Jordan
Dominican Republic–Central America Free Trade Agreement
Costa Rica
El Salvador
Guatemala
Honduras
Nicaragua
the Dominican Republic

PROPOSED BILATERAL AGREEMENTS

List of agreements currently in negotiations. Agreements that are so far only discussed without any formal action by the parties involved are not listed.

- Andean Community
  - India
- ASEAN
  - India
  - Australia
  - New Zealand
- Australia
  - ASEAN (negotiating alongside New Zealand for a proposed AFTA-CER)
  - United Arab Emirates
  - People's Republic of China (Australia-China Free Trade Agreement)
- Canada is currently negotiating or planning bilateral trade agreements with:
  - Andean Community
  - CARICOM
  - Guatemala, El Salvador, Honduras, and Nicaragua (Canada Central American Free Trade Agreement)
  - Dominican Republic
  - Jordan
  - EFTA (negotiations concluded, preliminary agreement reached)
  - EU
  - Panama (Canada-Panama Free Trade Agreement)
  - South Korea
  - Singapore
  - Japan
  - Joining the Trans-Pacific Strategic Economic Partnership

- Caribbean Community (CARICOM) - Canada to be negotiated, after Canada finishes their Central American Free Trade Agreement agreement.
- Caribbean Community (CARICOM) - EU (on-going negotiation on the EPA) ("Economic Partnership Agreement")
- Caribbean Community (CARICOM) - MERCOSUR (Open for discussions in May 2005)
- Chile is negotiating or is planning bilateral agreements with the following countries and blocs:
  - Guatemala
  - India
  - Nicaragua
  - Thailand
- People's Republic of China is negotiating or is planning bilateral agreements with the following countries and blocs:
  - Australia Australia-China Free Trade Agreement
  - ASEAN
  - Costa Rica
  - Pakistan (Signed on 24 November 2006 and has been executed)
  - India (proposed)
  - South Korea: China–South Korea Free Trade Agreement
- Costa Rica
  - EU
  - EFTA
  - Peru
  - Colombia
  - Singapore
  - South Korea
- Colombia is negotiating or is planning bilateral agreements with the following countries and blocs:
  - El Salvador

- Guatemala
- Honduras
- Costa Rica

- EU is negotiating or is planning bilateral agreements with the following countries and blocs:
    - ACP countries via Economic Partnership Agreements (EPA)
        - European Union Economic Partnership Agreement with the Pacific ACP Countries (EU-PACP)
    - Bosnia and Herzegovina Stabilisation and Association Agreement
    - CACM + Panama
    - Serbia Stabilisation and Association Agreement
    - Albania Stabilisation and Association Agreement
    - Syria European Union Association Agreement
    - Mercosur
    - Russia (EU-Russia Common Economic Space)
    - Andean Community
    - South Korea (European Union-Korea Free Trade Agreement)
    - European Union Central American Association Agreement (EU-CAAA)
- EFTA is negotiating or is planning bilateral agreements with the following countries and blocs:
    - Algeria
    - Albania
    - MERCOSUR
    - GCC
    - Ukraine
- Gulf Cooperation Council
    - EU

- Mercosur
- India
- New Zealand
- Turkey
- India
  - Australia (on negotiation)
  - Sri Lanka (separate from the South Asia Free Trade Agreement)
  - Chile (on negotiation)
  - New Zealand (on negotiation)
  - Hong Kong (on negotiation)
  - European Union (to be concluded before 2010 year end)
  - EFTA
- Japan
  - Gulf Cooperation Council
  - India (1st round of talks were held in New Delhi, and the 2nd round of talks are scheduled for Tokyo in April)
  - Australia (Conducting feasibility study as of 19 September 2006).
  - New Zealand - (Conducting feasibility study as of 14 May 2008)
- Jordan
  - Iraq
  - Palestinian Authority
  - Pakistan
  - Canada - (signed but not yet ratified)
- New Zealand
  - USA
  - South Korea

  - Japan
  - Hong Kong
  - Cooperation Council for the Arab States of the Gulf
  - Association of Southeast Asian Nations
  - Peru
  - Vietnam
  - India
  - Russia
- Peru
  - Mexico
  - Costa Rica
- Republic of China (Taiwan)
  - Dominican Republic
  - European Union
  - India
  - Singapore
  - United States
- Russia
  - European Union
  - New Zealand
- Serbia is negotiating bilateral free trade agreements with the following countries and blocs:
  - Ukraine
- Singapore is negotiating bilateral free trade agreements with the following countries and blocs:
  - Bahrain
  - Singapore - Canada

- Egypt
- Mexico
- Pakistan
- Panama
- Sri Lanka
- Kuwait
- Qatar
- United Arab Emirates
- GCC

- South Korea (Source: Ministry of Foreign Affairs and Trade, Minister for Trade - Free Trade Agreement Department) is negotiating or is planning bilateral agreements with the following countries and blocs:
  - Mexico (SECA 3rd round of talks in 14~16 June 2006)
  - Canada(10th round of talks in 23 April ~ 27 April 2007, Seoul)
  - India (CEPA 6th round of talks in 3 March ~ 6 March 2007, Seoul)
  - EU (2nd round of talks in 16 July 2007 ~ 20 July 2007, Brussels)
  - MERCOSUR (preparation study)
  - People's Republic of China: China–South Korea Free Trade Agreement(preparation study)
  - GCC (preparation study)
  - Japan (negotiations currently at standstill)
- Switzerland is negotiating or is planning bilateral agreements with the following countries and blocs:
  - Russia (Negotiations in preparation 2010)
  - Algeria (In negotiations 2010)
  - People's Republic of China (Joint Feasibility Study, Bilateral Switzerland-China 2010)
  - Thailand (In negotiations 2010)

    - Hong Kong (In negotiations 2010)
    - Vietnam (Joint feasibility study 2010)
    - USA (Bilateral US-Swiss Trade and Investment Cooperation Forum 2010)
    - India (In negotiations 2010)
    - Indonesia (Official Launch of negotiations: 07.07.2010)
- Ukraine
    - Canada
    - European Union
    - Israel
    - Singapore
- United States:
    - Colombia Trade Promotion Agreement (2008?)
    - Panama - United States Trade Promotion Agreement (2008?)
    - United States-Thailand Free Trade Agreement (on hold since the 2006 Thai coup d'état)
    - United States-New Zealand Free Trade Agreement
    - United States-Ghana Free Trade Agreement
    - United States-Indonesia Free Trade Agreement
    - United States-Kenya Free Trade Agreement
    - United States-Kuwait Free Trade Agreement (Expert-level trade talks held in February 2006) (part of US-MEFTA initiative)
    - United States-Malaysia Free Trade Agreement (next meeting on January 14, 2008 in Kuala Lumpur)
    - United States-Mauritius Free Trade Agreement
    - United States-Mozambique Free Trade Agreement
    - United States-United Arab Emirates Free Trade Agreement (5th round of talks are yet to be scheduled) (part of US-MEFTA initiative)

- United States-Southern African Customs Union Free Trade Agreement (on hold since 2006 due to US demands on intellectual property rights, government procurement rights and investment)
- United States-Ecuador Free Trade Agreement
- United States-Qatar Free Trade Agreement (on hold since 2006) (part of US-MEFTA initiative)

LATIN AMERICAN REGIONAL TRADE AGREEMENTS

Latin American Integration Association (ALADI)

Andean Community of Nations (CAN)

Central American Common Market (CACM)

North American Free Trade Agreement (NAFTA)

Southern Cone Common Market (Mercosur)

Union of South American Nations (UNASUR)

Free Trade Area of the Americas (FTAA)*

The Bolivarian Alliance for the Peoples of Our America (ALBA)

The Treaty of Montevideo (1980) established ALADI as a successor for the Latin American Free Trade Association (LAFTA).

The Cartagena Agreement was signed by Bolivia, Chile, Colombia, Ecuador and Peru in May 1969. Venezuela acceded in February 1973 and withdrew in 2006 while Chile withdrew in October 1976.

The General Treaty on Central American Economic Integration was signed by Guatemala, Honduras, El Salvador and Nicaragua in December 1960. Costa Rica acceded in July 1962.

The agreement was signed in December 1992, ratified by the three national legislatures in 1993, and entered into force in January 1994.

The four member states signed the Treaty of Asunción in March 1991.

The agreement was signed in May of 2008 after negotiations dating to the creating of the South American Community in 2004.

Talks began with the Summit of the Americas in Miami on December 11, 1994, subsequent meetings (Santiago 1998, Quebec City 2001, Miami 2003 and Mar de Plata 2005) have not been able to establish an agreement on the FTAA.

The first agreement establishing ALBA comes about through the Cuba-Venezuela Agreement signed in December of 2004. Susequently, the People's Trade Agreement was signed in April of 2006.

Argentina, Bolivia, Brazil, Chile, Colombia, Cuba, Ecuador, Mexico, Paraguay, Peru, Uruguay and Venezuela.

Bolivia, Colombia, Ecuador, Peru.

Costa Rica, El Salvador, Guatemala, Honduras and Nicaragua.

Canada, Mexico and the United States.

Argentina, Brazil, Paraguay and Uruguay.

Argentina, Bolivia, Brasil, Chile, Colombia, Ecuador, Guyana, Paraguay, Peru, Suriname, Uruguay y Venezuela.

Antigua and Barbuda, Bahamas, Barbados, Belice, Canada, Colombia, Costa Rica, Dominican Republic, El Salvador, Grenada, Guatemala, Guyana, Haiti, Jamaica, Mexico, Panama, Paraguay, Peru, St. Kitts and Nevis, St. Lucia, St. Vincent and the Grenadines, Suriname, Trinidad and Tobago, United States, Uruguay.

Antigua & Barbuda, Bolivia, Cuba, Dominica, Ecuador, Honduras, Nicaragua, Saint Vincent and the Grenadines, Venezuela.

* The following countries retracted from the FTAA: Argentina, Brazil, Bolivia, Chile, Ecuador, Dominica, Honduras, Nicaragua and Venezuela. When it was launched, ALBA had two member states, Venezuela and Cuba Subsequently a number of other Latin American and Caribbean nations have entered into this Peoples' Trade Agreement (Spanish: Tratado de Comercio de los Pueblos, or TCP) which aims to implement the principles of ALBA

www.ingramcontent.com/pod-product-compliance
Ingram Content Group UK Ltd.
Pitfield, Milton Keynes, MK11 3LW, UK
UKHW051509290926
15471UKWH00008B/1520